MIND
OVER
MATTER

D0836123

MIND OVER MATTER

*****

Loyd Auerbach

KENSINGTON BOOKS

KENSINGTON BOOKS are published by
Kensington Publishing Corp.
850 Third Avenue
New York, NY 10022

Kensington and the K logo Reg. U.S. Pat. & TM Off.

First Kensington Printing: May, 1996
10 9 8 7 6 5 4 3 2 1

ISBN 1-57566-047-4

Printed in the United States of America

What someone can do or cannot do is absolutely not proportional in any way to anyone else's belief or disbelief.

What you believe someone else can or can't do hasn't got beans with the doing. Or lack of doing. Just go back through your history books and you'll discover that just about everything you take for granted today in your daily lives *was absolutely impossible not so many years ago.*

—Martin Caidin

ACKNOWLEDGMENTS

First and foremost, I want to thank Martin Caidin. He has made more of an impact on me both personally and professionally than even he may be aware of. With Marty's friendship and mentorship, I believe I am a better writer, a better researcher, and definitely a better person. He has reminded me why I got interested in psychic phenomena originally, and has further opened my eyes and mind and heart to the true wonderment of the universe and human potential. His wife, Dee Dee, was also a major help with getting a handle on Marty's own telekinesis (and on Marty). We've also had the chance to adopt each other as "family."

Larry Loebig, too, was a big help. Larry has been my mentalism-partner in a show we've done (and will do again) called "Seance Fiction Theater" and is a player in the Internet/Web provider industry (Global InfoNet). Larry helped shape the style and flow of this book, and a few stands I took with my own opinions, with his very pointed advice.

I need to acknowledge a few others, without whom this book wouldn't be what it is (and may not have been at all). Special thanks to my agent, Linda Mead, and my first editor at Kensington (with whom I have enjoyed working at another publisher), Beth Lieberman.

Thanks go out to (in no particular order other than how their names pop up in my head) Barbara Gallagher, Jerry Solfvin, Guy Savelli, Jon Klimo, Kathy Reardon, Luis Gasparetto, Keith Harary, Marcello Truzzi, Uri Geller, Bob Steiner, John Barbour, Joan Borland, Andy Nicholls, Peter Jordan, Robert Morris, G. Harry Stine, George Weissmann, Jude Gerard Prest, David Abbitt, Chris Stier, and Rhea White. You've all helped with this book, whether you were aware of it or not (and some of you know how directly you helped).

Special thanks to Steven Youell and Dave Knapp for the great job they did with the Ronny Marcus investigation.

And to Gerry Griffin of California Magic & Novelty (1930 Oak Park Boulevard, Pleasant Hill, California 94523), for his help with the photos and with providing me with many, many items of magical interest (and for performance).

Finally, I want to thank some friends of mine for their support and understanding.

Donna Fitch and Michele Fuenffinger of the Los Angeles office and all the folks in the San Francisco office of my "real" job at LEXIS-NEXIS services were more than understanding and supportive as I wrote this book (and moved myself and my fiancée and planned a wedding).

My good friends Eric Brad, Petra Wingate-Brad, and Mark Pemberton not only have supported me mentally and emotionally in this project, but also made my fiancée-now-my-wife Julie feel welcomed and at home here in northern California. Oh yeah, and there was the moving thing they helped with as I also wrote this tome (and helped us plan and carry off our wedding).

Special thanks to Jojo Bagdadi for introducing me to Julie in the first place.

Most of all, thank you, Julie, for being all you are to me and more. I couldn't have done this given the schedule we had without you, your support, and your love.

FOR JULIE
WHO TRULY MATTERS TO ME

CONTENTS

Introduction

Can you move matter with your mind? Of course you can!

By the simple direction of your mind to tell your hands to pick up this book, open it, and page through it, you have performed a piece of "mind over matter."

When most people think of Mind over Matter, they typically think of TV or comic book characters levitating objects (or themselves) or throwing off bolts of mental force or perhaps bending spoons and forks (much to the disgust of restaurant owners). While all that may be part of what researchers in the field of parapsychology have been studying as "psychokinesis," the mind acting directly on physical matter or energy, there is much more to it.

And that "much more" is what this book is about. The "much more" of how our minds affect ourselves and the world around us.

As we near the end of the twentieth century, more and more of us have been looking outside as well as inside for "answers" to understanding our nature and improving our lives. At the same time one of the biggest political discussions today concerns the physical health of the citizens of the United States, and there is an increasing focus on the mind's interaction with the body to create good health.

Nowadays, we hear more and more about health care and medicine. Thanks to President and First Lady Clinton, the health care system in the United States has been in the news. We are clearly in crisis in this country. Rising medical costs, lack of insurance coverage, and the unwillingness of either the providers of health care or the insurance carriers to bend to some kind of compromise is forcing an issue out in the open that should have been there long ago.

Alternative medicine is the phrase covering methods of healing that stand outside of traditional "Western medicine," specifically that approved of and practiced by members of the American Medical Association. Insurance carriers and others who pay for health care are beginning to look toward treatment methods that have largely been ignored, undoubtedly because of the influence of the AMA and the pharmaceutical interests. These treatment methods include chiropractic (more accepted in some parts of the country than others), acupuncture, massage therapy, use of natural herbs, therapeutic touch, and a variety of mental healing methods. Even the National Institute of Health is getting in on the act by sponsoring research looking into alternative therapies.

Most important to "good health" appears to be a growing recognition that our healing processes are truly affected by our mental attitudes. It is now widely accepted that the mind-set of an individual can cause illness or healing, as well as dramatically affect performance of physical (and mental) tasks, from athletics to creativity.

On national and international levels, human performance, both physical and mental, is the subject of increasing attention and discussion. The media in all its forms has covered such topics as alternative medical and healing techniques, sports psychology, peak performance, firewalking, and conditioning the mind to achieve one's physical, emotional, and spiritual goals. The home video- and audiotape market has exploded with self-help titles covering all aspects of using the mind to help the body achieve better health and conditioning.

Motivational workshops which include methods for increasing self-esteem and personal power that may involve martial arts techniques and fire-walking are not only on the rise, but also have their own infomercial versions. Athletes help represent some of the techniques and products that have become associated with them, while making a point of discussing peak performance issues. In the athletic arena, sports psychology places much emphasis on mental attitude to achieve maximum physical performance, and this new branch of psychology is gaining more visibility every day in the media and the academic world.

Currently, there seems to be more and more media attention on how the mind can help and harm our bodies, how people can drive themselves to death or to physical near-perfection.

The issue at the heart of the human performance and mental healing movements is Mind over Matter.

While it may appear that this culture is just waking up to a new idea, as far back as Hippocrates, people interested in the healing arts have known that the mind and body have an effect on each other.

For many decades, much of the work done on how the mind affects its own body has been part of or connected to the work of researchers in and around the field of parapsychology. The "mainstream" of science and society at large has only recently taken note of the work conducted over the years in this field, because parapsychologists and healing researchers have also been involved in work on the effects of the mind beyond its own body, an idea more difficult to accept.

Parapsychology is popularly connected to a variety of topics, from ghosts to UFOs, from psychic detectives to the "lost continent" of Atlantis. In reality, parapsychology is the study of how the mind interacts with the environment and with other minds on a couple of levels. Extrasensory perception (ESP) was the term coined to cover the flow of information into and out of the mind.

Telepathy is commonly applied to the idea of reading another's mind, or of mental "talking" between two people, though this really works better in science fiction than reality. Telepathy is effectively defined as mind-to-mind communication, but it's rough communication at best, with concepts and emotions the main content of the "messages," rather than words.

Clairvoyance is the term applied to receiving information from a location or even outside the reach of one's "normal" senses. Researchers have done much work with this talent, most recently under the title of "remote viewing" or "remote perception" research, which has shown that just about anyone can receive information from distant locations (not just self-proclaimed psychics).

Precognition is the ability most touted in the media, since it not only covers information from another location or event, but also predicts events from a time in the future. Research has shown some success with precognition, but on a conceptual level, lots of scientists have problems with the idea that one can accurately predict a future that hasn't come about yet. In fact, there is much discussion about Time in research on precognition, and one framework says that it only works some of the time because a person is predicting what *might probably* happen, not what *definitely will* happen.

The other major area of parapsychological research has to do with the mind's direct effect on the physical environment. Psychokinesis is the term parapsychologists have applied to "mind over matter" since the early days of the work of J.B. & Louisa Rhine at Duke University in the 1930s. The definition of psychokinesis (PK) is the ability of the mind to affect matter, energy, and events without the use of the physical body. It is "mind over matter," the mind affecting material things at some distance outside the body (no matter how large that distance is). Another term often used is telekinesis, which means "motion at a distance," and is typically applied to the mind literally causing objects to move about (levitation, pushing objects, turning targets, etc.).

As used in Parapsychology, PK relates to a wide range of phenomena: levitation and movements of objects (as in poltergeist cases), interference in and creation of energy systems, materialization and dematerialization (and maybe teleportation), metal-bending, psychic (mental) healing of self and others, effects on photographs and audio- and videotape, and effects on micro-systems such as those in random event generators, computers, appliances, and other machines.

Together, ESP and PK are covered in parapsychology by the Greek letter "psi" (pronounced "sigh"), and research today has more commonly been called "psi research." Psychologist and psi researcher Keith Harary has also played with the term ESP, since really there is nothing "extra" about it (and perhaps nothing "sensory" as we normally use the word). The term "extended perception" has a better ring to it.

Parapsychologists also look at a third area, though generally this falls outside the laboratory. That area is one that got many of the early psychical researchers interested in psi to begin with. The idea that the mind or consciousness can survive the death of the body, in effect as spirits or apparitions or ghosts, and that it can communicate directly or through living people (mediums or channelers) makes up the third area of research, called "survival of bodily death" or "survival research" for short. While this area is of great interest to the media and the general public, it's been kind of tough to entice a ghost into a lab setting, so most parapsychologists interested in hard research tend to stick with ESP and PK research.

In the "early" days of psychical research, most psychokinetic events looked at were related to physical mediumship. In the seance room, the table would lift and move, objects would appear and disappear, things would float about, and people might feel physical effects of "something" touching them. While these events were often categorized as caused by spirits or as fraud, much has been done in the past to indicate that the "spirits" responsible for true PK in those settings were most likely those of living people.

PK as a phenomenon whereby the mind has an effect on the world outside the body is hard for many people to take. It means some kind of energy exchange that we have a hard time even conceptualizing, let alone explaining. It means our thoughts have an effect on the world around us, and therefore some responsibility to go along with it (a scary thought to many). That doesn't mean it doesn't happen, just that it's hard to accept.

But while psychics and parapsychologists (and the skeptics) think of PK as only outwardly directed, it is much more than that. In strictest definition, it is the mind's effect on matter in any way shape or form. That means, taken literally, my thoughts driving my fingers to type these words here at my computer is "mind over matter." The act of my arm obeying a mental command to move is PK. While we generally think of PK as directed outward, it is also our mental effects on our own bodies.

That's what this book is about: *Mind Over Matter* addresses how the human mind acts on the matter and energy of its own body as well as the evidence for (and examples of) how the mind may interact with the world outside the body. As you read on, you will get a feel for the range of effects the mind can have on the physical world, both positive and negative. I will directly address the "scary" implication of psychokinesis: that our minds not only have an effect (and therefore a responsibility) on ourselves, but also on objects, events, and even people around us. Taking responsibility for our own actions is hard enough. To many, the "scariest" implication of psychokinesis may be that we unconsciously have an effect on the world around us. That adds another dimension to personal responsibility.

This book will be a very personal perspective on Mind over Matter. Based on what I've seen over the years, what I've read and heard from very reliable sources, what has been supposed and hypothesized and theorized, we will explore Mind over Matter as it relates to ourselves and to the world around us, and the responsibilities such a connection has for all of us.

I will attempt to show why taking on such a psychokinetically responsible attitude can help bolster a person's confidence and self-esteem, and not add angst about having such abilities. Along the way, I hope you will learn much about what the "state of the art" knowledge is on ways you can affect yourself (and how you already do) through mental imagery and attitude both positively and negatively, as well as how you may be able to affect others and things around you through an ability that we all have and use (whether we're aware of it or not).

The idea of the Mind acting directly on Matter extends the idea beyond the body. Occultists and others trying to manipulate natural forces over the centuries have played at ways of using the inherent powers humans seem to have. Healing (and the opposite, attack or harm) is just one of the areas explored here.

Psychokinesis or Telekinesis or simply Mind over Matter is a reality. We can affect machines and technology and we can move objects with our minds, though this is often a subconscious process, as in the poltergeist experience. The evidence for Mind over Matter extends to moving objects and to metal bending, though the possibility of fraudulent effects must also be looked at, as with the case of Israeli psychic Ronny Marcus, who I, along with a couple of my magician buddies, investigated (and found fraudulent) in 1994.

But much of how we do with our minds and what we can potentially do is linked to performance issues. So, we will begin with human performance and progress to the "wilder" examples and uses of this ability.

I have personally experienced or witnessed a variety of Mind over Matter effects over the 16-plus years since I became involved in parapsychology (beginning with my graduate studies in 1979). Over the years, I have worked as a consultant to the American Society for Psychical Research in New York, have been on the faculty of John F. Kennedy University (Orinda, CA) since 1983, and have investigated a wide variety of reported psychic phenomena and abilities on my own and with the group I founded in 1989 (the Office of Paranormal Investigations).

The Office of Paranormal Investigations (OPI) is really an "office without walls," as perhaps is appropriate. OPI really consists of a group of individuals, mainly in the San Francisco Bay Area, who have some education or training in parapsychology, as well as some affiliated licensed counselors, psychic practitioners, and scientific or magician experts who are all interested in paranormal events. OPI mainly investigates cases of reported hauntings and poltergeists (essentially what come across as "ghost" cases) with the main intent to help the individual or family having the experience deal with the phenomena. In addition, we also do quite a lot of consulting with the media, and as an information and referral service. We get calls from all over the country, and since we have no funding that could allow us to fly all over the place to conduct investigations, we have a small referral network of investigators in places like Los Angeles, Seattle, Tucson, New Jersey, Pennsylvania, Florida, North Carolina, New York, St. Louis, and a few other locations.

During the investigations, we first look for "normal" explanations, whether physical or psychological, since one can't deal with or understand paranormal phenomena unless one separates it from normal (though perhaps misunderstood) happenings. As we help people with the situations, many of which turn out not to be psychic or ghostly at all, we do learn something about the experiences and the phenomena.

In reference to the OPI technique of not immediately labeling something psychic, I should also mention my perspective includes that of being a magician and mentalist. Since I got into learning the art of magic, I have performed professionally at Comedy Clubs, Corporate events, and in stage magic shows (and of course loads of private parties), and consulted as a magician with other researchers and even other magicians.

My perspective, therefore, has been to look for "normal" explanations first (though from the magician's perspective, "normal" may not always be the right word) before assuming any event witnessed or experienced is beyond such explanations. But there are many events, many feats performed by humans, many unusual abilities displayed that don't fit conventional explanation.

More than that, I was exposed to extraordinary human performance while growing up due to my father's connection to sports. As a producer and eventually vice-president for NBC Sports, my father, Dick Auerbach, has seen a lot of good and bad sports performances, his own coverage hitting just about every sport you can think of, from baseball and football to karate and skiing to the Olympics. Since leaving NBC in the early '80s, he has continued on with his connection to sports through his own international company, Videospec International.

While I have never been a sports fan (of any sport), I have always paid attention to the work my father did, and to the performances of certain athletic feats. Most interesting to me have been those situations I've seen or heard described to me (by my father and others, both on the TV and the athlete side) that have pushed the envelope of human ability.

To my mind, it all simply means we need to expand what we consider "normal" or "conventional." We can get on the road to do this by expanding our ideas of Mind over Matter to include the "normal" things that, so far, have eluded "conventional" explanation (such as miraculous healings, extraordinary athletic performance, and more, as you'll see).

Let me start you off here with a rundown of what you'll see in this book.

First, I want to discuss some basic ideas of the mind/body connection and the mind itself. From there, we'll move on to human performance.

From circus acrobats to Olympic gymnasts, from marathon runners to football running backs, humans have been pushing ourselves to greater and greater athletic heights since before the original Olympics in ancient Greece. Records are continuously broken. How much of the record breaking is done because mental limitations are overcome?

The idea of one's mind-set affecting personal performance is a fairly new one in Western culture. However, it is an ancient idea that is part and parcel of a physical tradition of the East.

For centuries martial artists have been capable of seemingly amazing feats that seem beyond the capabilities of the body. The philosophies behind the various martial arts have typically emphasized mind and mental control of the body and its energies as crucial to performance.

Are martial artists truly capable of surpassing "normal" bodily limits or does it just seem that way? Can anyone learn this? What is the place of mind in the martial arts? What is the role of the energy in humans, called "Chi" or "Qi" in the arts? What is the connection to healing (yes, there is one)?

Stories of the "powers" of martial arts masters abound. We'll explore the Mind over Matter connections in the Martial Arts.

Of course, throughout the ages, we have stories of incredible physical performances by many individuals, some mythic and some real. Some of the "powers" attributed to individuals down through time have been called psychic and spiritual, miraculous and even demonic.

In Chapter Three, we'll take a look at the reported powers and abilities of many spiritual and religious figures. The various saints and prophets from the Old and New Testament have been described as doing everything from levitation and teleportation to instant (and mass) healings. Whether God (or "gods") were responsible for these miracle gifts, they all have the look of psychokinesis, of the mind affecting the material world.

Over the centuries, such powers have been labeled as good or evil, or have been dismissed by more skeptically minded people as simply incidents of witnesses with hallucinations. More recently in time, demonstrations of these miraculous abilities have fallen into less religious contexts, as I'll discuss in looking at the physical (spirit) mediums from the 1850s to the twentieth century.

What about today? Are there people who do miracles in the late twentieth century? Or have such "miracles" fallen off in this century? Are there potential saints walking around today or are we learning more about both real and fraudulent psychic talents and simply labeling potential saints as superpsychics or as phonies? Are we all potentially capable of being saints if we choose the right path?

There are plenty of people who perform unusual and even bizarre feats, and can apparently teach them to others. From fire-walking to piercing the body with no pain, people perform (or try to perform) unusual activities all over the world, and even make them central to teaching other ideas such as motivation and self-esteem.

Fakirs and con artists in many cultures have used demonstrations of fire-walking, glass-eating, lying on a bed of nails, and other "fun" activities to gain money from their audiences. Today, Tolly Burkan, Anthony Robbins, and others have used fire-walking as part of their motivational trainings, and still others teach people self-esteem through fire-walking.

Is fire-walking easily explained? What about other "fakir" effects? Are they all fraud? If fire-walking is explainable, why do some people get burned and others not? Is there a mental "protection" at work?

Chapter Four will look at this and other "motivational" tools and how they may relate to both the mind/body and mind outside the body connections.

In addition, we'll look at some of the "normal" explanations for some of these things. However, be aware that not all unusual performance can be easily explained. While lying on a bed of nails has an easy physical explanation, there have been demonstrations of physical performance that run to the bizarre and appear to have little or no explanation.

We have all heard stories of people lifting cars or other objects off of loved ones during accidents. Is it adrenaline? Or is something else responsible?

What about people who have demonstrated bodily control by piercing their bodies with little or no bleeding? Or people who show stigmata? Are these mentally created and sustained effects? Are these abilities related to the healing process in us?

Healing is the next area to be covered, in Chapter Five. We'll look at self-healing and healing at a distance, as well as the arguments against them many skeptical physicians have raised. In this chapter we'll briefly look at a variety of forms of mental healing of others, including faith healing, psychic healing, therapeutic touch, pet therapy, distance healing, and psychic surgery.

As I have much experience in the field of psychical research, psychic healing, or healing at a distance, will be looked at a bit more closely in relation to how it might work, though this may seem to some more science fiction than science fact. Healers have apparently used more than just herbs and natural substances to help in the healing process. Many have shown, even in laboratory situations, the ability to affect the healing process of others. How psychic healing might work will be discussed in many contexts, from the self-named psychic surgeons to faith healers to shamans, voodoo priests/priestesses and "witch doctors."

I also want to introduce a buddy of mine, pilot/science journalist Martin Caidin, author of *Marooned* and creator of Steve Austin, The Six Million Dollar Man, who has experienced self-healing and Mind over Matter firsthand (he has, for example, healed himself after he broke his neck in an accident, much to the disbelief of his doctors).

The role of belief and disbelief will be discussed throughout the book, and specifically with healing, both in relation to belief in the process of self-healing and how belief in a spiritual power may augment (or even cause) self-healing/self-harm to work. Caidin believed he could get healed and he was. The mind-set of a patient is becoming ever-increasingly a focus of some medical treatments.

Finally, the prevalence and form of fraud (a consumer warning) will also be covered.

From healing, we'll move to its darker opposite: using Mind over Matter to cause harm to oneself or to others.

A focus of many religions in their dealing with "psychic" abilities is to say that they are "evil," that such powers are only going to hurt those who use them and others. But can psychic attack really cause harm to another? Does it work the same as psychic healing: is it dependent on belief to work?

Belief often seems to be the key in situations where people have harmful spells placed on them. Is there evidence that people can be attacked, hurt, even killed by the thoughts of others? Do gypsies really cast effective "curses"? Does voodoo or Santeria work to kill? What is "hex death?"

What about psychic attack by ghosts? If a ghost is the consciousness (or mind) of a dead person, then the effect they have on the living is that of psychokinesis or Mind over Matter. Can ghosts affect the health of people? Can they, as the tabloid talk shows would have us believe, rape and ravage living people?

In Chapter Six we'll look at a variety of opinions.

Of course, no discussion of healing and harm would be complete without looking at how notions called "occult" have come into play, as well as what the goal of such "magic" has been.

Over the centuries, people who believe in and practice various magical arts such as those related to witchcraft, voodoo, the Kabala, demonology, and the sorceries of other, more primitive cultures have set out to manipulate the natural world around them. From weather control to changing the migration patterns of wild animals to add to the food supply, using magic to affect physical change has stayed with us.

For example, just before a professional golf tournament in South Africa some years ago, the tournament folks hired a "witch doctor" to affect the storm that was, for all intents and purposes, almost on top of the location of the tournament. The storm suddenly veered off, leaving the tournament in good weather. Coincidence? Or Mind Magic?

Is "magic" a ritual-filled way to call upon our Mind over Matter abilities and to allow them to be applied to the natural world around us? Read on to Chapter Seven and find out.

But where is the field of parapsychology in all this? If things move around in a house (seemingly by themselves), it's not a sports psychologist or a doctor you call, it's a parapsychologist or psychical researcher. If someone claims to be able to levitate objects or bend metal with his bare mind, how do we know it's possible, that it is Mind over Matter rather than trickery? And can you learn to do this if it is real?

The latter part of our exploration into Mind over Matter will look at how our minds might truly extend themselves beyond the body.

Traditionally, besides a "live" sorcerer doing magical harm to people and objects, ghosts and spirits have been held responsible. But when people speak of "noisy ghosts," of poltergeists, what is really happening in such cases?

From the occult to ghosts, we'll look at the ultimate act of mind over matter: the psychokinetic temper tantrum. Poltergeist cases, in which physical objects such as books, pictures on the wall, glassware, and furniture move about and often shatter of their own accord, seem to have a common denominator: a living person who's generally around when things happen. Did you ever get angry and feel like you wanted to throw things, but didn't because it's not socially acceptable behavior? What if you could cause things to fly around and break without being blamed for it?

Chapter Eight will address the current model of poltergeist activity, that a living mind unconsciously directs itself outside the body to "let off steam." How this relates to psychological and physical stress, and therefore personal well-being, is the issue. We'll look at how this might work, including a possible connection to epilepsy, as well as the idea that "ghosts" (these being "minds without bodies") might also be players in this game. The main thrust of the chapter is to show the knock-down, drag-out poltergeist as an extreme, and rare, incident of the mind's ability to affect the outside world.

However, lesser displays by the mind and how they show up in cases investigated by the modern "ghostbusters" will be covered, including how living people sort of "help along" a haunting, when a ghost is not present.

What is the state of the art in field investigations of people's psychic experiences? What new devices and technologies are being used right now, and what is on the "wish list" of the modern "ghostbuster," especially when they are trying to "solve" a poltergeist case?

From here, we'll move more to other less violent subconscious PK effects and to purposeful attempts to affect matter by the mind. Can people mentally bend metal or is this fraud as many skeptics claim? Can we really affect objects at a distance? From levitation to teleportation, people have shown some extraordinary abilities with their minds throughout the centuries.

What's possible? That depends on how you look at Mind over Matter.

Has anything been proven in science? We'll take a very brief look at how the study of Mind over Matter evolved from looking at the physical mediums of the late nineteenth and early twentieth centuries to the laboratory researches of J.B. Rhine and his followers, as well as a discussion of the "hard" evidence for psychokinesis from parapsychology and other fields of science. In addition, I'll address the question of and speculation on whether this ability is a new one we are evolving or an old one we are rediscovering (though Martin Caidin also has something specific to say about this in Chapter Eleven).

Just for fun, I will also take a brief look at how TV, film, and literature (including comic books) have used Mind over Matter as a power for good and evil. After all, Yoda had some great advice for Luke Skywalker on Mind over Matter (in *The Empire Strikes Back*), didn't he?

Are these PK effects things we can all do? Are we already doing them? From the healing/harm of the body, we might extend our Mind over Matter influences to similar effects on technology.

Does your photocopier break down when you're stressed out and in a real hurry? Does your computer do strange things when you're in a bad mood? Does your car behave better when you talk to it?

Research over the past couple of decades has indicated that people have a real, though generally unconscious, effect on our machines and hi-tech equipment. Are you a "function-linked" person?

(Do certain pieces of technology work better for you? Can you "heal" a car just by touching it?)

Or are you "malfunction-linked" (Do things break down as you walk by them? Have a problem wearing watches?)

Chapter Ten will address everyday mind/matter interactions and how our mental attitudes seem to cause them (there's that belief thing, again).

Also to be discussed briefly are some ideas of how our minds could possibly exert some outside influence. (In other words, how could this work at all?)

From the discussion of what other people do consciously, what we do unconsciously and what's possible, we'll move to a way to try it yourself.

Can we learn to affect things consciously? The evidence says "Yes!" and this book will go over a method being taught to people by famed science fiction and aviation writer Martin Caidin. Besides his expertise on flying, the space program, and many other hard science and technology issues, Caidin has also become an expert on scientific anomalies and the paranormal. And his real-life accomplishments make Indiana Jones look like a wimp.

However, Caidin also has learned to do PK himself, and has been able to teach it to others. With comments from Caidin, as well as excerpts from his personal journal written while he was learning, we'll look at how you, the reader, can move objects yourself, based on Caidin's seven years of experience moving objects with sheer willpower.

In Chapter Eleven, contributed mostly by Martin Caidin, we'll explore his method by which you have a chance of experiencing Mind over Matter in a visual way, and how this might relate back to human performance and healing.

However, no fair treatment of the subject of Mind over Matter would be complete without discussion of the fraud that has been (and continues to be) perpetrated in the name of Mind over Matter.

So, in Chapter Twelve we'll take a look at the accusations of fraud leveled against so many physical mediums (and more modern psychics). People are often fascinated by the ways magicians and phony psychics can convince people they have miraculous power. We'll discuss this piece of the "psychology of deception," as well as some of the fraudulent mind/matter effects as uncovered by parapsychological researchers (including yours truly) and magicians. This will include a report on a phony psychic metal-bender who had less than limited success in convincing researchers of his abilities during a U.S. visit in 1994.

I will discuss some of the methods of fraudulent psychics, and throw in a couple of simple effects you can try out on friends. In addition, I want to say a word or two about what I *won't* reveal (the secrets magicians know) and why there's an ethical dilemma for a magician who observes psychic fraud.

So, as I bring this all back from the truly extraordinary abilities of so-called psychics to the perhaps extraordinary (though very explainable) skills of the sleight-of-hand artist, we are still left with the idea that the mind does in fact affect matter. The hard part for many to swallow is extending the effects beyond the body. But also hard to explain, at least right now, is *how* our bodies move when we tell them to, *how* we can initiate healing or harm on our own bodies.

And what does this all really mean?

What does an attitude of Mind over Matter really mean? From a basic level, it means that you, your mind, are responsible for your own well-being, both physically and mentally. You can bring about your own level of self-esteem and motivation. You can affect your own health, whether that means taking yourself to a doctor or mentally working toward healing yourself. You can also decide how to interact with others and how to treat them, whether to recycle or to mess up the environment, how to basically *be* in the world that we all share. Mind over Matter ultimately means taking personal responsibility for one's thoughts and actions, using your own *intent* to interact with people, places, and things, and to take the bad results with the good.

To finish our exploration of Mind over Matter, let's discuss the implications of Mind over Matter in all its forms as we know it today, and as it may develop in the future as more and more people accept it as real (and begin doing it consciously).

As part of our final discussion, I'd like to throw in a consumer-oriented discussion of how and why one must assess professed healing, fire-walking, and other mind/matter-type phenomena and methods.

And for those still thirsty for information after all that, I am including a brief resource list for further reading, organizations to contact, how you might get involved in the parapsychological end of the studies, and how the information superhighway is intersecting with our quest for answers.

Finally, there's a survey at the end of the book I'd like you to fill out. Have *you* experienced Mind over Matter? Fill this out and mail (or E-mail) your experiences and help us learn more about something we can all do.

My past three books have been, as one of my good friends put it, comprehensive in content, but not comprehensive in a way that shows what Loyd Auerbach has observed and concluded over the years. Since there are so many books out today that cover the mind/body connection, that touch on healing with its mental connection (such as the work of Bill Moyers, *Healing and the Mind*), what makes this book unique is not just the connection to what most people might consider "psychic," but my personal perspective, my training in parapsychology and magic, and my curiosity about human performance and unusual abilities.

So, this is not a book that's going to please the die-hard skeptics and debunkers (except in that it may give them ammunition to say I may be too accepting of what I see and hear). This is a book for those of you who want to explore the myriad ideas that come to mind when you hear the phrase "Mind over Matter" or "Mind Body Connection."

This is a journey of idea and thought. I think, therefore my fingers move to type. I think and a walk becomes a run. I think and I hit a baseball or golf ball farther and straighter. I think and I can kiss the woman I love. With practice, or under conditions of strong emotion, I can affect material objects beyond my body. My mind directs the matter of my body and the energy of my soul. The journey is from the way the mind acts on its own body to the mind stretching beyond the limits of the body to affect matter and energy around us.

So, let's move on to explore how the mind and body may connect. This will be a journey that will take us inside and outside ourselves, and certainly on an exploration of that vast frontier that goes from our left ear to our right.

Now, use that mind of yours to tell the matter of your fingers to turn the page and begin exploring. . . .

✳ **1** ✳

What Is Mind Over Matter?

Have you ever participated in a physical sport, say running, where you had to give yourself a little mental "push?" Did it work? Did you perform better, maybe run a little faster?

The human mind is the focus of the field of psychology. How the mind works, how it receives information and deals with it, how it communicates with the outside world, how it conjures up and displays emotions, how it functions properly or malfunctions, and how it changes and develops over the course of a lifetime are all topics of study for psychologists.

However, even though psychology as a field of science is over 100 years old, there is still no one consensus of how the mind works, let alone what it is. Depending on the "school" of psychology one subscribes to a person's perspective on the mind and behavior will be dramatically different. Freudians do not agree wholeheartedly with Jungians, even though they both deal heavily with the unconscious mind. Behavioral psychologists have a whole different approach, one that is more oriented to studying human behavior based on how the mind reacts to objective stimulation. Humanistic psychologists deal primarily with the idea of free will, where the conscious mind rules, rather than the unconscious or the physical environment.

And there are many more schools of thought other than those mentioned. In fact, while it appears we know so much about the functioning of the mind, by looking at the range of perspectives in psychology, one might come to the conclusion that the facts have been interpreted in dozens of ways, and that everybody seems to think his or her perspective is correct, and the other positions are wrong. We know a lot, but what we know has no real answer or consensus to it.

Of course, then there's the debate as to whether the mind is something separate from the brain, or if it's part of the brain's functions.

The human brain is a fascinating thing to study. We (meaning humanity and its accumulated science) know much about the workings of the brain, how neurons fire to activate certain signals in the body, how certain parts of the brain are more active during certain physical and mental activities, that damage to certain parts of the brain can permanently affect the mental and physical processes or might be rerouted by some kind of back-up system, and more.

But do we know all about the brain and how it works?

Hardly.

For example, memory is still far from completely understood. Our actual storage facility (where and how) for memories is still being searched for, and there are many theories concerning it. How some people are capable of retrieving seemingly any fact or idea they've absorbed and why some people are incapable of recalling a spouse's birthday is still a mystery. And how much memory we actual have (an identifiable quantity of storage, as with a computer) can only be speculated.

The brain's processes behind emotions are still far from understood.

How the brain allows for physical and mental multi-tasking is also not understood.

Multi-tasking is a phrase used much in relation to computers. It means that a computer is capable of performing many tasks at one time, hopefully without a loss of "quality" for any of them, with the added capability of switching from one task to another and back again. We know how a computer does that, since the computer was programmed by humans to achieve this state.

But what about people? Anyone who is doing more than one thing at a time, and is capable of redirecting one's attention from one task to another while doing them, is multi-tasking. As a friend of mine pointed out the other day, any mother of small children can tell you all about multi-tasking.

Think about this: while engaging a small child's mind (essentially trying to keep his or her attention), a mother might also be talking on the phone and cooking food or writing checks to pay the bills. My friend told me about many instances when she was holding her infant while on the phone (phone between shoulder and ear), and popping some food in the microwave at the same time.

Parents often learn to keep "one eye on the children, one eye on whatever one is physically doing, and one eye on the TV." How many of us grew up studying while watching TV or listening to music?

Doing more than one thing at a time, allowing our attention to cover many different tasks (both physical and mental), is multi-tasking.

Years ago, I worked as a bartender while attending graduate school. As I worked in a few very busy places, I had to be fast and more importantly attentive in order to keep up with the clientele. While mixing drinks (more than one at a time), I often had to take other drink orders, total up the cost of an order I was mixing, and at least pretend to listen to the customer at the bar trying to have a conversation with me. That's multi-tasking.

During graduate school, I saw a demonstration of multi-tasking by a man that, to this day, still amazes me. Luis Gasparetto is a "channeler" from Brazil. In an altered state of consciousness, some mild form of trance, he purports to be in contact with the spirits of artistic masters like Picasso, Rembrandt, Monet, and many more. With his hands (and sometimes his toes), using acrylic or oil paints, he quickly (often less than five minutes, sometimes as little as one minute) creates a painting identifiably in the style of the dead artist painting "through" him.

Is he really a deceased "master" painting through a living person? That's impossible to prove. However, the style in which he paints are undeniably that of each of the artists. Gasparetto has had no formal training as an artist. Most important is the ease and speed at which he creates original paintings, not merely copies of what we already know these artists have done.

Most impressive are the occasions during which he paints more than one painting at a time, one with each hand.

During the demonstration I saw years ago, Gasparetto asked for four sheets of paper, one for each hand and foot. Paints were placed on palettes near each appendage. He went into what looked like a light trance and began to paint. Each of the four paintings being created at the same time was in a different artist's style. And Gasparetto, his eyes closed, was also carrying on a conversation with the audience at the same time, relaying "messages" from each of the artists painting "through" him.

Absolutely amazing.

Is Gasparetto a case of a true spirit medium? As someone who studies ideas and experiences of life after death, I was and am more than intrigued by his demonstrations. But it's not proof of the existence of spirits. It could be "simply" an unusual case of mind over matter, multitasking at its best.

Gasparetto's creative abilities indicate that the human mind is capable of extraordinary multitasking. Now maybe Gasparetto is merely "wired" differently than the rest of us. Or maybe outside spirits are using their "minds" to affect his body. In any event, signals from his brain were telling each hand and each foot to paint, while at the same time, his brain was listening to what the audience was saying and asking, processing that, and responding with signals to the speech center.

His mind was directing his body in a way seemingly out of the reach of the rest of us. This is an extreme example of multiple-task processing.

But what is it that sparks the multitasking? What is it that initiates the firing of the neurons necessary to do that, or simply to order the brain to order your body to pick up the book you're reading.

It all boils down to the mind.

Psychologists and psychiatrists and even parapsychologists study the mind. Or do they?

In reality, to study something, one must have definitive evidence it exists. At least, this is the argument many of the skeptics of psychic phenomena use.

In studying the mind, scientists are really studying the outward display of mind: human behavior, human perceptions, human communication, and communication of subjective human experiences.

Is it really possible to study the mind? First we must define it. *Webster's New World Dictionary* (Second College Edition, 1986) says, a) that which thinks, perceives, feels, wills, etc.; seat or subject of consciousness, b) the thinking and perceiving part of consciousness; intellect or intelligence, c) attention; notice, d) all of an individual's collected experiences, e) the conscious mind and unconscious together as a unit; psyche."

This brings in the other term used for mind today, *Consciousness*.

The same dictionary defines *consciousness* as "1. the state of being conscious; awareness of one's own feelings, what is going on around one, etc." and "2. the totality of one's thoughts, feelings, and impressions; conscious mind."

One of the entries in Webster's defines the *unconscious* as "the sum of all thoughts, memories, impulses, desires, feelings, etc. of which the individual is not conscious but which influence his emotions and behavior."

Trying to find a definition of "mind" is not an easy thing. The best definitions point to the term "mind" covering mental processes. Many discussions of mind see it as a byproduct of the brain, while others separate it from the brain. Consciousness is often used interchangeably with mind, while others give consciousness the nudge beyond the brain, as incorporating the spiritual part of human nature.

But what *is* the mind?

The word *psychokinesis* is used by parapsychologists to indicate the mind's influence on material objects and events and on energy. Many scientists argue that psychokinesis (or PK) is impossible, that the mind can't extend its influence beyond the body.

But how do they know?

They may *assume* it's impossible because not all people can demonstrate PK beyond the body, and even those who claim they can do it can't do it with any real regularity. They may talk about there not being an explanation for such an influence in physics, therefore it doesn't happen.

However, there are two problems with assuming PK to be impossible based on such assumptions.

First of all, science cannot define the mind except in terms of behavior and reported subjective experience. There is no physical evidence for the existence of a mind or consciousness (unlike the evidence for the brain's existence and processes).

Secondly, physics is always expanding as we learn more and more about the physical universe (which includes us, of course). We may have no explanation for this today, but perhaps tomorrow we will.

So, to say mind can *not* affect matter outside the body is silly, considering one must know the limitations of mind before saying what it is ultimately capable or incapable of.

I also find it interesting that the main problem people have with psychokinesis is the idea that our minds can influence matter and energy *beyond* the limits of our bodies. Again, we don't really know what limits the physical body places on our minds. However, most people do accept that our minds do have a real effect on our bodies.

But what *is* the mind? That's still the major question of the day.

Throughout this book, as we discuss "mind over matter" we will explore not only psychokinesis, influence at a distance, but the greater, more encompassing notion that the mind affects matter and energy from the inside of the body to the outside world. In essence, without placing limits on the mind and what it is apparently physically connected to (brain and body), it's easier to see how any decision made by the conscious or unconscious mind can lead to some influence on the physical world of our bodies and that around our bodies.

And when I use the word mind (and occasionally, perhaps, the word consciousness), especially in connection with its affect on matter, I am referring to an *intent* of the conscious and unconscious mind to cause an effect, whether that effect be to lick one's lips or levitate an object. Intention, decisive direction, is the thought that initiates the action.

Parapsychologists have studied a wide range of effects under the umbrella of psychokinesis, yet most involve the influence of mind beyond the body. While it is recognized that self-healing is psychokinesis (at least by many parapsychologists), this is usually left to people in the medical field.

The definition of what parapsychologists study involves direct mind contact or connection with either information not perceived by the "normal" senses (also known as extrasensory perception—ESP—or, more recently, as *extended perception*), or with influence by mind directly on outside events, objects, and physical processes (that's psychokinesis). It also involves the study of evidence of the survival of human personality (mind, consciousness, spirit, soul, or whatever else you want to call it) beyond the death of the body, with that evidence indicating the personality that survives is capable of both communication and interaction (the latter being, of course, mind over matter).

In the Introduction, I mentioned a few subjects of parapsychology such as levitation and psychic healing, as well as mental influence on technology such as computers, watches, and even cars. Parapsychologists, in their process of labeling the phenomena for study, have grouped the effects into two categories for experimentation. Effects you can see, such as movement of objects, bending of spoons, and levitation are considered "macro-PK," whereas effects too small for the human eye to see, such as effects on the inner processes of a computer, the decay of some radioactive material, or even healing (working on the processes of the body) would be categorized as "micro-PK." Effects on energy (such as electricity) fall in there, too. Micro-PK effects take place at the microscopic or even atomic or subatomic level, requiring sophisticated equipment to keep track of them.

Of course, this "sophisticated equipment" can also include human perception. When a person is being "healed," one can often see or test for the effect of the healing, but there is also the subjective perception that one is feeling better.

Micro-PK studies have for the most part been conducted with random event generators (REGs), which are devices that internally include a truly random system, such as a piece of radioactive element that gives off particles randomly or perhaps a device that generates random signals, and externally have some mode of providing feedback to the users. Since the random system will stay random, the goal is for the user to try to cause it to be nonrandom, to affect the system (kind of like trying to convince a coin to turn up heads more than tails in a long series of coin tosses). The feedback may be a sound signal or a visual display (a light or even some kind of picture on a computer screen).

Micro-PK studies are popular among parapsychologists because more trials can be run in a shorter amount of time and that makes the results more subject to statistical analysis. In addition, the possibility of experimenter error or of subject fraud is very low compared to, say, an experimenter handing a spoon over to a "psychic" who then proceeds to misdirect the experimenter's attention and bend the spoon with purely physical force.

However, there are studies of macro-PK going on out there (more on these in Chapters Eight to Twelve), and can be much more interesting (and fun).

Macro-PK effects are not just object movements. There have been many reports of teleportations, of materializations and dematerializations of objects, of mental effects on photographs and even video- and audiotape, and even the destruction of objects (such as a vase or glass seeming to explode or implode).

Macro-PK effects are at the heart of the poltergeist phenomenon. While the movies and some folklore typically puts an evil or mischievous spirit as the cause of the events (as in the movie *Poltergeist*), the working model of parapsychologists places the unconscious mind of a living human as the causal agent. There is often an element of extreme stress in the makeup of the agent, making the poltergeist outbursts of PK more like a psychic temper tantrum (as in the movie and book *Carrie*).

While parapsychologists typically consider only these apparent displays of the mind influencing outside objects and events to be mind over matter, I believe that in every level of mental influence— from athletic performance (pushing the body to its limits) to self-healing, from causing the body to limit damage to it (as with people who walk on hot coals) to causing an object outside the body to move—the key factor is the mind, or some part of the mind, making a decision to cause something to happen, in the body and out.

It's all Mind over Matter. Call it psychokinesis, telekinesis, mind over matter, or simply force of will, the mind affects matter.

Ultimately, if we can truly affect our own bodies and the outside world, our minds may be a lot more powerful in shaping our lives than we, as humans, have typically accepted.

There is much power here. Unfortunately, all power can be applied in a positive or negative fashion. While accepting that we, that our minds, can truly affect change in ourselves (and outside ourselves), we also have to accept some responsibility for the thoughts behind our actions.

The athlete who believes he can push himself to break the world record he's going after can just as easily convince himself he can't break the record, that it was a fluke, that humans weren't "meant to do that."

The student who goes into a test (having fully prepared with appropriate information, of course) can succeed marvelously because of her belief that she really knows her stuff, or fail miserably because she questions her memory.

The martial artist about to break ten stacked boards will either do it, or not. Failure, however, may be based on her not believing she, personally, is capable of breaking more than eight boards.

Western medical science has been, for a very long time, based on the idea that intangible forces, such as the mind, had little or no effect on the body. As the social science of psychology (and its offshoot, psychiatry) developed, as people such as Freud and Jung brought up ideas to challenge this underlying belief in medicine, doctors have had to make some changes to their attitudes, but those changes have typically been minimal or slow in coming.

Today, we know our mental states clearly affect our bodies and therefore our health. Mental and emotional stress can cause severe physical repercussions, from muscular problems to ulcers and possibly even some forms of cancer. A patient already ill can be adversely affected if he or she gives up on getting better (or, worse, believes that getting sicker is the only thing that will happen).

Doctors have long recognized that a will to survive and/or a desire to be healthy can speed up recovery (or cause recovery to commence in the first place). But do they know *how* that really works? No. But this mind/body relationship is accepted as fact.

Studies have been conducted with actors purposely evoking emotional responses in order to see if those emotions are "real," whether there are any subsequent changes in the brain/body. The results are quite telling, that there is a physiological response.

Many have said we're in the midst of a mind/body revolution, as Western science may be having to rethink its position on the question of the mind itself. Eastern medicine has long seen that a balance between mind and body must exist in order to have good health.

Healers in many nontraditional (from the Western perspective) disciplines, from the acupuncturist to the psychic, have also recognized the need for mental cooperation by the patient. Psychic healers, for example, often mention that there can be no effect on the client if the client doesn't want to be affected.

Conversely, that would lead one to the conclusion that one can't be adversely affected by whatever process a psychic uses if the "target" doesn't want to be hurt or made ill.

Strangely, one does not have to believe the "power" actually comes from within oneself to achieve excellent physical performance or perfect health or levitation. God (or various gods) or spirits or Fate or other mystical powers are often believed to be the power that heals, or blamed as the power that harms. For many (maybe even most) people, to believe one might be able to heal or harm oneself (or others) can be rather scary, so it's far easier to place the responsibility with an outside power or intelligence, a force of nature or a deity.

And who's to say that the power on which our minds draw doesn't come from divine or mystical source? I can't, for sure.

However, for the duration of this book, I ask you to give some power to the human mind. Let's assume a few things and see where that leaves us at the end of this book:

Mind over Matter means any effect of the mind on matter and energy, whether that matter and energy be in the body or outside.

Mind over Matter requires some conscious or unconscious desire or need, a bit of *intent* that something happen for it to occur.

Mind over Matter requires some *belief* in the effect actually coming to pass for it to occur.

Mind over Matter does not depend on whether the intent or the effect is considered *positive* or *negative* for it to happen.

Mind over Matter means you can affect yourself and, to a lesser degree, the world around you.

Mind over Matter applies to all sorts of effects, from raising your hand to pushing your body seemingly beyond the limits of "normal" athletic performance.

Let's start there, shall we.

Outstanding Human Physical Performance

Sports and Other Mind-Body Performances

The professional golf player steps up to the tee and stares down the ball. She places the head of the club next to the ball, then raises her own head, turns toward the direction of the green, and, in her mind, "sees" a dotted line drawn from the tee, through the air, to a point just near the green, yet not quite on it. She "sees" the ball in her mind's eye following that pathway.

Her face turns back to the ball, she swings, and follows through. The spectators watch as the ball flies through the air, the player smiling inwardly to herself as the ball follows exactly the path her mind had "drawn" for it.

The pro quarterback pulls back from the line, looking for an opening to throw at the right teammate. One of the men waves his hands. He's clear. The quarterback pulls his arm back and lets the ball fly, just as he is hit by the other team.

The ball is knocked slightly off course by the tackle. It flies in the general direction of the intended receiver, but it looks like it will go off to the side, into the waiting arms of one of the opposing players. Both the downed quarterback and the targeted receiver call out to the ball, mentally.

Just as the ball looks like it will drop into the hands of the wrong player, it veers off in what looks like a ninety-degree turn, right into the grasp of the right receiver. After a moment of shock experienced by everyone on the field (and in the stands), the receiver takes off for a run and a touchdown. He looks at the ball and shakes his head, wondering just how a long pass could act as it did.

The runner mentally reviewed the facts. Roger Bannister had broken the unbreakable barrier: he beat the four-minute mile.

Incredible, thought the runner. *No one* could beat that record. But Bannister did. That means I could, too.

The runner took off at the signal. All he could think about was the fact that the maximum limit to human speed was no longer what everyone thought it was. Bannister proved it wasn't impossible. As he thought about this, he realized that time itself seemed to be slowing down. The seconds seemed like minutes, but he knew he was moving very fast.

Then, just as the finish line was in his field of vision, he felt like he'd been shot out of a slingshot as time sped up to normal. He passed the finish line almost immediately after.

The crowd cheered and his coach slapped him on the back, congratulating him for also beating the unbeatable barrier of the four-minute mile.

After more than a couple of years since I'd last gone bowling, I was doing it again, this time in Florida with my author buddy Martin Caidin and a friend of his. My first game didn't even top 90, the second just over 100. Now in the third game, I was back into the "spirit."

I stepped up to the ball return, and pulled out the bowling ball with my hands. I readied myself for the throw. All I tried to think about was that feeling I used to get when I was a kid, that feeling of detachment from myself, a connection with the ball that meant the ball would go exactly where I wanted it. I stood still for what seemed like minutes (but which I knew, based on the sounds from the other alleys around me, was merely seconds). I felt a sense of calm come over me as I stared at the pins down the alley.

Suddenly, I felt as though I was truly detached from what I was doing. I watched, almost as a dispassionate observer, as my feet started moving, and my arms geared up for the throw. As I approached the line, I watched as the ball flew from my hand, bounced once, and headed straight down the alley. I turned and walked back toward Marty and Ken without even thinking about what was happening behind me, merely listening for the strike of the balls on the pins.

Marty and Ken stood up as I heard the pins go down. I knew all of them were over.

"Perfect strike," said Marty. "Now *that's* telekinesis!"

While I was unable to achieve that same sense of detachment throughout the game, my score jumped to 183, thanks to some warming up, and a bit of Mind over Matter directed at myself (and at the ball).

*

Roger Bannister broke the four-minute-mile record back in 1954, and was followed soon by dozens of others. Once the impossible is no longer such, others try and succeed. The limits we put on physical performance are seemingly only one part physical, and one part mental. With some appropriate *intent* and the ability to ignore or shrug off the limitations others place on us, what is impossible becomes quite possible.

Sports psychology explores the limits we place on ourselves, and the ways the mind can be used to achieve desired levels of performance. Not all are accepting of some of the work in this fairly new subfield of psychology, but the power of positive thinking, how an athlete "psychs" himself or herself up for a performance, has long been a recognized part of the preparation for whatever athletic performance one is after.

For years, golfers and other athletes have used mental imagery, such as described at the beginning of the chapter, to help get their minds set for a specific goal. Athletes and coaches all over the world have become more and more aware that the proper mental conditioning and preparation can help—or hinder—their performance. To push oneself beyond the boundaries or limits of performance—

what's possible—one must first overcome the very idea of those limitations.

Over the past fifteen years or so, the "power of positive thinking" has evolved into an emphasis on using the mind to help push oneself further and further on the physical level, both for the professional athlete and for the "weekend warrior." A recognition that limitations are just as tied to psychology as to physiology has led to coaches and trainers focusing on the mental preparation for peak performance, and the downplay of any sort of set limit for just what human beings can do (before they get tired or hurt themselves).

Consequently, more and more books, both of an academic nature and for a general audience, focus on mind/body relationships in athletics. Sports psychology has become an exciting specialization for psychologists and professional athletic trainers.

There is just so much one can do with sheer muscle power. However, whatever one does with that muscle, speed, and agility is completely controlled by the mind. For athletes in training, the conditioning of the physical body must include a conscious focus on how to do, how to perform, until it becomes nearly a reflex.

A hockey player has no time to think an action through before blocking other players who have suddenly gotten control of the puck. A pitcher has to make a near telepathic connection with a player about to steal a base, so he can throw the ball without thinking, at the same time the player takes off for the stolen base. A martial artist must automatically anticipate a forthcoming blow in order to block it.

Part of the preparation for athletic performance is purely physical. Exercise and repetitive movements to train the body, as well as practice of the actual movements needed for whatever sport of physical activity one will participate in is essential. The body needs to prepare itself, to "learn" the movements so they come free and easy.

The athlete must learn the mental state and attitude, as well, to bring out the best physical performance. The mental part of the preparation may include relaxation exercises, meditation, and guided imagery. Imagining oneself "winning," beating the performance limits, helps one's mind-set and are essential.

Studies have been conducted that show that imagining, or visualizing the actual movements one will go through in the athletic performance, will actually help prep the muscles for the actual movements. Physiological measurements taken during studies of such visualizations has revealed that there is actual activity in the muscles, even though they're not actually moving.

When I first read about this, it was in the context of an application to doing magic (as in sleight of hand). An article I read suggested that the studies conducted with athletes could be applied to the physical and mental preparation required in practicing sleight of hand. By running a hand movement repetitively through the mind's eye, the muscles themselves would gear up for the actual activity.

For me, as interested as I am in how the mind affects all forms of matter, this was an experiment I could try, even though (or perhaps especially since) I don't do a lot of sleight of hand. The performing I have done as a magician has pretty much fallen into a couple of broad categories. I mostly do comedy magic, whether close up, at a private party or on stage. What that means is that the magic I perform hopefully occurs with a funny theme or outcome. Some of the effects require some dexterity with coins or cards or ropes, but most have built-in structure so that one can focus on the presentation rather than the handling of the effect. In other words, you're not likely to see me do a lot of fancy flourishes or manipulations of a deck of cards.

The other form of magic I do comes under the heading of mentalism, or mental magic. This is a category that involves the entertaining presentation of effects that appear to be supernatural or psychic in nature. Some sleight of hand is involved with mental effects, but for the most part the really tough sleights surround the handling of coins, cards, ropes, and other similar items.

The idea of using visualization to learn to as an aid in learning a new movement for magic was interesting for a lazy person like me (some magicians practice handling cards hours a day. I mentally "practiced" a few card movements, and found that I was able to do what I thought were difficult movements fairly quickly.

I also recall a situation in which I tried again and again (and failed again and again) to learn a particular rope trick. I "got" the effect in a flash of insight while watching a fellow magician perform the same trick, picked up the ropes I had had no success with, and performed it perfectly. My mind suddenly caught on, followed immediately by the correct actions of my hands. If that isn't Mind over Matter, I don't know what is.

So, I tried visualizing my hands going through the directed motions on a card effect and a coin effect. I deliberately avoided physical practice (except for the first time I tried it in order to see what motions I had to practice). I mentally practiced the effects for two weeks, a few times each day, then picked up the physical props to try the effects.

I surprised myself with how well I actually did the effects. After the two weeks of mental "practicing," I was doing the effects better, I thought, than I could if I had practiced them physically. To this day, when I work on physical manipulation in my magic, I spend more time on the mental preparation than on physical rehearsal (and believe I am a better performer for it).

Athletes not only take part today in such deliberate mental preparation as sports psychology teaches; they also recognize the mental and emotional states they can spontaneously get into when they perform well.

In 1978, Michael Murphy and Rhea White wrote an excellent book called *The Psychic Side of Sports* (Addison-Wesley Publishing Company). The book is, I believe, a milestone in looking at how mind and body come together to produce peak performances. Filled with anecdotes and examples of how athletes push their limits through achievement of various states of mind and consciousness, including states that appear quite mystical or spiritual, the book has long been out of print and difficult to find. However, I was pleased to see that a second, updated edition of the book, now retitled *In the Zone: Transcendent Experience in Sports* (Penguin/Arkana, 1995) was just published as I was working toward this very chapter (wonderful synchronicity, that).

Murphy and White are eminently suited to write this kind of overview of such experiences. Murphy is one of the founders of Esalen Institute, and is author of a number of books relevant to the study of the mind/body question, and to sports, including *Golf in the Kingdom* and recent massive tome on mind/body questions, *The Future of the Body.*

Rhea White has had a longtime connection to the field of para-psychology. She has been editor of The Journal of the American Society for Psychical Research and runs the Parapsychological Sources of Information Center (PSI Center) on Long Island, NY. She is also founder of the Exceptional Human Experience Network and publishes a journal that should be of great interest to readers of this book, Exceptional Human Experience (see Appendix A for information on the journal).

Many athletes have used the phrase "in the/my zone" in referring to that mental and physical state in which they can achieve (or surpass) peak performance. The key with all such experiences is a lack of doubt, a lack of the fear of success, and an accompanying self-confidence that what can be attempted can be achieved. There are often various shifts in how they are experiencing themselves and the world around them. They may experience detachment, watching their own bodies work almost without conscious direction. This may even go further to the athlete having out-of-body experiences, essentially experiencing the event as though watching their bodies from a vantage point outside themselves.

Often there is a build up of excitement before the event, but athletes often report feeling quite peaceful and calm during the athletic achievement, the excitement of success hitting afterward. Murphy and White also report other states of experience, including a sense of unity with others and with the environment around them, or an overwhelming sense of awe at what is happening, or that ultimate ego-place where the athlete may feel in total control of the entire situation and the environment in which it's taking place.

In addition, athletes have often reported an awareness of the environment in which they are performing that seems to go beyond ordinary perceptions. While it is true that we all perceive much more than our conscious minds will "admit," and while such subliminal perceptions can trigger a physical response, athletes have reported many circumstances in which it would appear that their perception has extended beyond what can be considered anything pulled in by the "normal" senses.

A pitcher may have an immediate reaction to the base-stealer behind him starting to move, without being able to see him even with peripheral vision. A quarterback may somehow "know" what the defense is going to do well before they even come back to the line of scrimmage. Athletes are no different from the rest of us when it comes to ESP, or what psychologist Dr. Keith Harary has called *extended perception.*

One of the more interesting mental "spaces" athletes find themselves in relates to alterations in perception of time and space. As with the runner's example at the beginning of this chapter, a shift in time, usually with time slowing down for the performer, may take place. Or perhaps the distance between two points a runner is running between or a trapeze artist is "flying" between, shrinks, so the physical power and speed needed to get there is well within the athlete's grasp.

For anyone doing something athletic or physical, achieving a goal depends on both physical ability and on mental attitude and intent. The former, however, may be stretched a bit, as we all tend to have reserves of energy and power that we can only seemingly tap into in emergencies or under conditions that encourage us to do something physical. Our strength may temporarily increase or our speed of movement shoot up, but that may be simply because we haven't tried to find our limits before. For those who continuously try to reach and surpass their limits, the reserves may be less a matter of "not knowing one's own strength" but more a matter of "I think I can," like the children's story *The Little Engine that Could.*

The big question, then, is how can some athletes and other individuals seemingly do things that appear to be well past their limits? How can the power weight lifter lift so many more pounds than the tensile strength for which muscle and ligament would apparently allow? How can people still perform their athletic feats after an immediately preceding injury, which they may not even acknowledge until after the goal is reached? How can people like Michael Jordan seemingly leap into the air, yet look as though they are floating, when it should be just the athlete's perceptions that are altered, not the spectators?

Currently, there is a consensus that the mind affects athletic performance. Positive, self-confident attitudes and mental states, which reinforce the "no limit" idea can positively enhance an athlete's performance. Believing one cannot perform a certain action or beat a record, or worse, that one can't perform well without artificial enhancements such as drugs (which do their own damage to the body, and only make the mind dependent on them for any sort of good performance), creates limits that may be impossible to beat.

Mind seems to affect body in a way that allows for physiological energy/power/speed/strength reserves to be tapped. Mind also seems to be able to, in certain situations, reach beyond the body and bring in energy and attributes that allow an individual to surpass what the body is physically capable of. For us all, this means that if we can constantly reinforce the "I think I can" attitude, visualize the activity and make it easier for the body to do the action, we may reach a point where physical activity is easy and where limits can be reduced to moot points.

Beyond this, though, are the situations in which the body is no longer in contact with the object that is performing so well. Granted that there is a definite affect that the human body has on a golf ball, a bowling ball, a football, or a baseball. The right, or wrong, spin on the ball, or the right/wrong amount of power applied to cause the ball to move can send it on many right or wrong pathways.

Psychokinesis, Mind over Matter, is not merely the province of the psychic. We all have this ability, and that would include athletes. Under certain circumstances, which appear to involve the athlete's mental state and belief in the existence/nonexistence of the limits of performance, there are situations in which the mind of the athlete appears to be affecting the matter of the ball (or even other athletes).

Over the years, I had heard about psychokinesis from athletes and TV personnel I knew. My father, Dick Auerbach, was employed by NBC Sports in a variety of capacities (mostly as a producer and later as a vice-president) from the early 1960s to the late 1970s. He worked on a wide range of sports, from producing the baseball and football games of the week, events involving skiing and karate, Wimbledon tennis, and the 1964 and 1972 Olympics.

During his tenure there, I met a number of athletes, and even got to work as a "runner" at some of the baseball and football games in New York and Chicago. Sometimes my interest in parapsychology would come up and I would often hear a story about something "strange" that had happened on the field during a game or event.

It became clear to me, after hearing these again and again, that the players sometimes were able to "give a little push" to the ball, whether they were golfers or pitchers or quarterbacks. Other players related being able to grab whatever kind of ball it was from the air, even though it looked to them as though the ball's angle, distance, and velocity would absolutely preclude that. I saw footage at one point of a football taking a right angle turn away from an opposing player into the hands of the intended receiver.

These "weird sports stories" go far beyond what are thought to be limitations of human performance. As do many extraordinary physical achievements.

The Martial Arts

A number of years ago, I worked at the American Society for Psychical Research. My half-time position was that of a consultant on Public Information and Media (a sort of public relations position), yet I also participated in some experiments performed at the wonderful location the ASPR has on the Upper West Side in Manhattan.

One such series involved work with a martial arts master and teacher from Kirtland, Ohio, who claimed he had psychokinetic and telepathic abilities.

Master Guy Savelli claimed to be able to do a number of things that came from his martial arts training. Many of them involved physically affecting people and objects at a distance based on moving "energy."

Several tests were set up for him by Dr. Karlis Osis, research director of the ASPR (now retired) and researcher Donna McCormick. While I had little to do with the setting up or running of the experiments, I was there during one experimental series in which Savelli attempted to "break" an infrared beam (as used in security devices) without physically doing so. He focused his attention on where he was told the beam was, then pushed his open palm in that direction (this from several feet away from the beam). He was able to cause a break in the beam in most of the repeated trials.

In addition to the infrared beam, strain-gauge sensors, which can sense small physical movement, and temperature sensors were used to check for disturbances in the area of the target (the beam).

Savelli achieved strong movements of the strain-gauges, and some weaker indications that temperature was affected. His son, Bradley, who also attempted to affect the targets, had better success with the temperature measures.

Savelli then attempted to teach a brief technique to Donna and myself. For me, the experience was both frustrating and finally exhilarating. I recall his guided visualization quite vividly, as it was not a "peaceful" visualization, but rather one you might consider was more in keeping with the martial arts.

He asked that I visualize myself as a hunting animal (I chose a wolf) and that I was hunting someone or something I disliked, that I "see" myself stalking this target through a forest or jungle, thinking all the while how much I disliked or even hated the target. Then, I was told to visualize catching up with the target, leaping and striking. At the moment of the strike, Savelli instructed me to throw the "energy" of the attack, of the emotion, at the place where the infrared beam was.

A number of images flashed through my mind at the time, however none with any real negative emotion attached. All I learned was that there was little I really hated (and this included people). It was frustrating, and Savelli could see that.

So, he told me to use that frustration as my negative energy, to build on that, to visualize situations that had caused me great frustration. Nothing. Then Donna McCormick piped up with "what about the ASPR documentary project and the board?", something I was very frustrated by at the time.

I felt intense emotion, opened my hand at the location of the beam, and was immediately told the infrared beam was interrupted. Success!

So, for some, frustration can cause a "negative" emotional response that can be translated into an "energy." This makes sense, as frustration is a stress-related reaction. In this case, I directed the frustration outward. For many people, the outward direction of frustration is done through physical activity (everything from athletics to chopping wood to, unfortunately, beating someone). For others, it may be directed outward in other ways involving Mind over Matter issue (see Chapter Eight on poltergeists). In many situations, it's directed inward, and may cause damage to the body.

The philosophical component of the martial arts can be a way to relieve stress, or better, to redirect the energy of the emotions. While most people think of martial arts as purely physical in nature, the various martial arts, in their pure forms, rely heavily on the mind and its manipulation of life energy, whether used in conjunction with the body (throwing blows) or, as Savelli demonstrated, as energy that can with little or no physical contact.

According to many true masters of the various martial arts, it is the use of the mind in controlling the life force energy, the *chi* (pronounced "chee," also spelled *ch'i* or *qi* in the Chinese usage, and *ki* in the Japanese usage).

By properly utilizing one's chi, by using the mind to focus one's energy, blows struck can break things normally unbreakable, damage to the body can be minimalized or prevented, and pain is next to nonexistent. While all martial arts training, to be somewhat effective, must include much of the same performance-confidence relationship that all sports do, doing what may be considered "extraordinary" feats requires much more mental work than physical. As in all performance of the body, if the mind does not back up the body, damage will occur to the performer, to the person throwing the blow, as much if not more than to the target or "enemy."

The philosophy of most martial arts in relation to the use of chi is not strictly limited to using it for defensive or offensive fighting. If you have been watching the reincarnation of David Carradine's martial arts show now in syndication, *Kung Fu: The Legend Continues,* you've seen the grandson of the original character Kwai Chang Caine, also a Shaolin priest, throwing blows that affect people from a distance and even through walls or other barriers. But you've also seen him use his chi to open locked doors, to manipulate physical matter, and to heal (the healing side of the martial arts will be discussed briefly in Chapter Five).

In motion pictures and on television since the 1960s, there have been probably hundreds of films and episodes of television series that have martial arts demonstrations. While most have involved the fighting prowess of heroes (as portrayed by people such as Bruce Lee, Brandon Lee, Chuck Norris, and David Carradine) and villains, every once in a while one sees more than just a good fight as the martial artist displays some unusual abilities, whether related to stealth, fighting, or healing.

I have always believed there was something "more" than pure physical training happening in the martial arts.

In a film clip I once saw a hand breaking a brick shot at one thousand frames per second. It looked like the brick broke *before* the hand struck it. I have no idea where that film is, however I have heard of other such films and tapes that apparently show targets breaking before being struck, as if the hand is preceded by some energy that does the damage. (I have even heard debunking of the idea of some "energy" or "force" breaking the target; the debunker claimed that if the target really broke before being struck by the hand, it was because of a buildup of air pressure due to the velocity of the hand, and that the pressure wave broke the target. Sure, that makes so much more sense! I think not!)

If one goes through David Chow and Richard Spangler's book, *Kung Fu: History, Philosophy and Technique* (Burbank, CA: Unique Publications, 1977), one will react with either increased interest or with disbelief. Sure, we all see martial artists in films and on TV doing all sorts of amazing things, but that's "fiction." To see some of those actions described in a serious text on Kung Fu is quite another thing.

In the book, there are descriptions of the use of one's chi to affect objects and people at a distance. Descriptions include injuring an adversary at a distance using the palms of the hand or a single finger to project energy, altering one's body weight so as to walk or run lightly across the ground without disturbing a grain of sand or a blade of grass, leaping vast distances from a standing position, and climbing a wall (with your back to it) with simply the pressure of your hands and heels.

While we tend to see such activities in fictional representations, many of the martial arts traditions teach that these otherwise extraordinary skills can be achieved by the proper balance of one's mind/body state and the chi that flows inside both.

Reading books by martial artists provides a good background in what the "masters" of these arts claim are possible achievements both with physical prowess and with appropriate mental conditioning and perspective. Murphy and White's *In the Zone* also provides examples of extraordinary achievements by martial artists, but only through watching displays by "masters" of their arts, especially those who truly understand and practice the philosophies of the various martial arts, can one get a good idea of what the mind is capable of pushing the body to do, as compared to those who just use the power of the human body (generally Western practitioners of the martial arts who are mostly into the fighting and competitive side of the arts).

The origin of martial arts is surrounded by legend and controversy. There are descriptions of various fighting techniques in a number of historical sources, from the Bible to the records of ancient Greece. However, the history of what are truly labeled martial arts is wrapped up in the development of fighting skills in India and China.

Some sources give credit to Tai Chi as the first of the Eastern martial arts, while others cite a form of boxing as developed by Shaolin monks in China as the founding technique, which evolved into Kung Fu. Many are unaware that there are martial arts in India that are quite similar in style to that of Kung Fu (such as Kalaripayat), and the history of the arts seemed to be tied to a legend that would tie both nations together.

Legend has it that an Indian Buddhist monk named Bodhidharma came to a Shaolin monastery in China in the early part of the sixth century, A.D., there to introduce a philosophy that became Zen Buddhism, a more meditative form. Long meditations required some physical exercise that could help keep the balance in the body. In addition, the monks needed ways to defend themselves against attackers in the mountainous area of the Temple. These exercises and breathing techniques evolved into a Kung Fu.

The spread of the philosophies of Buddha and Confucius throughout the Far East led to the spread of the defense techniques. Both the fighting techniques and the internal, mental techniques and the philosophies that went along with them were culturally transmitted and taught as the ideologies also spread. As they came into contact with diverse cultures, there were changes or adaptations or evolutions in the techniques, and so developed other, apparently related, arts such as those in Japan (Judo, Nin-jutsu, Aikido, Okinawa (Karate), Burma (Bando, kick-boxing traditions), Thailand (Thai boxing, Karabi krabong), Malaysia (Bersilat), and Korea (Tae kwon do, Tang soo do, Hwarang do).

While not enough historical evidence really exists to come to definite conclusions about the origins of specific martial arts, there is evidence that the influence of India and China is at the root of the development of, or significant influence on the styles of these other countries. The most significant piece connecting these arts is the reliance on chi, called *prana* in the Yogic system of India, and the similarities between the ancient Indian fighting arts and those of the Shaolin in China.

In more recent times, martial arts have shifted and new "schools" of the martial arts have developed. Aikido, for example, is a very new art developed this century by Japanese martial artist Morihei Uyeshiba, a student of a number of martial arts styles and techniques. Aikido relies on throwing techniques, and in the use of ki (chi). In effect, Aikido teaches "harmony" with the universe, and a unity that allows the practitioner to connect with the universe. An opponent to the practitioner is, in effect, opposing the universe itself, and who can win against those odds. It is through use of the mind's control of ki that one connects and becomes "one" with the universe.

Other martial arts styles and "schools" have developed, and the arts continue to evolve. Bruce Lee developed his own style, a synthesis of many other martial arts, called Jeet Kune Do. Lee himself was legendary in his abilities, which included demonstrations such as being able to knock an opponent across a room from a standing position, close to that opponent (with no room to pull back for a momentum gathering power punch).

Other martial artists continue to evolve their styles and techniques, often combining from several diverse traditions and schools of training. Yet the place of the mind in the arts is emphasized among the best of them, both in developing the abilities to size up and anticipate an opponent's abilities and actions, and in bolstering what the body is actually capable of.

Of course, there can also be much in the way of legend built up around the martial arts, and in the past, martial artists have actually encouraged superstition and supernatural prowess associated with their abilities.

We've seen much in the way of portrayals of the Ninja warrior, how they reputedly can do amazing physical acrobatics, can appear to hide in the shadows so effectively as to be invisible, can use almost anything as a weapon, and vanish as soon as they are "done" in a location. Other talents have been attributed to the ninja over the centuries including vaporizing into smoke, breathing underwater, changing shape into animals, flying, and even hypnotizing an enemy.

Ninjas seem to fascinate the public not only in this country, but in many others (and certainly in Japan, where Ninjas have even been transformed to cuddly animated characters). Ninjutsu (also spelled Nin-jutsu or Ninjitsu), the art of the Ninja, has been translated to mean variously "the art of stealth," "the art of espionage," "the art of persevering," and "the art of enduring."

While we, today, may think of the Ninja as an assassin or hired spy, that was apparently not the original intent of the art. According to some experts like Ninjutsu instructor Stephen K. Hayes, the art of the Ninja developed in Japan centuries ago as a way to protect locals from the armies and warriors of the feudal lords. The idea of being "hired killers" actually evolved from the alliances that people would make with those in power (as opposed to working as mercenaries). But according to others, and certainly to legend, Ninjutsu warriors developed as assassins or spies, and hired out to various lords.

In any event, the Ninja developed as a sort of "one man army."

Rather than develop or adapt one's body or life to an art form, Ninjutsu revolves around adapting various principles to one's own body and life, in effect to allow one person to make use of many disciplines.

This kind of comprehensiveness in a fighting/defensive art has shown many advantages, and display that one can achieve much with the body and mind. The "legendary" powers of the Ninja show this, as Ninjutsu involved learning to use a variety of devices as weapons, and to be able to adapt one's fighting style to the immediate surroundings. In addition, those "powers" show the ingenuity, as the Ninjas learned to use a breathing tube while hiding under water, pontoon devices on the feet to effectively "walk" across water, and smoke devices and misdirection to make it look as though they could vaporize. Various substances such as poisons or hallucinogenics were apparently used to create various physical and psychological effects in victims (and probably bystanders). These added to the stories of the Ninja's supernatural abilities.

Misdirection, which is of course also the province of the stage and close-up magician, was essential to the Ninja's "power" to be stealthy, to not be seen or to be able to effectively disappear from a scene without notice.

Ninjutsu, as with other martial arts, rely on that mind/body connection in order to be truly able to make the best of what one has.

However much legend and superstition has grown up around the martial arts, it's very clear that the emphasis of balance between mind and body, and the exercises that strengthen both that the various arts teach, do accomplish the goal of giving the practitioner the ability to know his or her physical capabilities better, and the knowledge that such limitations are really transparent, that they can be surpassed by using that which is in the body and mind, the life force or chi.

What's very interesting is the very notion that these fighting arts evolved together with ideas of spiritual enlightenment. The philosophies and spiritual emphasis of much of the teachings of the martial arts provides both for killing and healing, for incapacitating an opponent without harming him as well as for easing the pain of another, and for influencing opponents.

Going back to martial arts master Guy Savelli, other research conducted with him when I worked in New York, as well as subsequent information from him demonstrates the importance of mind in the martial arts.

When we did research with him at the ASPR, Savelli claimed to be able to influence people at a distance, so Osis and McCormick set up a situation in which a subject (that would be me) was to be influenced by Savelli, who would be in an isolation room watching the subject on a video monitor.

In order to determine whether there was more than a subjective suggestion reaction going on, the protocol involved me moving forward, backward, to the right, to the left, or up and down at signaled intervals. The movements were randomly assigned to time intervals, and Savelli was given the instructions and list of scrambled movements once he was inside the isolation room. I, too, was alone in the target room, which was being monitored by the researchers from a third room.

Basically, Savelli was to read the list of movements and at each specified interval, was to focus his energy on me (while watching me on the monitor) and somehow get me to do the movement.

As each interval was called out over the intercom to me, I went with my gut instinct as to what direction to move. One basic problem with the protocol was that I might have been using my own psi abilities (which we all have to some degree) to unconsciously access the list so I would know which way to move. However, I distinctly felt a force pushing or pulling me in particular directions during a number of the trial intervals. In fact, I felt myself pushed back during several trials in a row, the last of the series of pushes feeling hard enough to cause me to lose my balance.

I later learned that the random assignment of movements had resulted in several backward motions in a row, which Savelli said he used to really give me something to think about (and feel).

Our overall hit rate was over 50 percent, by the way. Much greater than what chance would expect (only about 20 percent, or one in five).

A few years later, Savelli sent me a couple of videotapes. One dealt with his healing work (actually helping people to heal themselves), the other was a demonstration of the techniques of Kun Tao, which he had taught to some army officers. Three soldiers, all who identified themselves as sergeants, appeared on the martial arts demo tape.

The tape was seemingly done for others in the military, to show what kinds of things one can do after only some, not extensive, training in Kun Tao. The emphasis, however, was all on mental attitude.

We've all probably seen martial artists breaking boards and even bricks or concrete blocks with their hands and feet on television, both for demonstrations and in the slightly exaggerated format in Kung Fu films, and you may have even seen people do this in person. I've certainly seen people do some pretty incredible things as demonstrations of martial arts skills.

What I saw in the demo tape Savelli sent me was a bit different. The emphasis was on the conditioning of the mind, rather than the conditioning of the body. The soldier narrating and doing most of the demonstrations constantly reiterated that fact, that he and his buddies had gone through no hardening of the hands by hitting sand or rice, that it was all in the mind.

The first technique they demonstrated was called "the whip," based on the whipping motion of the arm and hand at a target. Hands were whipped out at boards, both held in the hands of another and falling in midair. The fingertips would strike the boards and break them, rather than the full hand contact one's used to seeing in such demonstrations. Using "the whip," one of the soldiers broke off the top portion of a bottle he had just placed on a stand, shattering it, without disturbing the bottom portion.

Keeping his fingers stiff and straight out, one of the men broke through a pine board, then penetrated a watermelon with the same straightened fingers. No damage to the hand, much damage to the board and the watermelon.

One very interesting application of "the whip" was a slapping motion at a watermelon, the open hand hitting the side of the melon. No damage was done to the outside rind, but when it was cut open, the inner flesh of the watermelon was mushed. This blow was likened to a "dim mak," the legendary art of the "delayed death

touch (or blow)," in which the martial artist is able to strike someone with a blow that causes internal damage that may not cause
severe injury or death for hours or even days (leaving no outer evidence of the blow). Such a blow is supposedly less related to the
force used (how hard) and more to a transfer of energy, or *chi,* into
the target.

The lack of damage to the striking hands and fingers was related
to the mental conditioning, that with enough of a belief, the mind
tells the hands it can do the breaks and still not receive any damage. An extension of this was next, that the mind could tell the body
not to receive damage when struck.

The soldiers demonstrated this with what they called "the shield,"
again with more than a bit of mental conditioning. I watched the
demonstration tape, enraptured, as the soldiers struck each other
(or Savelli stepped in for the blows). A thick wooden dowel was
broken over one of the soldier's stretched-out arm, a 2x2 was broken across the back of the neck (took two blows to really break
the wood), and a metal pipe was bent across the chest. Each time
the "victim" looked as though he had been slapped with a feather,
no pain and no damage.

The conditioning and training Savelli had put them through focused on the philosophy and conditioning of the mind.

Using the mind to affect the body's energy or chi to shield the
body is sometimes called the "iron skin" technique because the skin
of the individual becomes near impenetrable, or like iron. By mentally changing the flow of chi so as to effectively *be* the skin (kind
of like visualizing a force field as part of the surface of the body),
weapons slide off of have little or no effect on the individual.

One can also change the flow of chi so as to become rooted to
the earth. If one visualizes (with proper training, even self-training)
one's chi flowing into and from the ground, a connection can be
established that might be very difficult to shift. A Chi gong master
who appeared in an episode of Bill Moyer's *Healing and the Mind*
series became an immovable object by shifting his chi. A number
of his students found it impossible to move him at all once he established his connection.

The use of chi to shield the body, to create an "iron skin" that cannot be penetrated, or to use chi to become an unmoving object, is not just limited to the "fighting" martial arts. Chi gong (or qigong) is more closely allied to the healing side of the martial arts. Chi gong involves the manipulation of energy, both inside and outside the body (internal and external chi). According to Paul Dong and Aristede H. Esser:

Chi gong . . . is an ancient Chinese system of "breathing" or "vital energy" mind-control exercises. It has a remarkably positive effect on health. It can prevent and cure diseases, increase strength, resist premature senility, and ensure long life. In ancient China it was called a method for "warding off diseases and prolonging life."[1]

Chi gong is what one sees many, many of the Chinese people practicing as exercise in films and video of mainland China, and it was prominently featured in the aforementioned *Healing and the Mind*.

Chi gong, besides being merely a form of exercise, is truly a healing art that involves the movement of energy for balance within one's own body and aiding the movement of energy in the bodies of others. Through the movement of *external chi,* one can heal or harm another (as with the delayed death touch, the dim mak).

Other martial arts also involve healing, which is the side of martial arts we rarely see, and will be further addressed in Chapter Five.

Chi gong, according to Dong and Esser, is acknowledged as a way to develop one's psychic abilities, those involving information flow (ESP; becoming *one* with the world certainly means tapping into the flow of information) and those affecting matter and energy (PK). A chi gong master can supposedly achieve many of the same affects as those in other martial arts, including knocking an opponent down without touching him, and becoming an immovable object (demonstrated in the Bill Moyers show with a standing elderly chi gong master who a group of people were unable to move).

In philosophy and deed, the martial arts (and here I am including chi gong) teach that unity of the mind and body, and an awareness of the vital energy of life in the body (chi), can push people beyond what is considered "normal" limitations. The mind/body techniques of the martial arts are not unlike the more recently developed techniques of sports psychologists. The more aware one is of the balance inside, the better one will be able to perform.

Setting limitations on one's capabilities limits one immediately. The philosophies inherent in the martial arts allow one to go past such supposed limitations. Breaking a brick is more than striking with strength and speed. It is "seeing" the end result, going past the brick with the hand as though the brick is not there. Focusing on the strength of the material one is to break, or on the strength of the hand (when opposed by a hard substance such as wood or stone) may bring up doubts. Those doubts immediately set limits on what one thinks one can really do, and what may end up breaking is the hand, not the brick.

"The power of positive thinking" is much more than simply "I think I can." It's actually a knowledge that one can do it, an "I know I can" do something, or even an obliviousness to the possibility that one *can't* do something.

The martial arts clearly shows the mind's influence on the matter of the body, pushing back the boundaries of human capability. Martial artists, and the spontaneous experiences of some athletes, have demonstrated that the mind can also reach past the body and influence the outer world, as will effects on a football or the apparent thrust of energy that influences another individual or knocks down an opponent.

The unity of mind and body, the balance struck, allows people to tap into both their own power and to extend that power. But it all boils down to how one trains the mind to react to the impossible. If one takes limits on faith, the limits hold. It is only when the mind discards the limits that they no longer are limits at all.

From the parapsychological viewpoint, martial arts allow the full range of psychokinetic experiences, from healing to moving external objects. Yet more than this, the PK of the martial artist is nothing unusual, just a stage one can reach with enough learning, practice, and the right frame of mind. Accepting, in essence, what others claim as impossible to be more than possible, to be fact, allows the martial artist to perform "extraordinary" or "exceptional" feats.

One must look also look into the reported feats of martial artists. As with the lessons taught by the ninjas, who used superstition to build on their own reputation, one must look closer at the reported abilities with open eyes, for the misinterpretation of what may really be happening. Interestingly enough, while some claims just fade away, other claims and demonstrations of martial artists clearly challenge our Western scientific understanding of what humans can do.

Clearly, in sports performance and specifically in the martial arts, people are doing the impossible every day. While skeptics may claim it's just that rare exception to what we consider normal physical prowess, or the "placebo" effect that lets them do these things, people can learn techniques that bypass the "exception" explanation, and we have no explanation for the placebo effect.

In essence, belief, the mind's attitude toward accomplishing something, often allows for that something to be achieved, even though the body isn't supposed to be capable of such an achievement without causing damage to itself.

The martial artists have it right: This is a world of mind and matter, but both are the same. Creating the balance between mind and body, one can affect the matter all around. Humans can train themselves to achieve this, provided we accept that many limits are just psychological barriers, not physical ones.

* 3 *

The Powers of Saints, Prophets, and Other Spiritual Figures

Even without the training martial artists get, we see from time to time individuals who innately know that there are fewer limits than others might recognize. Some of these are star athletes and incredible performers of both physical and mental feats. Others are labeled as psychics or shamans or even saints.

If one looks first to various tales of ancient religions and mythologies, it's easy to find wondrous descriptions of human beings with marvelous or horrifying powers, generally given to them by the various gods of those religions. The powers may include incredible strength or the ability to fly or levitate others, the power to transform oneself (or others), or to make something out of nothing. Or perhaps the power to affect the weather, to project heat or cold. Or the power to heal or harm with a thought.

We can find desires for godlike abilities in the tales of all peoples around the world. In our society, such desires may lead to positions of power in politics and business, or even religion. But the supernatural powers seem to stay with the psychics or in comic books and science fiction.

But are all the ancient (and more recent) stories of psychic powers and supernatural abilities all stories? Is there any truth to them at all?

As with the ninjas, reality can be misperceived and reported inaccurately, with exaggeration. On the other hand, the site of ancient Troy was found by Heinrich Schliemann thanks to the writings of Homer, which had been believed to be complete fiction. Much in mythological writings is based on fact.

On the other hand, one cannot accept all ancient writings as fact-based either. Books today are labeled works of fiction or nonfiction. Of course, with some books, the author's "nonfiction" may be a very subjective thing, based entirely on the author's belief system. Then again, it's an extremely rare author who can keep his or her subjective perceptions of reality out of their work. Plato's description of Atlantis has been taken as "fact" by many, yet so far the closest relationship of the descriptions of that lost continent to reality has been to relate it to descriptions of ancient Minoan Crete, a civilization that crumbled as a result of a massive volcanic eruption on the island of Thera.

So, we can only rely on the writings of people of history so much as they leave for us, their descendants, descriptions of events and people with seemingly miraculous content. The closer in time we come to our time, the better the reporting techniques and technology. Otherwise, we are relying on the subjective interpretations of "witnesses" of the times.

One of the more interesting projects I did as part of my undergraduate anthropology work at Northwestern University was a comparison of two versions of the same historical event: the conquest of Mexico and the Aztecs by Cortes. The first was a compilation of translated records of the period written by Aztec witnesses (*Broken Spears,* edited by Miguel Leon-Portilla). The second, *The Bernal Diaz Chronicles* (translated and edited by Albert Idell), was written by a Spanish witness to the conquest, Bernal Diaz del Castillo.

The difference in the accounts is striking. To the Spanish, the Aztecs were savages, heathens, and barbarians. In the name of God, the conquest brought about the downfall of a proud people and the capture of much land and wealth.

To the Aztecs, who first saw the conquistadors as possible divinities returning as was foretold by their ancestors, these were greedy conquerors, who killed because their initial demand for gold and gems was not well received.

People perceive others and events in their own cultural context. Were an individual to display seeming supernatural powers, the reaction of observers would depend on their belief systems, much of which comes from the culture and religion of the observers. In past times, an individual showing such psychic proclivity could be perceived alternatively as a messenger from God (or gods) or as a tool of the Devil (as a demon or messenger of an evil god). Such reactions have led to some people in history venerated as prophets and saints, while others were stoned or hanged or burned to death as witches, sorcerers, evil beings, and the like.

Looking just at the vast religious literature of the Judeo-Christian traditions, one finds an enormous number of people who have displayed miraculous powers. Moses, given power by God, changed the Nile to blood, turned a staff to a snake, and, parted the Red Sea. While scientists today have come up with various explanations for the parting of the Sea (including Moses knowing the tides well enough to find a shallow place to cross or the Red Sea parting as a result of the Tsunami created by the volcanic explosion of Thera in the Mediterranean) and for other events described in the story of Moses, people all over the world accept the "powers" demonstrated by Moses as fact.

Jesus Christ, as described in the works that followed his life, demonstrated incredible abilities of his own, which have been offered up as proof of his divinity. Walking on water, the production of food to feed thousands, his healings, and, of course, his resurrection all point to a conclusion that he had "godlike" powers.

However, there have been historians of the Bible who tell us that if it goes back to the original texts of the times, to contemporary (or near contemporary) descriptions of the life and teachings of Christ, there are variations. Throughout the past two millennia, the New Testament has been written, translated, and rewritten, so that while basic stories are essentially the same, there are many different interpretations and spins in the different Bibles. [For example, reincarnation was part of the original teachings, but was excised by the Catholic Church in the sixth century].

Throughout history, people with uncanny abilities have been described. Is there truth to their abilities? In fact, unless we can uncover hard physical evidence (or enough indisputable evidence in the form of written records), or unless we can come up with a time machine that lets us go back and see for ourselves, everything is subject to interpretation. So, lets make a few parapsychological interpretations of several figures in religious history. After that, we'll take a brief look at people who could have been called saints or sorcerers if they had lived at a different time, the spirit mediums of the nineteenth and twentieth centuries.

Actually, coming from a Jewish background, looking at the material on people called saints in Christian theology has been a daunting task. Sure, I knew about a few of them, such as St. Patrick and driving the snakes out of Ireland. And I knew about St. Joan of Arc and the voices that led her to oppose the English occupation of her country. But I knew very little else.

The various books describing the multitude of saints in history describe the activities of these people who have been canonized by the Church. Many were made saints because of their devotion to their religion and to Christ. Others because of some heroic feat or political stance they took. Saints in these positions were often canonized because they became martyrs, dying for their faith (like Joan of Arc). Some were led to the path of devotion because of their being visited and advised by Christ or by other holy beings. Even a new form of Christianity has been spawned by such visitations. Joseph Smith, Jr., was visited by God and Christ and led to form the Morman denomination.

Still others became saints because of miraculous events that seemed to happen in their presence, such as levitation (though devotion to the faith is probably the major component of canonization). Or perhaps because of what happened to their bodies after death, such as the sixteenth-century Jesuit missionary St. Francis Xavier, whose remains have been certified by the Roman Catholic Church to be in a miraculous state of preservation.

In recent times, Pope John Paul II has eased up on the requirements for sainthood, with the two main categories being martyrdom and miracles. The miracles generally referred to may involve the appearance of the prospective saint as an apparition, showing up to guide the living. But most of the miracles involve healing, whether while the saint was alive, or because people were "miraculously" cured after praying to the religious figure.

Keep in mind, most saints were canonized well after their deaths. Today, healing miracles may be harder to prove because of advancements in modern medicine may yield dramatic cures without the need for divine intervention (though who's to say that God or gods have no hand in how well modern medicine works?).

Still, the most common "power" of saints over time seems to have been that of healing. Very often in the presence of these historical personages, miraculous (and some mundane) changes in the health of visitors would take place. People today still report such healings because of prayer to particular patron saints, or because of religious icons associated with saints who, in life, had the gift of healing.

I will deal with healing in Chapter Five, but let me say briefly that given that many of the saints were known for their devotion to their faith, and because people who wished to get healthy came to know of these figures, it's difficult to know whether any special healings that took place happened because of the saint's "power," because of the belief by the sick that the saint *could* heal them, or because God simply willed them healed by their visitation with such devoted people as the saints. The source of the healing, ultimately, would be God in this belief system, but whether the actual power to cause the healing was exuded by the saint or came from within the victims is impossible to know.

Healing saints included Gerald of Aurillac, Catherine of Siena, Nicolas of Torentino, and Melangell of Wales. People take the powers of the saints quite seriously, especially where healing is a factor. The British newspaper, *The Independent,* reported in 1993 that "Hundreds of pilgrims have made their way over the past year to pray beside the shrine of an obscure Welsh holy woman" (Melangell, "who is also the patron saint of hares.") (From "Pilgrims Find Hope and Inspiration at Reconstructed Shrine" by Oliver Gillie. *The Independent,* July 26, 1993).

Paola Frassinetti, canonized by Pope John Paul II in 1984, was another saint who did much healing in her life (she lived from 1809 to 1882). According to the United Press International (article dated March 12, 1984), her canonization ceremony was attended by a woman who was cured of a crippling form of arthritis in 1981, "after praying daily for six months to Paola Frassinetti."

Levitation of oneself was another common symptom of the divine. St. Teresa of Avila was one who levitated on occasion, including an incident where it occurred without her thought or desire.

The seventeenth-century saint Joseph of Cupertino, known today as the patron saint of pilots and astronauts, is the one saint in history who probably flew more often than the "Flying Nun." His levitations began shortly after he became a priest. Not merely content to float above the ground, he was apparently able to fly even with others on his back. Sources vary as to how often he "flew" for witnesses, with some saying as many as over 100 times. Perhaps the most interesting flight included his ability to pick up/levitate others in a way that indicated that this was more than mere lightness of thought.

> "During the seventeen years he remained at Grotella . . . the friars were building a cavalry. The middle cross of the group was thirty-six-feet high and correspondingly heavy, defying the efforts of ten men to lift it. St. Joseph is said to have 'flown' seventy yards from the door of the house to the cross, picked it up in his arms 'as if it were a straw', and deposited it in its place."[1]

It should be noted that while there were eyewitness accounts written at the time of his other "flights," the incident with the cross apparently was reported by witnesses after his death.

It should also be noted that St. Joseph did much in the way of healing. Both this and his levitations got him in trouble with the Inquisitors in Naples (no surprise there), who ended up sending him to a monastery.

Some saints, it has been reported through history, also had incidents of objects moving about them, though often for "good" purposes (unlike the messy or uncontrolled movements of poltergeist cases).

Another sign of the divine in saints has been the occurrence of stigmata, mysterious wounds or bleeding on the body, often in the same places Christ's body was pierced by the nails and spear at the Crucifixion. This phenomenon is still observed and reported today, though not all people who experience stigmata are to be considered candidates for sainthood. This will be discussed in the next chapter.

What's interesting is, if one looks at the historical (and story-telling) record of the last couple of thousand years, there are also many more tales of other, nonsaintly people who had apparent healing powers, could levitate, or move objects. The specific context in which these occurrences happened led to these people being avoided, expelled from their communities, imprisoned, killed, or revered.

In the case of the saints, many of them died as martyrs, or were imprisoned or killed by a church that, at the time, could not see past its own political bureaucracies and teachings. However, since many who healed (or perhaps floated) were themselves rather devoted to God, and did their "miracles" in the service of God, there was some acceptance of their abilities (or at least the eyes were turned elsewhere).

Were these people possessed of the ability of Mind over Matter?

If the situations happened as described, one could make a case for them being psychokinetic and having some degree of control of their abilities. Levitation, if and when it occurs without the use of "tools" such as those used by stage magicians and Fakirs, would almost certainly have to be either misinterpretation of an event by the observer (such as a slowed sense of time in observing someone leaping in the air—if time appears to slow down, from a subjective perspective, then the few seconds a leaper is in the air stretches to many seconds or minutes), or it is mind acting directly on the matter of the body to move it upward or in other directions.

As for the healings and stigmata, if another individual (a healer) is involved, it could be the healer's mind acting on the healee. But since so many healings happen spontaneously after prayer to God in the presence of (or in the name of) a saint, the healing factor is likely to be the mind of the sick individual acting on the matter of his or her own body.

Attributing "cause" or "origin" to these abilities often means declaring to others (and believing within oneself) that the power comes from a divine or spiritual source. As time has marched on, a person manifesting such abilities as healing or moving objects or levitation has typically either stayed with the divine, believing and stating God's will is behind the phenomena (a safe position to declare) or that spirits of other sorts (usually the recently departed) are helping the individual along, as with the case of mediums in the spiritualist era.

Strangely enough, those throughout history who have taken personal responsibility for their own extraordinary feats have been the most chastised or ostracized (or, in Western history, killed as witches and sorcerers). For if the outside, socially accepted power of God (or spirits, in the case of spiritualism) is not responsible, the power must come from some evil source, such as demons or Satan himself.

Anything to avoid acceptance that people, themselves, are capable of extraordinary things.

The mediums of the nineteenth and early twentieth century are an interesting lot to study. While the idea of a *medium* who could communicate with spirits and even call on spirits to create physical effects was an ancient one (still continuing with native peoples all over the world, as well as with the phenomenon of *channeling*), the spiritualist movement itself, the idea of a religion built around the contacting of the dead, was a new one in the 1800s.

It had a humble beginning, with Margaretta and Catherine Fox, two young sisters living near Rochester, New York. In 1848, they suddenly manifested and demonstrated some kind of spiritual "contact," during which rapping sounds were mysteriously heard in patterns that answered questions. Perhaps because the Industrial Revolution was underway, and science and technology were quite popular, spiritualism and its "experiments" in spirit contact allowed for science to be brought into religion.

Spiritualism swept the country and to Europe. It subsided for a time in the U.S. during the Civil War (people here being busy with that nasty business), then picked up again after due undoubtedly to the number of dead soldiers and civilians who had left survivors behind. These survivors, of course, wanted to make sure their deceased loved ones had gone on to a better existence. Historians of spirit contact also suggest that its popularity had something to do with the large number of people unaffiliated with a particular church here (people such as Abraham Lincoln, who attended a number of seances).

England was the other major site of interest in spiritual contact, and it was there that several scholars had their interests piqued enough to formalize study of mediumship through the Society for Psychical Research (the SPR, founded in 1882). A few years later, a U.S. counterpart, the American Society for Psychical Research (the ASPR) was founded.

The areas of study for both organizations in their charters dealt with a variety of psychic and related phenomena and effects, from telepathy to apparitions and hauntings, as well as the study of hypnotism and its effects. A central focus of the studies at the time was that of physical and mental mediums.

A mental medium was one who would (typically) go into trance and provide information from the dearly departed. A physical medium, on the other hand, was one who, in (or out) of trance, called on the spirits and their powers to physically affect objects (or themselves) in the seance room.

A number of physical mediums were studied throughout the nineteenth and early twentieth centuries. The most famous of them were undoubtably D.D. Home, Eusapia Palladino, and Margery.

Daniel Dunglas Home (pronounced "Hume") has been called by a number of people the greatest physical medium who ever lived. Reported abilities of his would have gotten him either canonized or burned at the stake under other circumstances. These abilities included levitation (self and of others), movements of other, often heavy objects, materialization, immunity to fire (and the ability to pass the immunity, temporarily, on to others), rapping sounds, and even the apparent elongation of his limbs and body (shades of Plastic Man!).

His abilities apparently first manifested themselves during his childhood, before the Fox sisters' phenomena caught on. Poltergeist-type effects occurred around him. During the 1850s, he was first picked on for study by spiritualists, and amazed them by being able to perform his feats often on command and in full light (most seances ended up in dark or semidark rooms).

He never charged for his "performances" (usually gifts and food and a place to stay came into it, though). His seances were often conducted in the homes of people he visited, making the idea of fraud difficult. The abilities he displayed during those seances, though not directed at contacting the dead, were attributed to spiritual origin by spiritualists, yet to Home himself by the scientists who studied him.

No one during the time of his life ever caught him at fraud. Researchers instituted various controls in their experiments with him, yet he still was able to produce effects. Of course, a very wily fraud or skilled magician might be able to get past such controls, yet Home was never shown to be either.

Thanks to very detailed notes taken by his companions and by witnesses, even today there is enough information to get a clear picture that Home was a most unusually gifted man. If he was a fraud, he was a genius at it and the best that ever lived, given the levitations and other demonstrations under conditions over which he had no control, in places where the light was more than enough to check for any apparatus.

What one can say about Home today is that those of use in the field of parapsychology interested in psychokinesis, wish he was alive or that someone like him was around, as his manifested abilities truly showed that mind can affect matter in a wide variety of ways.

With mediumship came a great deal of fraud. Con artists have always known how easy it is to fake out a bereaved individual. Mediumship was a perfect venue for such trickery. Consequently, as the researchers dealt with their studies of physical and mental mediums, they also had to deal with the uncovering of fraud. In fact, fraud became so prevalent that one could say there was almost more focus on fraudulent mediumship than on true spiritual contact and power (except by the devout spiritualists, whose beliefs, by their very nature, ignored fraud much of the time).

In 1888, the Fox sisters confessed that their spirit rappings had been caused physically, by them, through a clever trick of cracking the knuckles of their fingers and toes. Later, one of the sisters recanted that confession, but the damage had been done. With scientists and magicians uncovering fake mediums, it was a difficult climate for any new mediums to come forward.

Even so, Eusapia Palladino came to prominence beginning with Italy in that same year of 1888.

Another physical medium, unlike Home who "performed" seated or standing (or floating, as it were), Palladino preferred the seated seance. Included in the phenomena of a typical Palladino seance was the levitation of the seance table, spirit rappings, moving objects, blowing curtains, unusual light effects, and manifestations of spirit hands. Also unlike Home, Palladino's seances took place in a semidark or dark room.

Palladino was, in fact, caught several times at fraud. However, that didn't stop the researchers. Apparently, she was also able to perform while under controlled conditions, such as having her hands and feet held while the table rose and fell.

One of the more interesting effects noted during some of Palladino's seances was that at the end of many of them, she appeared physically exhausted, and often appeared to have lost weight. In fact, this was a measurable quality of some of her seances, and in one she reportedly lost many pounds (kind of the psychic diet, I guess). Such a factor was apparently not present during the seances where she was caught at fraud.

It has been thought that Palladino learned to do fraud because the *real* phenomena took so much out of her (even literally). Where she could cheat (since it was easier and less tiresome), she did. When she couldn't the physical toll on her body was evident.

Skeptics will say that because a person is caught cheating once, everything they do is suspect. That may be true. However, when one can control against the cheating, and the effects still happen (usual in a more impressive fashion), can an inquisitive scientist afford to throw out all sessions?

Palladino, while claiming to be in contact with spirits, evidently had true powers of Mind over Matter. As with Home, under other societal or cultural conditions, she, too, might have been a saint or a sorceress (most certainly the latter if she had been caught at fraud).

Harry Houdini made the search for fraudulent mediums quite famous, although dozens of others, magicians and scientists alike, had uncovered fraud before Houdini turned his eye toward spiritualists. Houdini was just much better at publicity.

In the early part of the twentieth century, Mina Crandon, the young wife of a Boston physician, performed her spiritual antics as the medium "Margery." Margery also manifested physical effects, all with the help of spirits. Margery also became the focal point of an investigation that tore apart the ASPR.

Margery could produce a number of effects in a darkened seance room; everything from levitations of objects (and the seance table) to glowing ectoplasm, from ringing bells to the linking of wooden rings. Margery also became the target of much commotion, undoubtedly due to the number of staunch supporters she gained from the ASPR.

When investigated by a committee sent by *Scientific American* magazine, the verdict was anything but unanimous on either side. The conditions under which Margery performed seemed daunting for anyone thinking fraud, with Margery seated in a wooden box with only her head sticking out. However, the idea of a spirit cabinet was not a new one, and even though mediums had been tied up before, during, and immediately after the seance, fraud could be accomplished (magicians/mentalists Glenn Falkenstein and Frances Willard perform a spirit cabinet routine today all over the country, with Frances securely tied, yet with all sorts of seemingly impossible physical manifestations occurring).

The dissenters, including Harry Houdini and psychologist William McDougall, claimed Margery was faking it all. Houdini even took the elaborate step of duplicating her feats, including those produced while she was seated and sealed in the wood box.

The dissent between the members of the committee sent shock waves throughout the psychical research community, and has been cited as the cause of trouble within the ASPR and as one of the factors that drove McDougall and young protégé J. B. Rhine away from the medium's parlor and into the laboratory.

Some supporters of Margery claimed that Houdini was unable to actually catch her at fraud and took it upon himself to duplicate her feats in an effort to "frame" her. To this day, the controversy continues, as writings left by members of the committee suggest both perspectives may have been true.

The idea of spirits entering someone as a vehicle to move objects or heal or levitate is, as I said, an old one. For the physical mediums, this was their "out," a way of avoiding personal responsibility for the physical manifestations. However, the evidence for Mind over Matter (as well as the literature of fraud) indicates that whether real events or special effects, the medium was somehow responsible for the physical phenomena occurring in the seance room.

Psychokinesis works often through the subconscious. The late British researcher Kenneth Batcheldor formed a theory of PK that accounted for the spontaneity of the effects and for some psychological factors that helped or hampered.

In essence, we all have an *ownership resistance* to having extraordinary "powers" or abilities. Unless we are encouraged to excel, to outperform others, to essentially separate ourselves from the norm (as athletes often are), most of us are quite content to be like everybody else. Having an ability like PK, which parapsychology posits *is normal,* is still something outside the accepted range of what's normal. Therefore, for most of us there is a resistance to having, or *owning,* such an ability.

In addition, we all have our own problems merely witnessing such events. *Witness inhibition* is another point Batcheldor made.

He postulated that under appropriate conditions, where the people involved could be in a *safe* setting to witness unusual events (like a seance parlor) as well as in a setting where anything that happened was attributed to an outside source, such as spirits, or demons, or gods, or aliens or whatever, the chances of something happening went up. Ownership resistance would be down because the setting said that something or someone else was responsible (with the saints, that would be God). Witness inhibition is not a problem because the setting is one in which one *expects* odd things to happen (like people expecting to see a miracle from a saint whose reputation states "miracles happen when s/he is around").

Experiments conducted with Batcheldor's ideas have shown that the subconscious minds of the people involved (since he modeled the experiments on the seance room, they are called "sitters") play along with the setting, supplying PK effects in some cases. One of the best known *sitter groups* was the Philip Circle in Canada, who "created" a fictional entity named Philip to more or less give responsibility to when anything happened. There'll be more about this later on.

In general, the specific setting or the cultural context in which apparent miracles and psychic events happen have a lot to do with how often they may happen and how they are perceived. People who still follow their native traditions (what some call "primitive traditions") may include belief that higher powers can work through the body and mind of an individual and produce wondrous (or terrible) effects, from levitation to healing to death.

What I have learned over the years is that any apparently psychic event that can be seen or experienced can be perceived and received in a number of ways. For many people who have such experiences or merely witness them, reporting them means being labeled a "flake" or being socially ostracized. For others, it may mean being personally seen as someone in contact with the divine, with God(s).

What's most interesting is that the very thing that the skeptics complain about (rightly so) that makes such claims of miracle powers dangerous is the very thing this book, and the field of parapsychology, is all about: Responsibility. If all such reported events and abilities were considered as normal as the exceptional ability of a great athlete, we would see both more incidences of such abilities showing publicly in people, as well as a lesser need to revere—or fear—that miraculous person.

Today, such miracles as those of the saints and those of the great physical mediums have fallen off in their incidence in the Western world. The reasons are numerous. One is that people became more interested in the marvels of science and technology than those intermittent ones of the spirit. Another is that with scientific knowledge has come a new "religion" of sorts, one that worships the materialism of science. There is little room for spirit, for the mind's interaction with matter directly, if one comes from the perspective that we are nothing more than biological machines.

This is not to say, of course, that all of us buy into the "humans as only biological machines" idea. In fact, based on the fact that the majority of humans practice some form or religion or spiritual practice, it's more than fair to say that most people have a great interest in spirit and higher consciousness, in there being something more to human existence than the flesh.

However, there are a number of people who may believe in divine power, yet still not accept the idea that humans have something aside from a mind/consciousness that may be created by and reside only in the brain. Many who have a spiritual belief still have a hard time accepting that our bodies and minds can be affected by spiritual forces, whether divine or from within ourselves. And many very religious people hold that we have no effect on our own bodies, that any positive or negative impact is due to God or some higher power. The issue becomes where the responsibility for action following thought lies; do we heal or affect ourselves or is the thought merely a form of prayer that is answered (or not) by spirits and divine entities outside ourselves?

If one looks at Christian Science, which posits that all healing comes from God, one will find situations that have reached the courts where parents or spouses refused medical treatment for a family member because of their religious beliefs. People live or die by God, not by humans cutting into them with surgical instruments. Medicine may work for such people, but it's not the *right* treatment, the one that their beliefs allow for or wish.

In more traditional Eastern religions, we are part of the divine, and therefore it is ourselves that must take responsibility for action.

More and more people are opening to this idea that we are more than the sum of our biological components. More and more Westerners (many in the East have had this down for years) are opening to the perspective that mind affects body directly, and are looking for more and more ways that this is demonstrated. The ideas of Eastern philosophy and religion have been an overwhelming force in the so-called "New Age Movement," whether preached by the living or by spirits speaking through the living.

Some of these ideas follow along with the concepts in the "new" physics, which is establishing interconnections between matter and energy on the quantum level and on our own level of reality.

But Western society as a whole has a ways to go. Thankfully, people are more and more interested in "connecting" with the world around them, and with their own bodies.

From the mind/body connection, one can be led to how the mind affects things outside the body. That's where we're headed with this book.

The Unusual and the Bizarre

Unusual Human Achievements

We've all seen people doing things a bit out of the ordinary, whether in films, on television, or in person. The Indian Fakir lying on a bed of nails, for example, looks perfectly happy where he is, but the rest of us wouldn't even consider touching such a surface, let alone lying or sitting on it.

People do very odd things in all societies. In many places around the world (the United States, included), people have various parts of their bodies pierced, both on an ostensibly permanent basis (for earrings, etc.) and for temporary ritualistic/religious reasons. One of my students at JFK University spent more than a little time studying this, and providing other students in a class on altered states of consciousness with information on the activity and its context.

People have hooks and slivers of metal and wood driven through their skin, their cheeks, their hands and feet, as part of religious ritual or as part of a ritual that may simple show it can be done. People hang from hooks and strings attached to their bodies, or pull carts or other weights attached to the strings. Blood, if it does flow at all, is minimal. Pain is apparently near nonexistent.

How is this possible? Why do people do it?

From one perspective, people do such things to prove to themselves that there is more to life than just what we see around us. In many cultures, lying on a bed of nails or having the body pierced or eating glass or walking on hot coals is a way of proving that one's devotion to whatever divine or supernatural power one believes in is real, and that the higher power can protect those who believe.

This is, in fact, a common belief in most religious belief systems. Whatever power one believes in protects those who believe. While body piercing and fire-walking may be extreme, we see examples of the basic belief system all around us. Millions of people believe that if they behave a certain way they will be rewarded or punished after death, and many believe that their behavior toward or on behalf of the divine power can bring good or bad to their lives right now.

While many of us in Western religious traditions find such activities that involve self-mutilation or risk-taking strange or something we can't imagine doing ourselves, people who walk on hot coals as part of their belief system may find going to church every week or giving up much of one's earnings or attacking "nonbelievers" physically or verbally just as alien. Fasting can be a mode of proving to devotion to a deity, or it can lead to a physical and mental state in which one has a vision of the divine. To many people, going to synagogue or church and worshiping is the highlight of the week, with much gratification both in the social setting of worship and in the very act of prayer itself. On the other hand, people who walk on hot coals (without harm, mind you) or endure physical and mental activities that would tax the health of others get just as much from their religious practices.

One of the lessons I learned in my undergraduate cultural anthropology studies at Northwestern University was that there is a seemingly infinite diversity in the beliefs held by human beings, especially where such beliefs relate to a connection with higher powers of the universe. What is right for one person or group may or may not be right for another. It really is up to the individual to decide for him/herself what the correct "path" in life is.

When it comes right down to it, there are often physical explanations for how a particular otherwise dangerous act may cause no lasting harm and no pain to the participant. For example, people who have their skin pierced may experience little bleeding and little or no pain because of where the needles or hooks pierce the skin. Pinching the skin can help squeeze out local blood vessels, and provided a vein or artery is not pierced, little bleeding *can* occur. For someone to be held off the ground by hooks piercing the skin, one can look to how much skin has been pinched, and how many hooks are in the body (the more hooks, the better the weight is distributed, and the less one would feel the tugging of the individual hooks).

This is akin to the "levitation" that we've all probably tried as kids. One of us in a group lay down on the ground, then four or six of us would stick just an index finger from each hand under the body. As long as the person "thought light thoughts," he or she was easy to pick up. The weight of the person was distributed among a number of index fingers, so that the load on each was relatively small.

The main mental component with the body piercing is the ability to not feel pain. Our bodies are covered with nerve endings that feel pressure, temperature, and relate pain signals (which means that something's wrong). When the skin is pierced, one should feel pain, but this is not always the case.

First of all, the entire body is *not* one big nerve ending. During the Middle Ages, witch-hunters used to use this fact to "prove" that an accused person was guilty of witchcraft. They would stick the body of the accused with a pin all over the place until hitting a spot without a nerve ending (therefore, no pain). This spot, often called the Devil's Mark, was a sign that the accused had made a pact with Satan. However, we all have a few of these on our bodies.

Secondly, one can be in a state of mind whereby pain is ignored. Ever been told by a doctor that if you look away, the needle won't hurt as much when you get a shot? Ever focus your attention on some other body sensation or some other thought when getting drilled by the dentist? The pain is not so bad (and may even be nonexistent).

Hypnosis can clearly be used to alleviate pain in many people, even though it's not been proven that hypnosis actually creates a specific altered state of consciousness. People can be talked into feeling no pain by others, and therefore can talk themselves into this state as well.

This is clearly Mind over the Matter of the body (in this case how the body responds to damage, with pain signals).

However, there is another mental component to the "levitation" and to the hanging by hooks. As with an unconscious person seeming to be heavier than a conscious, cooperative one, state of mind is important. Somehow, we are able to make our bodies harder to pick up by willing ourselves to be somehow heavier (but not as far as a scale is concerned). A relaxed individual is harder to pick up because the muscles are limp, a "ready" individual's body helps us pick him or her up (the difference between picking up a one-pound bar of metal that's long and thin and a long, skinny balloon filled with water weighing the same—the metal bar is much easier to handle than the floppy balloon).

So, we cannot only control experience of pain by mental control, but also the state of the body. Mind over Matter.

In doing "impossible" or "dangerous" feats, people are often doing them to accentuate their belief systems, to prove to their God(s), to themselves, and to others that by sticking by the "right" beliefs, one can do seemingly impossible things and beat the normal laws of the flesh. But religious belief is not necessary. Just belief in the effectiveness, in the end result, of the *reason* why one shouldn't be hurt or feel pain may be enough. This could be a belief in the scientific explanation for lack of bleeding and pain rather than the religious one.

One might also say that belief in the *power* of science and its explanations is itself a religionlike dogma. Instead of placing the power in the hands of a divinity, the scientific faithful place their trust in the body of knowledge we call science and technology and that the explanations are the right ones.

However, sometimes the "scientific" explanations may be, themselves, wrong or bogus. Yet the individual can still come out of the dangerous situation with little damage and certainly without pain.

In many cultures, such as India, people often learn to impress others with their "supernatural powers" through demonstrations of control of their bodies. Or they use such controls to show that they are wise individuals (like the yogi who has learned to control his body functions so well, he can slow his heart to a crawl and make it appear that he has no pulse). Or they use such talents to make a buck.

Some of the bizarre things that people do to themselves show up in the entertainment circles. Fire-eating, sitting on a bed of nails, sword-swallowing, and resistance to continuous bites of poisonous snakes are among the wonderful things that people do to themselves, in the name of God(s) or in the name of entertainment.

Harry Houdini published an exposé of the methods of people who do such things back in 1920, which included all of the above and more. These methods are hardly paranormal or supernatural, but they do often take a good deal of understanding of the principles, practice, and guts. They may also involve a bit of masochism on the part of the performer.

A more recent book on the history of bizarre performers is *Learned Pigs & Fireproof Women* by magician Ricky Jay (which also ended up as a TV special awhile back). This wild book covers quite a bit of history of the unusual performers out there, as well as going into things like people resisting fire (remember D.D. Home from last chapter).

People can do amazing things, of that there is no question. Houdini himself had such muscular control as to be able to swallow a small item, such as a lock pick, keep it in his esophagus, then regurgitate it when he needed it (say, after he was strip-searched and locked up). Mind over Body . . . Mind over Matter.

As with the chi gong master who cannot be moved by a number of people, individuals have shown the ability to somehow resist being picked up. While there has been no explanation in Western science of this, there are explanations in the East, such as anchoring one's energies (chi) to the earth itself. Whatever the subjective explanation, people can do this. It is an illustration of Mind over Matter.

But perhaps the epitome of the Mind over Matter connection here is really more a matter of Mind over Mind.

To perform any sort of "stunt" such as holding a hot coal or eating glass or swallowing a sword, besides any physical preparation, there has to be a lot of mental preparation. Most of us have the innate concept that fire burns (that's from experience, something we learn growing up) and that extreme heat is dangerous. We know that sharp objects can cut us. We know things like this on both the conscious and unconscious level, and there's undoubtably some degree of instinct at the primal level (after all, animals also know to fear fire, whether they've seen it before or not).

So the idea of fire-eating brings with it a nonintellectual reaction that this is not something one should really do. You may understand that the chemical used in fire-eating is one that burns at a low temperature; it looks like a hot flame, but it may not be. You may know that consciously, but there is still an instinctive fight-or-flight mechanism that may prevent you from trying it.

Unless, of course, your mind overcomes the instinct built into the body. Mind over Matter. One's belief that one can do something, can push past the limits, can easily bypass the reflexive move-away actions. The development of any physical skill requires learning, whether learning the moves or learning to bypass other, more reflex, reactions. Mind over Matter.

Then again, some of the things people try to do they may do because they don't consciously (and maybe even unconsciously) know something is dangerous. A native of a group that's never seen an electric stove may have no concept that the coils on top glow red because of heat, and may try to touch it (the heat will cause an almost instant reflex action to move the hand away).

And, too, in some instances a person may perform an extraordinary act in the heat of the moment, not thinking how impossible something looks.

I think we've all heard about people who have been in accidents and lifted the car off a loved one. How can this be possible? An adrenaline surge due to the immediacy of the situation allows the body to tap into reserves of energy and strength that one might otherwise never touch. However, there's a problem.

Can adrenaline cause the muscle tissue and the bone to increase its own tensile strength so as not to be damaged? Not quite.

A power weight-lifter does need to do some body preparation.

While much of power-lifting is in the mind, the body needs to be in a condition that can avoid damage from the stresses put on it by the enormous weight.

I was at a friend's house a few years ago for a small, afternoon party and barbecue. At the party were two doctor friends of my host, and we naturally got to talking about the "weird stuff" I deal with. I asked them about whether they had heard of real instances of a person lifting a car in an accident.

They both said yes. One, an orthopedic surgeon, said he had examined a woman who had saved her child's life in such an accident. I questioned him further about the weight load on the woman's body. He confirmed that the human body can only stand up to so much stress without there being damage to bones, ligaments, and other muscle tissue.

I asked whether there was any such damage to the woman's body. He said "No, just some bruises and cuts from the accident."

I asked how she could have avoided any internal damage from lifting the car.

He said she couldn't. But then he agreed that she did. He also agreed that he had no idea how that was possible. Yet it happened. To quote Martin Caidin, "It shouldn't be happening, but it is!"

So, in those cases where a person lifts a heavy object without the predicted damage to the body, just what's going on?

That's hard to say, because such things happen in the moment, and there's no way (ethical or otherwise) to get someone into such a state to find out for sure.

I have a couple of ideas I want to put out about that. First, it *is* possible that medical science has much to learn and we really *don't* know how much stress the human body can physically take under certain conditions.

Secondly, the mind of the lifter may have somehow protected, strengthened even, the body so damage did not occur. Or perhaps the mind made sure all healing systems were operating at full steam to heal the problem as it occurred (no, then the other cuts and bruises would also expect to be healed).

Or maybe there's something more at work here. People have been able to move objects with their minds. Psychokinesis. Maybe the car was actually being levitated off the child by the subconscious of the mother. Her hands on the car were necessary because of the problems of *witness inhibition* (most people would have a hard time understanding how a car can float in midair) and *ownership resistance* (most people would freak out if they thought they were levitating a car). So, by keeping her hands on the car, the lifter can believe she is doing something *normal* albeit out of the ordinary, thanks to the extra strength an adrenaline surge delivers.

What's the answer? The question needs to be better defined and looked at more closely. In any event, there is an extraordinary occurrence happening here that relies directly on what the mind allows the body to do.

The mind can also cause damage to the body as a result of belief systems. As mentioned in the last chapter, one of the signs that someone may have contact with the divine is *stigmata*. Stigmata is usually related to religious "wounds," mostly Christ-related. Bleeding from the hands and feet, bleeding from the forehead as though one was wearing a crown of thorns, and bleeding as though one's side has been pierced. Such effects may often happen at Easter. Among the saints that evidenced stigmata were St. Francis of Assisi and the aforementioned St. Catherine of Siena, whose stigmata began when an unusual light that appeared to come from a crucifix hit her at Easter.

More recently, the late Padre Pio evidenced stigmata, his bleeding beginning in 1918 and continuing until his death. Padre Pio was a healer and a prophet in Giovanni Rotondo, Italy. To cover his hands, which bled constantly, he wore fingerless gloves. His feet and his side also bled. When he died, however, there was barely a trace of the wounds, even though they had been clearly witnessed by others throughout his life.

Religious figures are hardly the only ones to show stigmata. Many people around the world have started bleeding spontaneously. While not all stigmata correlates to the wounds of Christ, not all stigmatics are Christian. The belief system of the stigmatic is intimately connected to the phenomenon. In fact, some sources state that Christ's left side was pierced, others that his right side was pierced. The stigmatic who bleeds from the side bleeds from the side that he or she thinks Christ was wounded.

Another interesting point: The Romans pierced the wrists in crucifixions, not the palms (although depictions of the crucifixion usually show Christ's palms as pierced by the nails). People apparently bleed from places shown in paintings and crucifixes in their own churches.

So what's happening here? If the wounds don't even correlate to historical reality (unless that's different from religious reality), how can they still happen?

From a psychological perspective, such things are plainly possible, though the biological mechanism is hardly understood (or even identified). Hypnosis has been used to rid people of warts. Physical illness can come on a person because of emotional or mental stress, or because one believes one is sick. People can affect their own bodies, both to heal themselves (Chapter Five) and to harm themselves (Chapter Six).

This effect one has on one's own body seems to be mainly a function of the subconscious, though people can consciously learn, as with biofeedback, to affect their own physiology. In Chapter Eight, you'll run across a rather dramatic example of how belief, coupled with fear and trauma, can visibly affect even the outside of the body (it's a case of a woman who claimed she was being strangled by a demon, and had the marks to prove it).

Mind over Body . . . Mind over Matter.

Religious faith brings with it strong belief and much emotion. People who look for a sign from God or Christ or whoever they worship may get that sign, if their belief kicks in whatever switch it is in the body that allows the mind to affect it. While there is nothing mystical, paranormal, or psychic about this, it clearly demonstrates how little we really know about ourselves and how the mind and body interact.

The key is strong belief. Overcoming or altering one's beliefs can lead to different reactions in the mind and body. Overcoming one's idea of limitations can lead to greater confidence and motivation.

This last idea is one that is played on with the fire-walking groups.

Fire-Walking and "Motivational" Tools

Fire-walking is a tradition among many cultures and religious groups around the world. From the South Pacific islands to Greece, from Japan to Sri Lanka, walking on hot coals or rocks is an activity often used to demonstrate faith or belief or devotion to a higher power, or simply to demonstrate one's belief in oneself, that the "odds" can be beat and limitations overcome.

Here in North America, fire-walking is often used as the climactic event after some form of motivational or self-esteem training (although one alternative to that seems to be walking on broken glass, as shown in an infomercial). There are a number of issues surrounding fire-walking, with the main controversy being whether there is a mind/body issue there at all.

Clearly there is an aversion to even trying to walk on hot coals. Getting past that takes a bit of self-mind-control. In addition, any pain or the sensation of heat can be affected by one's mental state. In fact, pain control may be the main mind over matter effect, as there are other explanations for the lack of burned skin on the walkers' feet.

First of all, it's important to note that the materials used in fire-walking can produce less heat than one thinks, even though the temperature registers quite high. For example, if you were in Phoenix on one of those days when it's hot enough to fry an egg on the sidewalk, the air and ground temperature may be the same, yet the egg will cook only when it hits the surface of the sidewalk. Air is a lousy conductor of heat. Water is better, and other materials, such as aluminum or steel, are even better.

The surface of most burning charcoal is very hot, but doesn't transfer heat very well. If it's covered with ash, then there is essentially a layer of insulation against heat transfer (but the temperature of the coals is still hot enough to cook something held over it for a time).

Human skin is somewhat resilient to heat. Have you ever touched a hot pan, removed your hand quickly, and found no burn (even though it hurt a lot—there's that pain thing)?

For someone to walk quickly across hot coals has been said to be like touching the hot pan quickly (though the coals transfer heat less well than the pan). As long as one doesn't simply stand still for too long in the coals, there's little chance of getting "cooked," or so the explanation goes.

In many places around the world, fire-walking may involve some kind of lotion or substance rubbed on the feet. There are a number of substances that can protect one against heat for a time (as discussed in Houdini's and Ricky Jay's books). In fact, moisture on the soles of the feet can protect one against burning soles.

This effect is called the Leidenfrost effect, and is cited most often as the explanation for fire-walking without injury. The best way to demonstrate this is with drops of water on a hot skillet. If the skillet is hot enough, the surface of the drop vaporizes, creates a cushion of air, and the drop dances on the surface until it completely evaporates.

Several antifire-walking advocates have stated that moisture on the soles of the feet (from the ground or simply from sweat), is enough to create the Leidenfrost effect and protect the walker from serious burns. However, looking more closely at this as the explanation makes it evaporate like the water droplets. People are significantly heavier, and with the lengthy fire-walks (some over forty feet) that many have done, the Leidenfrost effect may help the walker, but not protect them completely from the heat.

But if you couple the Leidenfrost effect (which helps a little) with the low heat-conductivity of the coals (which helps more), and if the walkers are careful not to stand still too long (or get hot embers between their toes) and actually step across the coals fast (that helps even more), you have a pretty good start for a physical explanation for fire-walking.

This is not to say that everyone can do this because of simple physics. In fact, people do get burned during these fire-walks (though rather infrequently, and often, I'm told, because of hot embers sticking to the skin). The skeptics have a problem with fire-walking in its motivational incarnation because it is suggested that people have special "powers" after taking a workshop from people such as motivational speaker Tony Robbins and fire-walking advocate Tolly Burkan.

I visited the tail end of one of Tolly Burkan's workshops for fire-walking instructors in 1994 up in Twain Harte, California. The Fire-walking Institute for Research and Education (F.I.R.E.) conducts workshops for motivational instructors and for others interested in beefing up their own self-confidence. The idea of fire-walking as an illustration of self-esteem is interesting (and not unlike the uses of the ritual in other cultures). After a bit of walking on hot coals, believing in oneself may be a bit easier, and facing what may have been intimidating tasks in the past is not so tough.

I spoke with a number of the instructors about the "specialness" of the training, and they all seemed to avoid any issue of special powers. Instead, the fire-walk just told them that they had control over their own bodies.

As I was up there for a TV shoot (and actually I was really there for minor commentary and to observe), the real stuff happened between skeptical southern California Physicist Bernard Leikind, an expert on fire-walking, and Tolly Burkan. Leikind was quite gracious, yet unyielding when it came to his analysis of what goes on when someone fire-walks. In fact, without any prep, he walked across the coals without a comment.

He also tried a few experiments for the camera, including strapping steaks on his feet to show that they, too, could avoid getting burned. In addition, he placed two aluminum oven racks in the coals to heat up, suggesting that the higher heat conductivity of the aluminum meant burnt flesh. This he showed with a touch of one of the steaks to the rack. It did show a bit of cooking.

However, a brave volunteer stepped on the racks as well. No cooking, no burning, no apparent pain. Must have been that idea of touching the hot pan quickly without burning (the steak obviously didn't know better).

People have reportedly stood in hot coals for many seconds. In some parts of the world, hot stones, which may be better conductors of heat than coals (depending on the type of stone), are used. People rarely get burned. More importantly, people feel no pain (unless they are burned).

Tony Robbins and Tolly Burkan have used fire-walking as the endgame of their motivational, self-esteem trainings. Skeptics claim this is dangerous, yet I saw nothing but respect for fire among fire-walking instructors at Burkan's F.I.R.E. workshop. To my mind, while there is inherent danger in fire-walking, the act itself is not something that will cause problems for the participants in the long run. To the contrary, people tend to see this as a confirmation that they can do what they set their minds to do.

That's Mind over Matter.

In some reported cases, it would appear that there is an extraordinary resistance to fire and hot coals. People who merely stand around in the coals without being burned are experiencing something more than low heat conductivity or the Leidenfrost effect. And all fire-walkers who don't perceive the heat or any pain that may be associated with even a quick touch of a hot surface are utilizing the power of their minds to affect their bodies.

While fire-walking is a better ritual than an example of actual Mind over Matter, it does seem to bring out people's attitudes of self-esteem and confidence, or in many places around the world, confirm their faith in their God(s) or in the power of their God(s) to protect them. While fire-walking is more dangerous than simple prayer, if the skeptics are right and there is merely a physical explanation for it, then perhaps it acts as a psychological placebo for bringing out what lies within a person. As long as people are taught to respect the fire, and follow instructions exactly, there is, even as the skeptics admit, little danger in fire-walking.

Mind directs the body to avoid injury.

In the extreme I'll stand in the fire for a while examples, there appears to be something more going on. The mind controls perception of heat and pain, yet the flesh stays unburned. For these rare people, who may believe that what they are doing is harmless, they stay unharmed. Mind keeps the body safe, somehow.

That protection factor may be similar to the healing factor we all have. In all cases, belief in one's ability to walk across the coals with whatever explanation for the lack of burning skin is of the essence. Leikind's own belief in the physics of the situation precluding him getting burned may be what kept him from getting burned. After all, science says a placebo works, and that belief in placebos may be all that helps the patients heal themselves.

There are other motivational techniques, besides walking on hot coals, that are in use.

One of the most common motivational tools is visualization. Whether conducted in a calm, peaceful setting, with dimmed lights and soft music playing, or in the setting where one normally works, visualizing the goals that one wants to achieve (and often the actions needed to get to those goals) or seeing oneself operating at peak efficiency (or beyond) aids in getting physically set for physical activity, in framing what one really wants out of life or in particular situations, and in motivating oneself to go out and try to achieve those goals.

Fire-walking is used to "prove" that one has the mental (if not physical) "stuff" to achieve, to reach a goal. One might try other things, however, to reach a lofty goal. For example, some people might learn juggling in a motivational workshop, which for those of us who are terminally uncoordinated is a clear example of learning a mind over matter technique. Others might go into martial arts training as a method of self-discipline that can be applied to everyday life.

For some motivational trainers and speakers, running people through an obstacle course until they can do it right (with lots of positive reinforcement and visualization to help them) is the way to motivating people, to getting them to know that they can achieve something if they set their minds to it.

Others might go the route of Billy Crystal and company in the film *City Slickers,* whether that means running with the bulls in Spain (much more dangerous than walking on hot coals) or heading out to bring in a herd of cattle. Most people wanting this kind of excitement might choose a white water rafting trip or skydiving to achieve that "I can do it" spirit.

All of these things take a force of will, a determination to try and do something that one might otherwise assume is personally impossible (even though many others can do it). That mental resolve, followed by the actual achievement requires the attitude that you can do something otherwise out of the question, that your mind can push your own limits to achieve something physical.

With most of these techniques, unlike fire-walking, there is more of the mind-pushing physical endurance than a potential mental "shield" that may need to be there to protect one from hot coals. However, as with athletes pushing the limits of what they can do physically, people in extraordinary (for them) physical situations again and again demonstrate that their will to achieve overcomes perceived physical limits or shortcomings (though, let's face it, there can be some limits that even the mind can't overcome).

Motivation can be mental or physical in nature, and the techniques used to motivate can incorporate both. However, whether the goal is physical or mental achievement, the process of motivation is primarily a mental one. And while the muscles can "learn" certain things so as to make certain actions easier, the mind is always involved in that learning processs. Then, utilizing the mental motivation, the belief that one can do what one sets out to do, the physical becomes easier.

Our minds, properly motivated, can push our bodies to do seemingly miraculous things (even if the miracle is only in the way we look at ourselves). Whether that means achieving juggler status, or walking across red-hot coals, we set our minds for a goal, and our bodies come in line with that.

By the way, I didn't do that fire-walk myself. Before you say "oh, he's chicken," I have to say that I had not gone through any training for it, I didn't buy the physics-only explanation for the fire-walking, and I have tendinitis in my left heel (which unfortunately means I'd have had to limp a bit across the coals). He who hesitates, I was told, gets burned.

I avoided the walk because I didn't really want to have to test that next example of Mind over Matter, self-healing. That's next.

Mental Healing: From Self to Psychic

We are in the midst of what many have called the *alternative medicine revolution*. Western medicine is apparently under siege because of rising costs of health care and less and less money to pay for it. Many are seeking alternatives to what is often termed "traditional Western medicine," and interestingly those alternatives have much longer traditions than most of modern medicine. Herbal remedies and body-energy techniques as well as a focus on the mind to heal the body are more and more coming into acceptance in the U.S., though not without much struggle. The range of techniques and the politics of medicine are enormous issues today.

While I hope to give you an understanding of many of the issues in this chapter, there is no way a single chapter in a book like this can do the whole subject justice. So, I will focus more than a bit on what has been called anomalous healing (also remote mental healing and psychic healing), with some discussion of other areas. There are dozens of new sources on spiritual healing and alternative medicine out there now, and here I hope to just whet your appetite, with the end result being that you will *want* to know more about healing and the mind/body connection.

Many of these techniques of alternative medicine and alternative therapies are finally being looked at in this country by the National

Institute of Health's Office of Alternative Medicine. For example, researchers at the University of Texas School of Public Health at Houston and M.D. Anderson Cancer Center received a three-year, $730,000 grant with which they plan to use to evaluate herbal remedies and other biological materials being touted as treatments and remedies for cancer.[1]

Other studies funded recently by the Office of Alternative Medicine have included those looking at the uses of meditation techniques and hypnosis in treating drug addition, insomnia, and chronic pain. Research is being funded to look at the effectiveness of acupuncture and homeopathy. Studies are looking at shifts in diet and lifestyle to help stave off heart disease.

"For example, the Preventative Medicine Research Institute, in Sausalito, California, conducted a recent clinical study that, according to its president, Dr. Dean Ornish, demonstrates that severe heart disease can be reversed by changing one's diet and lifestyle. The findings were published in the September 1995 issue of the *Journal of the American Medical Association*.[2]

Essentially, what is happening is a shifting of attitudes toward health, at least in Washington, D.C., so that emphasis is being placed on the health of patients. Can people be kept healthy or cured of diseases? Are there other techniques that have been out there for a long time that really work, as the claims state? The Office of Alternative Medicine is interested in getting alternative therapies scientifically evaluated, to see if they really work.

Some may work as they claim, others may not. But at least there is money flowing now to objectively evaluate alternatives.

In Appendix A, I have listed some resources for further reading and exploration on more general issues of the mind and healing. In particular, let me refer you to the work of Dr. Larry Dossey, Dr. Deepak Chopra, Dr. Andrew Weil, and Michael Murphy of Esalen Institute.

∗

As long as there have been people there have been people who have attempted to hurt and heal others. Animals are often observed

to aid their young and their mates when injury occurs, and social-
ized animals may even help others in the group.

Our ancestors utilized a variety of techniques to help the diseased
and the injured. Some of these techniques involved prayer and ritual, imploring God or the gods to help cure the victim/patient. Some
techniques put the power of healing in the hands of the shaman or
witch doctor or holy person. Other techniques involved the use of
natural substances, from roots and herbs to parts of animals and
other living things, to minerals found in the earth.

In a few cultures, forms of surgery may have been performed to
remove foreign substances or diseased tissues, or to repair torn tissues or set broken bones. Some cultures practiced a primitive form
of brain surgery, to relieve pressures on the brain or to allow spirits to enter the brain to effect a healing.

Over the centuries, as sophistication in healing rose and fell, there
were some techniques that evolved into others, and some that
stayed the same. In general, we in the world today seem to have a
couple of major philosophies or viewpoints when it comes to healing.

On the one hand, Western medicine has evolved into a very
mechanistic science. The body is a biological machine that can be
altered through a variety of means, mostly physical, from surgery
to the introduction of scientifically identified or designed substances.

On the other hand, Eastern medicine traditionally involved a
variety of techniques, some mechanistic, and others designed to restore *balance* to the body and to the mind. In fact, while many techniques, such as acupuncture rely on restoration of balance in the
body, the mind is still a vital component of that balance.

Western science has traditionally ignored the idea that intangible forces, such as the mind, have an effect on the body. With the
rise of the field of psychology (and the medical discipline of psychiatry), there was some recognition that the health of the mind also
may affect the health of the body (and vice versa). One of the best
documented mind/body effects in medicine has to do with how the
mind accepts certain statements about healing.

The *placebo effect* revolves around a substance with no re-
deeming medicinal value (or perhaps some other form of physical

therapy) being given to a patient. The patient is told (and hopefully convinced) that the substance, perhaps a sugar pill or vitamin injection, has curative powers. The patient, accepting this, then goes on to be healed.

Of course, the placebo effect doesn't always work. One can't simply give out sugar pills for all ailments and expect some kind of restoration of all body functions. But in some cases, especially those where the influence of the mind may have actually spurred on the illness to begin with (and of course, in those cases where the patient is completely imagining his or her illness), the mind works its wonders based on the belief that the medicine is doing its job. In other cases, where the illness is very real and not necessarily tied into the mind at all, patients have recovered, apparently through their belief in whatever placebo was given to them.

Doctors of Western medicine have come to believe a truism that has been accepted in other parts of the world for centuries: the patient's *will to live* is often a crucial piece in the healing puzzle when the patient is critical. Expanding on that a bit one comes to the conclusion that the patient's *will to be healed,* which is undoubtedly a big part of the equation in the placebo situations, is necessary for many, if not all, medical situations.

What has been very obvious to Eastern medicine (and, to many Western doctors, by the way) is nearly a revolutionary idea here in North America: the mind and its emotional states must be brought back into medical science.

Medical science in the West has become quite compartmentalized and specialized in nature, with doctors dealing with small parts and functions of the body instead of the whole person. The mind is seen as a separate entity from the body, and often doctors may overlook the idea that the person seeking medical help is more than just the body, but a combination of mind and body.

My own doctor (the general practitioner who I have to see first through the HMO I am a member of) is, I believe, a rarity. Whenever I have gone in to see him, unless the problem is an actual injury (such as hurting because of a car accident), he listens to what I have to say, then asks me whether there are additional stresses on me at that time, from work or personal life. He asks about my emotional states. He talks that out with me, trying to relate what's on my mind to what's happened to my body.

He also asks for my gut feeling as to what I believe would be the best line of treatment for me (of course, as the doctor, he's not going to let my "gut" lead me down the wrong pathway). I always feel as if *I* am being taken care of (the *I* that is both my mind and my body).

But based on my experience with many other doctors (both as patient and in social contexts), this doctor is a rare being.

In Western medicine, there seems to be the kind of attitude one might expect from an auto mechanic. The body of the patient is just another "heap" that needs repair. In fact, while this is definitely undergoing change, *repair* seems to be the main focus rather than *healing*. While there is more and more emphasis on preventative medicine, suggesting ways for the patient to be healthier so as to prevent any future illness, the idea of helping people achieve balance through a multidisciplinary approach, effectively dealing with the whole person instead of just the mechanics of the body, seems to be still very new to doctors.

In the East, one can observe traditions and techniques of healing that have survived for hundreds if not thousands of years. Chinese medicine has survived because it apparently works, because its track record is a good one. Herbal remedies are used by people because the results are good, not because of the understanding of the chemical properties of the herbs, roots, and other substances.

Chinese medicine is based on a philosophy of energy in the body and mind, and on creating or maintaining an appropriate balance. Techniques such as acupuncture, which are based on affecting the flow of energy, or *chi,* in circuits (meridians) throughout the body, do work effectively and are even used routinely in situations where more Western techniques such as invasive surgery are also in play (acupuncture is used in such situations for anesthesia).

Massage and the specific form known as acupressure are used to also effect a balance in the body, a balance that may restore temporary or permanent functioning to the body.

But the mind is a vital part of the process of health and healing in China, for it has been said that mental attitude and belief is the major factor in affecting good or bad health.

How can this be? one might ask. If disease is caused by the spread of bacteria or viruses, how could the mind be that important?

If one considers our own immune system as capable, under certain conditions, of fighting off most disorders that infect the body, and one considers the effect the mind has on the body appears to include an effect on the immune system, then it's not such a stretch to consider that the mind can actually help fend off invaders of the body.

However, no technique seems to be foolproof, and it would appear that a combination of mental and physical treatments seems to be the best of all possible worlds.

When the body is physically injured, such as with a broken bone or a deep wound, the healing process may need some help to effect the cure. A broken bone, not set properly, will either heal incorrectly or not at all. A deep wound not stitched up may cause too much blood loss for the patient to initiate his or her own healing processes.

On the other hand, it would appear that people can initiate or speed up the physical healing process of even broken bones and wounds with the right mental attitude.

Author and pilot Martin Caidin has learned over the years to directly affect matter with his mind. He practices his "telekinetics" on small targets, getting them to revolve even when placed in sealed chambers. Caidin, who will share much about mind over matter with us in Chapter Eleven, has had more than his share of bad physical incidents in his life. In one situation, he had a break of his neck that left a spur on a nerve. He was told that unless he had surgery in thirty days, he'd become parapalegic.

He decided he didn't want to go that route immediately, since there were always risks in surgery. Money was not an issue, as the surgeon, a good friend, was going to waive his fee (and most of the hospital fees).

He focused his attention on himself and on mentally "seeing" a reduction of the spur while doing his target turning. He would give himself what he called a "self-hypnotic suggestion" that a "wind" would blow across the spur (the same mental "wind" that turned the targets) and erode it. To the surprise of his doctor (and the hospital) 95 percent of the spur disappeared over the next month, leaving the need for surgery a very moot point.

According to Caidin, when he works on himself with his "mental wind" or other relaxation techniques, the relaxation part of it is quite dominant.

I must caution the reader that this is not something that we can all apparently call on. If you have a physical ailment, it is good to mentally work on yourself while under the care of a doctor or other health practitioner, but for most of us it is not a good idea to rely solely on the power of our own minds to heal ourselves.

In China, many people practice preventative exercise to keep the balance of the body and mind. Much of the exercise people do there owes its form and practice to various martial art forms.

Tai Chi Chu'an is practiced to keep the flow of *chi* in the body going and balanced. Much has appeared in the world press about chi gong (pronounced either as "chi gung" or "ki gung"), a technique of body movement that revolves around moving energy in and around the body. While we in the West often question even the existence of *chi* (let alone affecting its flow and balance), it is accepted as much as blood flow is accepted in Chinese life (and this is by no means limited to the Chinese, as many all over the world believe in "life-force" flowing through the body).

Chi gong masters have put on some amazing displays of mind over muscle, as mentioned in Chapter Two. In chi gong, it is not use of muscle that wins over an opponent, but the manipulation of energy that wins over muscle. This energy is manipulated by both mind and body.

The rise of alternative healing here in the West appears to be the result of a number of factors. I am by no means an expert in the sociology of the medical system, but there have been a number of rather obvious influences on healing and medicine here that have at least contributed to the interest and practice of alternative therapies (even if they are not mitigating causes).

First of all, over the past thirty years or so, there has been an increasing awareness of mind- and body-altering substances and techniques. People have increasingly been questioning the status quo in all areas of their lives, from government to work ethics, from the way they entertain themselves to the way they worship (and what or who they worship). It's no shock that how they keep healthy or get healed should also be a focus of attention.

The rise of so-called "New Age" thought and philosophy (much of which comes from very old, tried and true traditions and beliefs . . . it's just "new" to many people in Western society) has brought with it a focus on the mind/body connection, and by extension, how the mind heals/harms the body and vice versa.

People, dissatisfied or frustrated by failures or incompleteness in healing and health with the current system, have sought out other means for getting healthy.

Some of the frustrations also apparently surrounds the rising costs of medical treatment in this country. Let's face it, it's cheaper to go to an herbalist than it is to visit a doctor (and certainly *much* cheaper to seek alternatives than to go into the hospital for some kind of treatment). Without appropriate insurance (and even with it), money can be a real issue, and can even be the deciding factor for some people who need treatment as to what kind of treatment they may seek and receive.

In fact, the continually rising costs of traditional Western medicine has cause more than a small stir in the insurance industry. Insurers have had to take a close look at how much treatments cost, and pressure has been put on both patients and medical providers to go for lower-cost treatments. So-called "alternative health" practices are being explored as a means to provide lower-cost treatment. Some insurance plans cover chiropractors or acupuncturists or other health alternatives in an effort to bring down costs of health care.

Of course, there is much controversy inherent in such alternative health practices, again because of several factors. Acupuncture has not been accepted by traditional Western medicine because the basic tenet, that it affects the flow and balance of *chi,* is itself an alien concept (given that there is no physical evidence for *chi* and given that the AMA is big on physical evidence and testing). The same goes for other techniques.

When Dr. Jacques Benveniste, a researcher with a national research organization in France, took on homeopathy as a research project and found, surprisingly, that continually diluting a solution until the solution contains mere molecules of the original substance, still has an affect, he was met with shock and accusations of fraud. That a team came to check his lab out for fraud rather than calling for independent replications (apparently because the result that homeopathy *might* actually work was an affront to Western science) is very telling (the team included James "the Amazing" Randi—why include a debunking magician in a team investigating what basically amounts to a biochemistry exercise—an inclusion that is very telling as to the motives of the team).

Where was the scientific curiosity? Western scientists, especially, it would appear, medical scientists and doctors, and pharmaceutical companies have a vested interest in keeping certain techniques, practices, and philosophies out of Western medicine. For some, it is a matter of belief and conviction that alternative therapies are ineffective or perhaps dangerous (and some are—the same can be said of unnecessary surgery and many medical treatments in specific cases). For others, it is a matter of protecting one's financial interests.

The current trend to question medical treatments and to explore alternative therapies and practices is a very good one. Many of the techniques may prove useful, while others worthless. Many may simply be found to have more than a little placebo effect component that explains why they work.

But if the question is the health of a human being, does it really matter whether one technique that works for a person is "alternative" or nontraditional? Is health of the human being the real concern here, or is it abiding by the ritual of a particular healing practice that is more important?

The mind as healer is becoming more and more a part of our focus as a society. There is no question that this is a good thing. How the use of what we have considered alternative therapies (but others around the world have relied on as primary healing practices) is acknowledged by people here in North America remains to be seen. Acceptance may happen because of curiosities in these techniques being piqued, because the AMA sees an inevitable swing of public opinion headed in that direction, or because the insurance carriers, looking for lower-cost treatments, start pushing for such acceptance.

But if any of the techniques work, from herbal medicine to acupuncture, from homeopathy to aromatherapy (the use of aromatic substances to help effect changes in the mind and body), from therapeutic touch to biofeedback, it is important that medical science grows and matures enough to really take a look at them and consider accepting them.

After all, doctors prescribe placebos from time to time. They know they work. They don't know *why* or *how* they work. Results may need to be emphasized over knowing how and why something is effective, at least in the short term (though the search for explanation is and always should be part of the process—that's science).

One technique for allowing the display of mind's effect on body that is generally accepted is that of biofeedback. The idea of this is of course to allow some kind of feedback device (other than your own perceptions of how you're feeling) to show that you are actually effecting changes in some bodily process.

In a full-scale biofeedback setup, you may be hooked up to monitors of your heart rate, blood pressure, brain waves, temperature, respiration, and other measures (such as galvanic skin response, or GSR, which checks activity of the sweat glands on the fingers or palms, activity which is highly reactive to emotional and mental states).

Biofeedback monitors provide either visual or more typically auditory feedback that tells the user when he or she has relaxed themselves, slowed or sped up one's pulse, raised or lowered blood pressure, or even put oneself into a particular altered state of consciousness (and the accompanying range of brain wave activity).

Generally, biofeedback is used to train people to get into the right mental and emotional state that brings on a desired physical state. Once a person is capable of doing this repeatedly and consciously through use of the devices, that person can typically bring on the state without hookups, in their normal lives.

Certain visualizations may be used with biofeedback, or there may be more focus on actually bringing forth certain remembered feelings or memories of certain physical states. The benefit is that one can become less stressed, calmer, and even effect change that could mean giving up certain medications.

Martin Caidin has written about a blood pressure-control technique for pilots in the professional aviation literature. The wrong blood pressure readings can ground a pilot. His technique involves relaxation and visualization. Success has followed pilots trying the techniques. Many pilots, under a doctor's care, using the technique are off their blood pressure medication (according to the many, many letters he's received).

Many others teach techniques that revolve around meditation and relaxation and visualization in order to bring the mind into the process of consciously connecting with the body.

By the way, while brain waves are usually not included, when one is hooked up to a polygraph (commonly called a lie detector), measures of a variety of physiological processes can be used to give a trained technician enough information to determine if one is telling the truth (insofar as the person knows or believes what he or she is saying as the truth). One must wonder, given successes with biofeedback, whether polygraph examiners ask the question "have you ever taken any biofeedback training?" before relying on the information the polygraph presents to them.

For your own "play," I should mention that biofeedback devices are available (some expensive, some cheap) to the general public. Tools for Exploration, a company in Marin County, California, sells a number of them, as do other places around the country (check Appendix A for resources). In fact, Radio Shack sells a biofeedback device, a hand-held GSR that gives off a changing tone, the shifts based on your emotional state (the more relaxed, the lower the tone).

Others have taught people to use visualizations to help mentally enter the fight against one's diseases or to help spur on the healing process. Much has been written about Carl Simonton's use of guided imagery techniques in helping cancer patients. The technique, pioneered by oncologist Simonton and his former wife, psychotherapist Stephanie Matthews-Simonton in the 1970s, has been used in a number of contexts, and not limited to cancer treatment. Guided imagery involves suggestions from a health practitioner or an audiotape that helps the patient relax and visualize positive mental images. Suggestions that the white blood cells are actually knights in shining armor, then guidance with that image to have the "knights" attack the cancer cells and tumors might be used to help reinforce the "will to live" and somehow switch on (or speed up or strengthen) the body's natural healing process.

The mind, using such imagery, somehow passes instructions on to different systems in the body, possibly the autonomic nervous system, which does control functions such as regeneration of healthy tissue (healing).Coupled with such a technique may be a regimen of exercise and/or a change in the kinds of foods one eats.

Some skeptics have attacked such techniques, claiming, among other things, that visualization is just using one's imagination, and that the imaginings that one is feeling better may be what's going on. However, our imagination can in fact cause responses in the body. If one really lets go with visualization (which could also include imagining "hearing" pleasant sounds or "smelling" certain scents; in essence, any of the senses can be "visualized"), there are often responses in the body. If you imagine (well) the smell of fresh baked bread, you may salivate or feel hungry (possibly with accompanying rumblings of the stomach). You may sweat if you imagine feeling hot, or shiver if you believe it is very cold.

In addition, there have been a number of medical studies that have shown that guided imagery has an effect on the body, though not necessarily a complete healing from a ravaging disease (it may be simply a slowdown of the disease's progress, rather than a remission). There have been seemingly "miraculous" turnarounds for many people, whether they used such visualization techniques or simply *chose* to get better.

The mind affects the body.

Visualizations are used in healing the mind and healing the body. It may be that one can shift one's emotional state through visualization (causing, then, appropriate shifts in the chemistry of the brain and the rest of the body. For example, imagining one's anger compressing into a ball of energy, which can be thrown away, may leave a sense of calm (this is a technique I have used, taught to me by martial artist Guy Savelli years ago; it works, at least for me). Such a technique may be useful in "throwing off" any negative feelings associated with an illness or injury (such as the pain) and reinforcing the positive healing "energy" in the body.

If one talks about visualizing a change in the body's healing "energy," we might relate that to Chinese medicine's concept of restoring the balance in one's own life energy, one's *chi*. Martial artists may both utilize and teach techniques of healing, an idea that most people will certainly wonder about, given the typical connection of the martial arts to fighting skills. Keeping in mind that the martial arts involve doing things one might consider outside the range of what's normally humanly possible on a fairly consistent basis, it's no real surprise that whatever the "force" or *chi* is that allows for such performance may be applied to healing oneself. If you have seen episodes of *Kung Fu: The Legend Continues,* you will see much healing done (though not as much as the fighting, since that's typically what draws ratings).

Belief, *knowing,* is again a major part of this, though the *knowing* that something will work may be a very subconscious thing. Knowing *how* is not as important as knowing or believing or wanting that it will work, that healing oneself can happen. Healing on any level may fail because of the patient's own desire or willingness to be healed, and self-healing may fail because one doesn't want it to work, rather than because there is a lack of understanding of how it works.

Guy Savelli, whom I discussed in Chapter Two, is a martial artist in the Midwest interested in mind over matter in more than just the fighting arts. For years he has engaged in spiritual healing, using his blend of martial arts and spiritual beliefs to work on others and, more to the point, in helping people heal themselves.

One area of real success is in pain control, which can be extended to try to effect real healing. Different martial artists may have differing views on how to help people learn to heal themselves, and some may use their own *chi* to help heal others, but many of the techniques can be taught so that one can continue to work toward a healing even without the martial artist.

I recently rewatched a videotape Savelli sent me a few years ago of a couple of sessions he had in his school in Kirtland, Ohio. In the first session, he helped a gentleman with some intense back pain.

He told him that it's important to "Say thank you, say your sorry [for anything you may have done wrong], and ask for help" from whatever higher power one believes in.

Visualization is an important part of the process, and being able to visualize in color and in three dimensions makes the process that much more effective. "To work with this power, you have to picture it. . . . As you believe more, the picture becomes clearer."

Savelli first asked the man to picture an open Japanese fan in front of his face. Then, he had him visualize the fan becoming a funnel, the point of the funnel going into him. As the man was Catholic, he had him picture Christ standing at the open end of the funnel. For other belief systems, it could be another religious figure or figure of power, or simply a "power" at the other end.

Savelli asked the man to "see" a beam of light coming from the Christ-figure through the funnel and into him, "swirling around and around" in his body. As the man had a lower back pain, Savelli directed the visualization so that the man directed this light down his shoulders, down his spinal column, dripping and swirling around it, and down to where the man's back pain was.

"Picture all of that and say thank you, say you're sorry, and ask for help."

Then he asked the man to both picture and feel the energy as heat or warmth being applied to the place of pain.

The man, at first, related that the pain had lessened. Yet over the next few minutes, as Savelli reinforced the visualization, the man spoke of the pain being gone.

The next step, of course, would be to attack the cause of the pain, to use that same energy to effect a self-healing.

Years ago, Savelli had told me something I've since heard from a few other martial artists I've spoken with. People can heal themselves if they just tap into their own energy. Sometimes they need help, either in getting in touch with that energy (through techniques such as I described above) or in initiating the healing process. If the latter is the case, it may be that they need the energy and aid of others.

Healers of all sorts have existed throughout time. While some use herbs and other substances, physical therapies, or objects such as acupuncture needles, some have used their own "energies" to heal others. Whether through the laying-on of hands or simply praying for another, people around the world believe that there are those who can heal others through their thoughts, beliefs, and faith.

In many traditions, the healer is effectively channeling healing energy from a "higher" power, such as God (or gods). The healer may firmly believe this, or may believe that the power of healing is a gift from the Supreme Being(s) that must be used to help others.

If one removes the "God" element from the healing, the healer may refer to their psychic abilities as the source. Psychic healing, or perhaps more correctly "remote mental healing," firmly deals with the mind/body connection and the connection of one mind even beyond the body. Remote mental healing typically involves a designated healer who claims to be able to manipulate another's physiological system to positive result.

For example, a healer, whether he or she lays hands physically on the patient, focuses his or her attention on the patient's illness. Psychics speak of a variety of steps they might take. They might visualize energy going from their bodies into those of the patients, destroying the unhealthy tissues or energizing the patients' healing processes. Some might visualize the illness leaving the patients' bodies and being absorbed into their own, where they can better cause it to be destroyed.

One psychic I knew years ago told me that she would absorb the illness into herself, then move it up and out of her body, as though she's simply discarding it like a torn sock.

Some healers believe they directly affect the injured area of the patient's body (as through psychokinesis). They might visualize changes in the body structure of the patient, essentially forcing physical changes in the tissues, whether sped-up growth of the healthy cells or the destruction of the unhealthy one.

Still others believe they telepathically influence the patient to kick in their own healing abilities. A healer may also simply assume that the patient's belief in his or her abilities is the trigger for the self-healing, this going back to the placebo effect.

Many alternative therapies deal with an improvement of mental attitude. Others deal with physical manipulation. Still others relate to "energy work," such as acupuncture and techniques taught in the martial arts. In such energy work, the therapy purports to manipulate the energy system, the chi, of the patient's body, which is out of whack. Acupuncture, for example, is used to unblock or alter the flow of chi through the body, so the natural balance of the body is achieved. With balance in the energy system comes health.

Therapeutic touch, possibly the closest therapy to "psychic healing," is used by nurses all over the U.S., and purports to allow the therapist to manipulate the patient's energy without the need to physically touch them. Nurses using this form of therapy learn to "feel" (subjectively) the energy being given off by the patient's body, and to stroke their hands along the lines of energy, pulling off bad energies and throwing them away, and enhancing the good, healthy energy the body needs to stay healthy. By manipulating the energy of the patient, the physical body follows along to health.

In 1982–83 I was fortunate to work with the late Alex Tanous at the American Society for Psychical Research in New York. Dr. Tanous was there as a subject in experimental series looking at out of body experiences. However, his own talents also ran to working on haunting cases, working with law enforcement, and working with terminally ill patients at a New York area hospital.

Alex's work at the hospital was not a solo practice. In effect, he was "prescribed" as a method of treatment by a doctor for patients who had no other recourse. Alex had some success in his healing practice, and there were both temporary remissions of the illnesses treated, and in a few cases, complete turnarounds. While Alex related to me that he believed his own abilities connected with the patients using a psychokinetic influence to kick-start the healing process again, he also told me that he really couldn't discount the possibility that he was nothing more than a placebo. In effect, he said that for a patient who believes in such forms of healing, an actor well-cast to play the part of a healer may be enough to restart the healing process.

In dealing with research on the effects of the healer on the patient, eliminating a psychological effect of the patient's attitudes and moods on health is difficult, if not often impossible.

Parapsychologists and people outside the field have conducted a variety of types of healing experiments throughout the twentieth-century. Many of these experiments have shown significant results, both based on the subjective experiences of those being healed (the "patient") and evidence of physical changes being apparently caused by the healers.

Some of the best experiments conducted over the years have been those of Dr. Bernard Grad at McGill University in Canada and his work with a retired Hungarian military officer, Oskar Estebany. These were well-controlled experiments that, unlike what one would expect in psychic healing, did not use human subjects.

Instead of subjects who could respond to a placebo effect, Grad first utilized mice as his patients.

In one experimental series, Estebany was to retard the grown of goiters in mice given an iodine-deficient diet. Without touching the mice directly (only the cages they were in), Estebany worked on a subject group of mice, while other, control groups, were either left alone or given a heat treatment. The result was that there was a significant difference in the growth of goiters between the group Estebany worked on and the other two groups.

Grad also did a little surgery on the mice in another series of tests. A small patch of skin was removed from the mice (and covered). Estebany was to work to heal one group of mice. Again, the group Estebany worked on showed a difference from the control groups, the patients healing significantly faster than the others.

Next, Estebany worked on plants. A saline solution was poured on seedlings to inhibit the growth. Estebany, rather than working directly on the plants, worked on samples of the solution. With the plants watered with his treated solution, the seeds sprouted, grew faster, and weighed significantly more than the control samples. Whether Estebany had somehow, apparently, affected the solution rather than the plants (even though he didn't focus on the plants) is difficult to determine.

Grad went on to using others as substitute healers in similar experiments. These experiments showed that the attitude and mental states of the healer can affect the growth rate of the target plants. In one series, Grad's lab assistant did well with the plants while an individual suffering from a psychotic depression ended up with a sample of plants that were worse off than the control groups.[3]

Further work with Estebany was conducted with Sister Justa Smith, who had Estebany "treat" flasks containing trypsin, an enzyme at work in the human body. The idea that a healer might somehow speed up the healing processes in the human body (such as those involving enzyme activity) was one that had occurred to Sister Justa. After Estebany worked on a flask for a time, there was increased enzyme activity which was similar to that of a control flask exposed to high magnetic fields.

Experiments since those of Grad's have included subjects such as the late healer Olga Worrall, Dean Kraft, and other "gifted" subjects, as well as those involving "normal" people as healers have shown positive results over the years, whether the patients were samples of plants, laboratory animals, people, or samples of biological materials such as cancer cells or blood.

In one experimental series conducted by Dolores Krieger, Ph.D., one of the "founders" of the technique of *therapeutic touch* (more on that in a moment), who observed Estebany healing people to apparent success, involved the healer in an attempt to affect a change in blood hemoglobin. The results showed an unusual increase in the hemoglobin content of a blood sample.

Out of her work with Estebany and others came Kreiger's technique. Therapeutic touch involves use of the hands to direct one's energy to influence and affect a change in the body and energy of another. It may involve some direct laying-on of hands, but generally the hands simply sense and either are held over spots on the body or are stroked along above the body to effectively brush away "negative" energy that might inhibit healing (or cause illness in the first place).

Therapeutic touch is practiced by nurses and others all over the

U.S., as well as outside the country. Utilizing therapeutic touch by itself may not provide the level of healing one might need (though there are cases where, as with other healing techniques, people's health has gone from bad to better with therapeutic touch), but when used by a nurse in conjunction with other medical care, one may end up with a very winning combination.

Naturally, the groups of organized "skeptics" around the world have shown their opposition to this technique, given that the "energy" being ostensibly manipulated has no objective evidence backing up its existence. One reason they appear to be more and more opposed to this technique is the fact that it is being taught at nursing schools all over the U.S. and beyond (and that means funds that might go elsewhere are being used for what some skeptics have called "New Age quackery"). In addition, skeptics have expressed concerns about funding experiments to understand an effect that they claim doesn't exist.

While both sides dispute how much evidence there is that therapeutic touch actually has a real effect (and whether there is an "energy" that is even present, let alone manipulated), the subjective side of this, the patient's subjective state, seems to support that there is a positive benefit to the technique.

Patients generally respond to touch, as all people typically respond positively to being touched in a positive way. When in therapeutic touch, people still report that they feel less in pain or that their illnesses feel as though there's some relief, indicates that the techniques at least helps the patient's view of his or her illness (shifting it to or aiding in it being positive, which can only help the healing process).

One example I recall involves a TV news cameraman who was working on a couple of pieces for a series on the power of the mind. He and his crew were doing a couple of segments at the American Society for Psychical Research when I worked there in the early '80s, and they had just shot a piece on therapeutic touch. He had bad back problems, and he had volunteered for an on-camera treatment. After getting a therapeutic touch treatment, he said he felt a big difference in how his back felt and the pain was greatly reduced, even days later.

The debate over therapeutic touch and other alternative health therapies has only really gotten underway, especially with the federal government calling for more reserach into such therapies. Politics are involved, legal issues abound, and much money is at risk. Over the next few years we should all see much change in the choices of treatment are offered patients, and hopefully more research into just how and why such techniques actually work (although skeptics would claim this is all a waste of money since the techniques "obviously" don't work).

Of course, much of the alternative therapy out there deals directly with the mind/body connection, and is directed at getting the patient to self-heal (as with the placebo effect, an effect rarely challenged by skeptics undoubtably because the only unknown in its equation is the mind itself). Humans are not the only participants in the healing arts. One of the alternative therapies being researched is called "pet therapy," and involves the effect animals may have on the human mind and health.

A leading expert on mental healing research in the field of parapsychology today is Jerry Solfvin, Ph.D. He is currently co-director of the doctoral parapsychology specialization at Rosebridge Graduate School of Integrative Psychology in Concord, California. His background in the field includes work as senior research associate at the Psychical Research Foundation in the 1970s (during which time he was one of the investigators of the "Amityville Horror" hoax). He was visiting research faculty at the Parapsychology Laboratory at the University of Utrect in the early 1980s, coming later to John F. Kennedy University in Orinda, California to coordinate the Graduate Parapsychology Program (which no longer exists, I'm afraid).

At a presentation to the California Society for Psychical Study in Berkeley (which he has served as vice president) in May 1994, Solfvin discussed the role of healing in the animal world and new research on the role of animal-human bonding in healing. While this research is not specifically "psychic" in nature, it has incredible implications where healing of all kinds is concerned. [Note: the following information was also presented in my "Psychic Frontiers" column in *Fate* magazine, August 1994]

Solfvin has had a lifelong love of animals, and a few years ago he was able to begin to combine this with his intense interest in mental healing. He learned about "animal-assisted therapy" from the folks at the San Francisco Society for the Prevention of Cruelty to Animals (SF/SPCA). This form of therapy, also called "pet therapy," involves a bonding process between animals (usually dogs) and patients in hospitals and clinics. Such therapy programs have been going on for more than a few years, and often provides psychological enhancements to attitudes of people who are both physically and mentally ill, as well as to alleviate loneliness.

Looking into this form of therapy led Solfvin to look at the role of animals as healers both in societies around the world, specifically preindustrial peoples, and within the animal groups themselves. Preindustrial societies (and even more modern peoples) often look at animals as having some kind of spiritual power, or as just being representative of such power. Many peoples consider animals to have specific healing power, while others have certain totem animals in their local as representative "wise shamanic beings." The boundaries between animals and humans is often blurred (which has given rise to legends of such metamorphic creatures as werewolves).

In many societies, there are more defined boundaries and even specific culturally determined definitions of what is a "person." Hitler's Nazis, for example, considered Jews and Gypsies (and generally most non-Aryans) as "soul-less" or "not human," thereby allowing for an easier justification to kill them. In our modern society, animals are often considered to be "soul-less," without true consciousness, and therefore subject to humanity's whim.

However, if one looks at animal behaviors in their own environment, from wolves to gorillas and chimps to dolphins, there are examples of what looks like communication between individuals and their groups, as well as even some examples of what look to be morality systems. Dolphins, of course, may possibly be the most intelligent creatures on earth next to humans (possibly more so), and we learn, in small bits and pieces, more and more about their communication processes every year.

The main debate about animal behavior seems to be whether

their behaviors are programmed instinct, or examples of conscious thought. Are animals self-aware (and is that even a criterion for consciousness)? That's hard to say, since whatever the observer of the behavior believes going in may influence how they interpret the behavior. But there is much evidence, mostly anecdotal, that suggests many animal species are capable of learning "new tricks" that appear outside of what could be considered instinct (for example, the case of Koko the Gorilla, who over the past several years has learned American Sign Language with a large vocabulary, can put together sentences in ASL, and has even been caught lying). These behaviors appear to be evidence of some form of consciousness, which may therefore be able to interact with the consciousness of a human. Any pet owners who believe they have telepathic connections to their pets are already accepting of this.

Solfvin has been looking at the question of whether certain animal species have designated "healers" in their groups. Primates and other animals have demonstrated some instinctual "knowledge" of natural healing plants and other substances. In Africa, he told the group he lectured to, he had the opportunity to visit a preserve in Kenya where baboon behaviors are observed.

In asking about animals who were injured and whether other baboons helped heal them (which may only involve protecting the injured or sick group member, or more advanced behaviors such as bringing food, water, and comfort to the injured and sick), he was at first told that no "healer" behavior was observed. But after asking a few more questions, the observers began to realize that they had in fact observed such behavior, only they never thought to consider what it meant. In other words, the observers of the baboons hadn't labeled the baboons who paid attention to injured or sick members of their group as "healers."

Animal-assisted therapy is based on the act of bringing an animal and an injured or ill human together to improve the psychological (and therefore the physical) well-being of the patients. Animals are nonjudgmental, and there is often a relaxation effect of the body (and presumably the mind) when a pet is around. Studies have indicated that a person's blood pressure goes down (relaxation) when talking to a pet, yet up (stress) when talking even to a close friend.

Sometimes the effect may go beyond the simplistic. You may have read something about a project where autistic children are guided into a swimming area with free-free swimming dolphins. This particular therapy has yielded amazing yet controversial results in many cases. The autistic children often appear to react to the dolphin, focusing on the mammal and even reaching out, something that autism would preclude. Some have suggested that telepathy may be involved, others that the brains of the autistic children are "wired" in such a way as to allow for some kind of tacit understanding or at least recognition of dolphin communication methods, but most studying this phenomena would say it's too soon to even speculate.

Clearly, however, there is a medical benefit to animal assisted therapy, whether that effect is a psycho-physiological reaction or something more than that. Checking what the medical benefit is has led Jerry Solfvin to his current project. Based on some cases where coma patients have come out of coma apparently due to the presence of a dog or other animal, as well as other considerations, Solfvin began working as co-principal investigator of a project sponsored by the SF/SPCA to look at the effects of animal assisted therapy on coma patients.

One spontaneous awakening case that received some press involved an 11 year old boy named Danny Tomei who was hit by a car in 1991. He apparently emerged from his two-week coma when his dog, Rusty, was allowed to visit him in the hospital and "pounced on him."[4]

Animals are being more and more used in a variety of therapeutic contexts around the country in a variety of hospital and clinical settings, and Solfvin is far from the only one who has used animals with coma patients. ". . . a golden retriever named Chip, often goes to coma victims' bedsides. Some patients who have recovered say they remember the dog. One boy emerged from his coma, calling for his pal, Chip."[5]

According Solfvin, there are several reasons why coma patients are ideal for such a study. First of all, besides the amazing recoveries from coma that have made the press, the psychological effects of the presence of an animal on normal, waking consciousness is eliminated. Coma patients are in a state of reduced or minimal sensory awareness, often (though not always) with some neurological dysfunction involved.

Coma patients have typically low prognosis for survival, and after three or four days in coma, the prognosis goes down exponentially. In fact, there is often nothing to do for the coma patient other than to maintain the body through mechanical life support.

Solfvin and the other volunteers worked on this project in five Intensive Care units at two hospitals in San Francisco. After being notified by the hospital of a new coma patient, and after gaining appropriate permissions from the family of the patient, they tried to set up visits to the ICU as soon as possible. The team, composed of two to three people plus a dog, visits once or twice a day for approximately twenty minutes. Each visit was videotaped and the team had access to all medical records to see if any change is affected.

During such visits, the dogs (small, of necessity) are placed on the bed and are encouraged to interact with the patient. The volunteers will often pick up the patient's hand and stroke the dog with it, encourage the dog to snuggle with the patient, and generally try to observe any sort of reaction on the part of the patient.

Jerry has stated some degree of "success" in eight patients, though nothing as apparently instantaneous as Danny Tomei's case. One case, however, was very encouraging.

Late in 1993, a young man named Jerome, in a coma due to a car accident, had just been checked by the nurse before Solfvin's team visit. A check of optic reaction showed no dilation of the pupils of the eyes when a light was shined in them. "As many of you may know," said Jerry, "this is very bad." Such a lack of reaction in the eyes can indicate little or no brain activity.

However, shortly after a dog was placed on the bed, and his hand was placed on the dog, Jerome showed some signs that there was, indeed, "somebody home." Solfvin related his amazement when Jerome's arm began to move of its own accord and he opened his eyes. To the team's observing eyes, he was reacting to the canine. While the effect didn't last, there were similar reactions on subsequent visits. Jerome eventually came out of the coma (though not during a period when the dog was there).

As of this writing (fall 1995), Solfvin and his team has finished its data collection, and is in the process of tabulating and analyzing the data for their conclusions. Besides the observers' and doctors' notes and health charts of the patients, there are videotapes of the last couple of months covering the pet visits and any impact on the patients in the five hospitals they were working with. "We had good success on a practical level," said Solfvin, "but lots of problems working in the ICUs" and subacute care units." The only patient they had striking results with was Jerome, but there were indicators of positive results, which they are analyzing through "looking at the subtle medical indicators."

While this may seem "nonpsychic" or unrelated to mental healing research on the surface, there are major implications for such research here. If the coma patient is "not conscious," then what is the communication/interaction that causes either a reaction or even, in rare cases, an awakening? Is the coma patient still somehow aware of outside sensory input, but unable to react? Or is there some deeper awareness of the presence of the nonjudgmental pets?

We already know there is a psychological effect on sick humans when animals are present, but that appears to be conscious. With coma patients, Jerry Solfvin is attempting to control the psychological conscious effects. It will take further study and much speculation to determine just how the animals are "reaching" the patients in their comatose, unconscious states. Also, he has indicated that other questions to ask are "What makes a good healing dog?" and "What is the role of healer in animal social groups?" While a skeptic may say this research is clearly "for the dogs," the results are more and more coming into focus as a benefit to human health.

The implication may be simply that the mind is aware of its surroundings, whether physically conscious or not. The presence of the animals may be a calming influence on whatever spark of consciousness is aware of the immediate environment and the status of the body. Perhaps what the presence of the animal does is give a positive reinforcement on the will to live and the will to be healed;

an anchor, if you will, that the patient can use to pull him or herself into a healthier state.

Research such as this helps pave the way for nontraditional alternatives to healing. Perhaps once the animal-assisted therapy is clearly acknowledged to be helpful and healing, then we can step up to the idea that an appropriate human, designated as having "healing abilities" is an acceptable step to take in the healing process, and can be just one more tool in the medical community's "black bag."

Why animals, and not humans, can be more easily accepted and studied in this way may be a result of medical science's bias against the extreme claims of human healers over the centuries. Animals make no claims, and an animal participant is less likely to try to convince a doctor or patient that it has miraculous healing abilities. With no claims as to energy transfer or psychic abilities, researchers can, as they like to do, work out a more empirical research project looking at the healing rate of the patients in the presence of animals, rather than the healing powers of the healers.

In essence, the main implication is that there is healing going on, healing that has no "traditional" explanation, healing either caused in an unusual manner by the presence of an animal in a way that a placebo works (self-healing) or healing in that the animal somehow causes an effect on the patient, (like a psychic or faith healer). Which is it? That would seem to be a next step in research.

There is a lot of information available on human healers, but much of it is in the form of testimonials and anecdotes, and most of it exists outside any sort of "acceptable" scientific evidence. In other words, for the AMA and the Food and Drug Administration to accept everything from herbal remedies to psychic healing, there have to be empirical clinical studies of the positive and negative impacts the healing traditions and methods have. That's what the Office of Alternative Medicine is attempting to move toward, given that people are more and more concerned with the form and the cost of being healthy today.

Healers on the human level come in all shapes and sizes, from all belief systems, with all kinds of claims and theories as to how their healing works. A look into healing around the world, throughout all cultures and societys, shows a range of healers from the specialists we have in "modern" medicine, to the healers of the Australian Outback.

The techniques used by healers are often determined by the cultural and religious belief systems in which they exist, as well as what has worked in the history of that culture. The roots of modern medicine come to us from many of these traditions, though apparently medicaₗ doctors of today are only just starting to recognize some of the value in the older traditions, even those that are still around today (such as acupuncture).

Shamanic healing, or healing by a designated shaman, someone who connects with the supernatural and spiritual and divine worlds around us, is possibly the oldest form of healing. Shamans, sometimes called "witch doctors," "medicine men" or "tribal healers," exist in many cultures as they have for thousands of years. The term "shaman" comes to us from ancient Siberia, and refers to people who are able to communicate with the spirit world, often through some form of altered state of consciousness, such as trance, and utilize knowledge they gain from the spirits to, among other things, heal the living.

While the term itself may not be used by people all over the world (for example, "sangoma" is used in parts of Africa), this type of healer, one who gains knowledge from outside sources, is a prevalent one and reaches even into modern society. The famed clairvoyant Edgar Cayce would go into trance and receive information from the spirit of a deceased doctor, and then offer advice and even prescriptions for substances to help clients get over illnesses.

The spirits who are contacted by such healers (and sometimes the source of information is some deity) often provide knowledge on herbal remedies or physical therapies, or perhaps allow the healer to channel healing energies to help the patients. Some healers may pray to the spirits or gods for the healing to come directly from the source, rather than through the healer.

In other situations around the world, knowledge of herbal remedies has been passed down through the generations. Perhaps the original idea for the herbal remedies was credited to a spirit or god, or perhaps (more likely) trial and error on the part of the originators of the herbal remedies led to the knowledge (trial-and-error testing being part and parcel of the scientific methodologies used in drug trials today). Some herbal remedies may have been discovered by watching indigenous animals, injured or sick, who seem to get better after coming into contact with or eating/drinking plants and even minerals.

In fact, most people who are known as shamanic healers around the world may combine a number of healing techniques on a single treatment, offering herbal or dietary advice (and prescriptions) as well as spiritual treatments.

Today, ethnobotanists are studying tribal knowledge in many places around the world to catalog and understand the places and properties of plants in the diet and in the healing process of indigenous cultures such as various tribes in the rain forest of South America.

Other healing traditions, and the healers who use them, may involve a more physical approach to the body, such as acupuncturists, who use thin needles to change the flow of chi in the body to effect health (health often being adversely affected by a blockage or rerouting of chi). Others may use massage and pressure points to affect the change in the flow of chi (acupressure and shiatsu massage) to bring a healthy state to the patient.

Massage is an ancient tradition to manipulate muscles and body tissues to alleviate stress in the body. I know I feel good after a massage, and my body feels healthier. Massage therapists are another form of healer (though thanks to some inappropriate uses of the term "massage," many people unfortunately may bypass it because they erroneously relate it to some sexual practice).

With many forms of healing in the world, a cause-and-effect relationship can be clearly seen. An individual ingests an herb and feels better. The claimed medicinal properties of plants can be tested (as they are now), and the effect can be connected to the substance, rather than the healer himself. With physical manipulations such as massage or acupuncture, the healer is the vehicle of delivery of the treatment (like a surgeon is), but the healer has no special powers to effect the healing in the patient.

But some healing is related to the power of the spirits or gods, or even to the healer himself. The healing happens because, we are told by such spiritual and psychic healers, energy of some kind flows into the patient and causes the healing. God, gods, or spirits, or the energies of the healer work to heal the patient. This is not an easy cause-and-effect relationship one can empirically study, because nothing, so far, can detect the supposed energy doing the healing.

So in such cases, a major question to ask is "what is the source of the healing?" That is, if one really cares. If the issue is to make sure the patient is healed, perhaps that question is a moot one. From a scientific perspective, we should understand just what is going on in an interaction between a coma patient and a dog laying next to him/her. We should want to learn about the subtle energies that may (or may not) exist that allow healers practicing some kind of therapy, whether acupuncture or therapeutic touch or psychic healing, to help the patient get better.

But there are dangers inherent in alternative therapies, as there are dangers inherent in traditional medical treatment.

Doctors must go through enormous schooling and training before they are allowed to practice medicine. This in itself is enough to separate good healers from bad, or so one would hope. But doctors are human beings, too. There is much medical fraud and malpractice going on, some motivated because of greed, some because of misplaced attention, some because of sheer ineptitude and stupidity, and some because the belief system of the doctors will allow no other (than hard, medical scientific) viewpoints as they relate to healing the patients.

On the other side of the medical fence, one finds some practitioners of healing arts going through much training (such as those practicing acupuncture or therapeutic touch or biofeedback), and others who simply hang out a shingle and start whatever practice they want, from psychic healer to faith healer.

Psychics who also do healing have their own personal ethics to abide by, and their own beliefs surrounding how and why they can do the things they do. However, they do not generally go through any sort of training other than self-training, as the psychic ability to do the healing is generally something one has or doesn't have control of. In addition, a good, knowledgeable "phony" can convince a subject that he or she has genuine "powers" of other sorts (such as telepathy or predicting the future) and can use that kind of demonstration to convince the "patient" to pay for a healing.

Much of the subjective perception of "feeling better" can be real, and relate to a real healing going on. Much of it may be due to a desire to believe that the healer can truly help. Some people seek out psychic (and other) healers because their medical doctors have told them there is nothing wrong with them, even though they are positive there is. Such situations as those where a patient has an imagined illness might be best treated by a psychologist or other mental health practitioner, since the illness is truly all in the person's belief system, and therefore all in the mind.

But most people would rather seek alternative healing than seek out a counselor, for that would be an admission that there is really nothing physically wrong. Interestingly, some of the alternative method healers who are sought out come to the same diagnosis as the medical doctors, leaving the patient generally out there seeking some healer who will say "yes, you are really sick and I can help you."

The psychic healers I've met have often suggested that the best combination for healing is the situation where the patient is both seeing a medical doctor as well as the healer. However, don't let this statement lead you to believe that all healers who suggest that you also see a doctor are legit. Some healers may suggest this and still be able to take advantage of you.

In addition, while word of mouth is often the best way to find a doctor, it may not be the best way to choose a healer. There have been many frauds perpetrated on people who genuinely believed they felt better and then referred friends to the healer (who did nothing in the first place except, perhaps, to act as a placebo). One should always seek medical help rather than assume there can be a miracle cure.

Of course, it may be that the alternative therapy is the right one to pursue for a particular patient. In addition, some of the people seeking alternative therapies are doing so because of the inability of medical science to help them in a way that doesn't cause other illness or weakness (such as chemotherapy or radiation therapy to slow down the spread of cancer). The right Mind over Matter application, by the patient or spurred on by others, may be the right treatment for some, as a placebo is for others.

Many phonies claim extraordinary supernatural powers and the ability to cure some people instantly. They may ask their clients to keep quiet about the actual methods or they may claim to have discovered some either "new" or "ancient but lost" substance or method. Any healer who cannot adequately explain his or her method, or who wants to keep the method a secret from patients, should be suspect (although the secret may be kept because the treatment is blatantly illegal in this country, even though it may be acceptable, and real, in other countries). They generally charge large fees (though this is not necessarily the best indicator . . . note how much doctors and surgeons charge).

Most practitioners of alternative medicine are sincere and do have the patient's health as their main concern.

I don't want to scare you away from alternative treatments. I would just suggest that as one would want to get a second opinion when seeing a doctor, one should be knowledgeable about the alternative treatments and all its implications. Read up on it and maybe even seek out a second opinion.

One technique of psychic healing that has come under continual fire (and not without good reason) is psychic surgery. Hardly an alternative "therapy," psychic surgery occurs when the healer apparently either parts the flesh of a patient with his or her hands or through the use of a knife or scalpel. The healer reaches into the patient's body, rummages around a bit, and usually pulls out some organic tissue that may look like a tumor or simply a piece of a damaged organ. The wound is closed again, often without a mark left on the body of the patient.

Psychic surgery is practiced in the Philippines and Brazil and a few other places around the world. Undoubtably a descendant of certain "surgical" techniques carried out by primitive shamans and healers, it is illegal here in the U.S. Part of the issue is lack of sterile conditions during the "surgery" (especially with those psychic surgeons who actually draw blood), the other is out and out fraud. Psychic surgery is actually easier to fake than other healing methods. While sleight of hand is required for faking this, there is visual reinforcement to help create a convincing demonstration (such as showing the patient the "tumor" removed from the body). To convince someone of one's healing talents of laying-on of hands requires much in the way of verbal suggestion and convincing.

Some skeptical magicians, such as the Amazing Randi and my good friend Robert (Bob) Steiner (a mentalist and past president of the Society of American Magicians) have done much to expose the methods of fraudulent psychic surgeons. However, they seem to emphasize the use of magician's gimmicks to show ease of creating the fraud. As I've expressed to Bob in the past, such gimmicks are not necessary (or even available) for some of the phonies to do their work. One skilled at sleight of hand can do much without modern magician's tools, and people have been doing sleights of hand for thousands of years. This means that a psychic surgeon out in the boondocks some place, claiming that he had no training as a magician, or access to magician's gimmicks can still be held suspect.

However, there is some evidence that some psychic surgery is "real," in the sense that there is both a real aftereffect on the patient (which can, of course, be attributed to the placebo effect) and a real physical change during the time of the surgery.

In Brazil, for example, psychic surgeons seem to like to use sharp objects to cut into their patients. They reach into the incision, move something around in an attempt to apparently repair damage, and sometimes remove some tissue. The wound is often closed incompletely, though it heals inordinately fast over the next day or so.

Several years ago, while doing a radio show in New York, I spoke with another guest (a psychologist/sex therapist) who had been to Brazil to observe some of the healers there. She told me that one of the psychic surgeons worked on her, cutting into the skin of the throat (she had some sort of obstruction in her throat). The "surgeon" made the incision, worked on the throat a bit, and closed it up with his hand alone. She felt no pain, only pressure, through the procedure (which was being observed by a number of others), and there was almost no bleeding.

After the "surgery," the obstruction was gone. She removed the bandage on the incision, and told me that her colleagues checked it every couple of hours. It healed completely in less than a day.

So, here's a situation in which a person was actually cut into (though it may have been a shallow incision), the disorder (the throat obstruction) was cleared (though that may have been a result of self-healing), and the wound caused by the incision healed rapidly (again, this could have been self-healing).

Was this a worthwhile adventure for her? Yes, since it was handled so rapidly and without the risks of traditional surgery (from anesthetic, etc). Cost was negligible (in fact, one would have to wonder if the cost of the trip to Brazil might have been less than the hospital stay and normal surgery). The real risk was from infection because of the lack of a sterile environment or from the psychic surgeon's knife that could have "slipped" (a risk one may also take with a trained surgeon, though the odds are against that).

However, this is not to say we should all hop on a plane and head to Brazil for psychic surgery.

Even if there are some instances of real healing happening, there is much risk of fraud and of being taken for one's money here.

In essence, one must be a responsible consumer for all medical and psychological treatment. A lot is known in Western medical science as to how to treat people's illnesses and injuries. Other medical traditions, such as those in China, have a different philosophy behind them, yet they, too, appear to be effective. Adaptations of health therapies from around the world, especially those that involve the mind/body connection, are evolving every day.

So which is the right method for you? Hard, if not impossible, to say. Because Western medical science is a "given," this is possibly the best first choice (though don't forget that second opinion). Read up on the alternative treatments out there and see which ones go best for you. Ask your doctor (or other doctors) about them.

Hopefully, unlike what the organized skeptic groups and the AMA apparently desire, more research will be conducted into whether (and how) these alternative treatments might have a positive effect on people's health. Hopefully, that we don't understand just why a treatment works (from the Western scientific dogma) will not prevent it from being used when it has been shown that it does work.

Medical science is often hung up on knowing how and why something works if it doesn't already fall under the philosophical umbrella. Placebos work, though we know not why. Some pharmaceuticals work, though the actual process is not understood (and often the side effects are not uncovered) when the drug is released.

So why is it that something like acupuncture, which has centuries of successful treatment history behind it, is so hard to accept? Could it be that an explanation, any explanation, that involves something intangible or currently outside the area of "known" science (other than an admission that "it works but we don't know why") is too hard to acknowledge?

Let's take the idea of prayer and the power of God, for a moment. Faith healing is a big thing for a lot of people around the world. A number of Christian ministers have founded major followings based on their abilities to channel the "power of God" into them in order to heal members of their flock. And truly, some people are healed by these faith providers.

In fact, much of what may happen to audience members at a faith healing meeting may be actual healing, without those feeling healed ever needing to stand up with the healer himself. Such meetings reinforce people's connection to God and conviction that God will help them. Self-healing may be spurred on by such a strong reinforcement. Then again, I certainly cannot say that God doesn't heal them Himself.

But with every positive there are apparent negatives, and one must be aware of them as well (this is the "second opinion" on faith healers). There are problems with *some* of the faith healers out there, who apparently have more selfish goals than working with God to help others.

Have you ever watched some of these folks on television? Attendees at the Rev. John Doe's "Crusade" for whatever may include dozens of physically disabled, injured, or ill people. The Rev. Doe calls them down, one at a time, asks if they accept the "power" and lays a hand on them (often a slap on the forehead), announcing "you are healed!" Often the person is pushed over onto the floor (sometimes they show them getting up, sometimes not). Some people announce they are, in fact, "healed. Praise the Lord." Others are not shown with a response (the camera tends to follow the Rev. Doe unless there is an instant reaction by the patient).

Is this real? Clearly a lot of people believe in the powers of the faith healers. People with an illness or injury may in fact feel better and get on the road to a faster recovery after being "treated" this way. However, there is little evidence to show that such miraculous *instant* healings happen in the way they apparently are seen on TV (or even in person if you were there to observe one).

Rent the video of Steve Martin's excellent film *Leap of Faith*. This movie deals with the methods of the phony faith healers, methods that are at once both obvious and undetectable to most. The Amazing Randi, Bob Steiner, Alec Jason, and others have exposed fraudulent techniques used by faith healers over the past few years, including Peter Popoff and W.V. Grant. Through the use of electronic devices to listen in on communication between some of these "healers" and the backstage helpers who prompt them with information gathered about the "patients" and through the use of misleading information, they have shown how televangelists can fool just about anybody.

They might have had a hard time doing any of it without the help of Don Henvick, who might be legitimately called "the most healed man in America." Don is a postal worker here in the San Francisco Bay Area heavily involved with the Bay Area Skeptics. Working with the others, often in heavy disguise, Don was healed of many different illnesses (including, apparently, uterine cancer on one occasion while dressed as a woman) by faith healers who never guessed who he was (apparently God was not on their wavelength on those occasions).

This kind of mass fraud, where a televangelist can use his or her position to receive millions of dollars from viewers, where the sick and injured are on display and taken advantage of, is inexcusable. That Randi showed the good sense to gather all the very clear evidence to expose such frauds is commendable. Again, one must be an informed consumer when it comes to health, and judge for oneself the evidence for and against a particular treatment method (without dismissing it out of turn simply because it "can't work" or because there's "no evidence" for the how and why it works).

Health fraud occurs in all walks of life, from doctors to ministers, from psychics to herbalists. One must generally believe only in the power of oneself in healing, because with that acceptance of personal responsibility, one can usually better judge how a particular treatment might really help. But evidence does exist that the beliefs and prayers of others can actually help us.

You may have read about the work of Dr. Larry Dossey. In his bestselling book *Healing Words: The Power of Prayer and the Practice of Medicine* [6], Dossey discusses the empirical evidence that praying for someone who is ill can have a positive effect on that person's health. Looking at over 100 scientific studies he found in the medical literature, coupled with the anecdotal evidence he has collected over the years, Dr. Dossey has become convinced that the evidence is there, in a scientific format, that supports prayer as an alternative therapy.

Some of the studies conducted over the years involving prayer, like the studies involved in researching psychic healing, have involved nonhuman, though living targets such as fungi and bacteria. The indications are clearly present that prayer has a significant effect. In addition, by all indications from the laboratory studies, distance has only a minimal effect on the power of healing through prayer. None, by the way, seemed to indicate any sort of instant or miraculous healings, though the anecdotal evidence describes such cases.

While some studies seemed to indicate that people praying for the "target" closer (geographically) to the "target" got slightly better results, significant results (the target population healing faster or better or needing less care than the control, not-prayed for subjects) were still achieved with the "healers" hundreds of miles away.

In parapsychological research, distance has some but not much effect on certain types of experimental conditions. Remote viewing has worked over long distances. Remote influence (PK), while apparently not as effective when the target is an inanimate, nonliving object such as a random event generator, does seem to have an effect when the target is a living organism.

Dossey makes no special distinction for any particular form of prayer, nor a particular religious perspective that works better than any other. This perspective is undoubtedly what has upset certain religious groups about his findings. While one would assume that it would be the hard scientists who would have the biggest problems with the results of various prayer studies, it has been certain religious groups who have been loudest in their protests. "Some conservative Christian groups are willing to go to extreme lengths to defend their special ways of praying," Dossey said. "They are willing to toss out all of this data, to call it heresy and blasphemy . . . some religious groups are bent out of shape because you can put agnostics in the laboratory and show the empirical effect of their prayers—as long as they have empathic, compassionate, and loving concerns about the distant person in need."[7]

Such opposition is likely because they have a vested interest in a particular form of God and the *only* way to pray (whatever their way is). Along comes Larry Dossey, with evidence supporting prayer as an effective aid to healing, but also evidence that the form of prayer doesn't seem to matter.

Prayer works, and it apparently works regardless of the "faith" of the patient. This is counter to what many faith healers claim, again challenging the often structured form of healing particular individuals put forth as the *only* true faith or spiritual healing method.

But Dossey also cautions that one should not rely on a particular form of therapy as the only therapy. During an interview with Leon Harris on CNN News on February 24, 1994, he had this to say:

> I would say you ought to really be aware that prayer is another thing that you can put on the table as therapy. It should be seen as therapy. But don't get locked into any particular form of therapy. Don't try to do it all with prayer. Don't try to do it all with surgery and medication. We need to take a common-sense approach to this and use what works . . . if you've got appendicitis, you need an appendectomy, but there's no reason why you can't use prayer in addition, so let's keep all our options open here.[8]

One might liken prayer to *intent* of the healer that the healer should get healthier, should be healed. The person praying may call on whatever higher power they worship in their particular religious perspective, be that God or some gods or some other universal force (maybe even *The* Force, if one feels in connection with the Jedi Knights of *Star Wars*). In this way, the power of prayer is similar to any intentional healing thoughts a healer sends out to his or her patients/clients.

Psychic healers may work in ways that are similar to other spiritual healers, praying to a higher power for the patient, or they may directly intervene with their own energy. Some psychic healers I've spoken to over the years have told me that they may send out their own energy to interact with that of the patient, causing an initiation of a healing process or a speeding up of the process already underway. Others claim to take on the "negative" energy of the patient that is causing the illness.

One healer I spoke with several years ago told me she works more on an empathic level, absorbing the illness and negative emotions associated with it, passing it through her body and out. This method, she told me, can be difficult and even harmful to the healer.

On one occasion, she worked on a friend who had a spot on one of her lungs appear show up on a recent X ray. She worked on her friend, absorbing the illness into her own body. However, shortly after, while her friend felt better (and had a second X ray done that showed the spot gone), she felt a bit ill herself. This prompted her to go to her own doctor for a checkup, insisting on X rays of her own lungs. The X rays revealed a spot on her lung in the same place as that of her friend. She realized she had not adequately focused on passing the illness through her, and she ended up taking it on in her own body.

She spent the next several days working on herself (she felt it harder to work on herself than on others), until she felt better. A return visit (and second X ray) showed her problem also had vanished.

There are more than a few conceptual frameworks that may allow for healing to take place, and many different perspectives and differing belief systems on just how the healing works. Many believe that a higher power, whatever they believe that to be, becomes aware of the healer's desire to help the patient and intervenes, causing the healing, as with much shamanic healing. Others see the power in the substances, the roots, and other materials they give the patients.

Even psychic healers are divided on just how the healing happens. Some psychic healers believe they act directly on the body of the patient (as though the consciousness of the patient is irrelevant, as with "healing" flasks of enzymes or working on samples of bacteria). Others believe that they are a trigger for the healing mechanism inherent in the body of the patient, with their "energy" interacting with that of the patient to get things going (and this, of course, can also work at a great distance). Some believe that the consciousness of the patient, recognizing *something* in the healer switches its own healing capabilities into overdrive (with the distance piece handled by telepathy; the patient receives some kind of signal that the healer is working on him/her directly from the healer's mind, whether consciously or subconsciously).

Whatever the belief system, there seems to be a common piece: the patient has to want, at some level of their consciousness, to be healed. Just as some medications and surgery and other "normal" medical treatments require the "will to live" ("will to be healed" may be the better phrase), the cooperation of the patient, for the treatments to really work, with mental healing this may be more important.

One cannot apparently force another to be healthy. Granted, the evidence that *intent* of the healer can affect biological materials of other sorts indicates that there is a direct effect of mind on matter, when one deals with human beings, one is dealing with an additional factor: the mind of the patient and its own desires and goals. No matter how good the healer, if the patient, deep down, has a desire or reason not to be healed, little healing will occur.

The placebo effect completely relies on this factor, that the belief in the "medication's" ability to positively affect the patient is the key that initiates the healing process. No matter how convincing the doctor might be when describing the effects of a placebo, without that belief factor there will be no cooperation from the patient's own immune system.

In fact, people have died because they willed themselves into that state. People can become ill because of their mental or emotional state and their belief that they are truly ill. So, no matter how potent the healer, whether physician or psychic, there needs to be cooperation from the mind of the patient to either allow his/her healing to take place. Keep in mind that there could be a consciously expressed desire to be healed, yet a subconscious, deep seated reason why the person doesn't feel deserving of being healed.

Because of this factor, a doctor sometimes needs to be a good "reader" of his patients. Unfortunately, medical training today rarely instills this in the current graduates of medical school, and many physicians don't always see the need to develop such skill. People with psychic abilities are typically more connected to their clients, and can often pick up not only physical ailments but also unconscious desires (though not always, since many psychics have their own belief systems and agendas).

In addition, even the best of the phony psychics can "read" a person well, often uncovering what the client really wants and reflecting that back. In the case of the phonies, unless we're dealing with a fraud who means well (and there are not too many of those people out there in the world), any healing that happens after a session is strictly due to the placebo effect. Unfortunately, there is generally a downside to any such sessions, even though there may be a positive health effect in the long run: the wallet of the client is often severely weakened.

Regardless of the healing method one chooses, it is undoubtably wise to do as Larry Dossey suggested, and not rely on any one form of therapy. Today, seeking a "second opinion" may involve finding an alternative treatment therapy, whether acupuncture or ayurvedic medicine or psychic healing in addition to traditional medical treatments (amazing how "traditional" is used with the more recent techniques of medical science, while "alternative" is used with techniques that may be thousands of years old).

The developing interest in alternative medicine can only be a good thing in the long run, contrary to what many doctors and skeptics may state. For if there's anything to them, only through research will we really know. If there's nothing to them, again, only through research will we really know.

It is very clear, however, that the trend in alternative and traditional medicine to include the mind's effect on the body is a good one. Medical science has developed a specific field of research called psychoneuroimmunology (PNI), which looks at just how the mind and emotions affect the immune system of the body, and whether one can "train" the functions of the body to respond to mental and emotional states and commands. According to Kenneth R. Pelletier, Ph.D.:

> Although PNI research is still at an early stage, it is already offering strong support for the observation that there is an intimate interaction between mind and body at the heart of health and disease. That idea, however, is hardly new. Since the early part of this century, clinicians have known that the psychological conflicts and difficult life events—what we generally think of as stress—could affect the body's hormones and cardiovascular system and could increase the risk of illness. More recent discoveries in PNI have brought a higher level of precision to the research process, suggested more sophisticated possible explanations for the mind's role in certain diseases, and raised a host of new and provocative questions.[9]

It is clear that our minds affect the matter of the body. Our minds may also help others with their healing. Consequently, there should be some development of caring, of compassion for others, and a general emphasis on all of us wishing others well. Provided the individual needing healing *wants* to be healed, there can be nothing but positive effects.

However, what about situations where the reverse is the situation, where an individual wishes another to come to harm? We can certainly cause a negative effect, an illness or health problem, in our own bodies. Can there be a negative effect on another? Can the mind of one person *harm* the body of another?

Psychic Attack

As the director of a small group that investigates reported paranormal events, I get a variety of calls dealing with all sorts of bizarre experiences. With a name like "The Office of Paranormal Investigations," the calls include our mainstay of ghost and poltergeist cases, questions about psychic experience and about psychics, reports of UFOs (which we refer out to others), possible (or should I say perceived) "satanic" groups, requests for help in proving the government (or some other shady organization) is either intently watching the caller or is affecting their mental or physical health with some form of weird technology (which we also refer out or simply explain that it's not part of our job description), and requests for help in dealing with a curse or psychic attack. I should mention that many of our referrals are to licensed therapists and counselors or appropriate local, state, and federal agencies.

The reverse of psychic or mental healing is the use of the ability to harm or attack another person. The belief that one person, through psychic or magical means, can harm another is not an uncommon one, nor is it a new one. In fact, looking at the beliefs in supernatural powers attributed to gods, demons, and magic wielders (like shamans, witches, druids, and others), the idea of psychic harm is as old as that of miraculous healing. Basically, as old as we have had some form of belief system.

Anthropologists who study magic and sorcery beliefs among cultures (today and in the past) have found a wide variety of uses of the "magic" forces in causing harm. However, as mentioned in the last chapter, magic was and is generally used by a culture or society to heal, to protect, to help crops grow, and for other positive gain. The application of whatever forces one considers supernatural or psychic for negative outcomes is generally rare within a culture.

However, that does not hold true in looking at how an outsider to a cultural group perceives the magical activities of that group's magic wielders.

Let's face it, people are typically xenophobic. Human beings have an abiding fear of the unknown (not everyone, of course). More fear, followed often by violence, happens because of a lack of understanding of the beliefs of strangers than because of the actual beliefs themselves. Rather than trying to understand and appreciate the diversity of beliefs of others, we often turn away in fear or lash out at those we don't comprehend.

What happens with such a lack of understanding is a false perception of what's going on. Wars have started because of misperceptions. People have died because others feared them for being different.

"Magic powers" may even cause fear within a culture. Putting too much stock in the supernatural abilities of a culturally accepted magic wielder can cause people to attribute power-hungry, greedy, and even evil attributes to that person. All because the perceivers are unwilling (or incapable, mentally and emotionally) to try to get to know what that person is really all about.

Of course, some individuals throughout the centuries have taken advantage of the "power" attributed to their magic. Many a royal or court astrologer or magician in the history of the world used the perceptions of others to get to a power position (or to stay there). Some did it through creating trust in their abilities (even if the trust was based on misconception), and others, such as Rasputin, through creating fear.

During my college years at Northwestern University, I studied cultural anthropology, my central focus (of a couple of classes and lots of research papers) was supernatural beliefs. I had a couple of classes on both the anthropology of witchcraft and sorcery beliefs and on the history of witchcraft in Europe (actually dealing with the reactions and overreactions to belief in witchcraft). I did a lot of research into the beliefs of the Rom people, also known as Gypsies, because of opportunity (a professor who had lived with gypsies for a time) and because of the traditional association with the supernatural. Because of the association we perceive they have with magic and fortune-telling, much "power" is often placed with them for foretelling the future and curing or cursing people.

What I found interesting in what I learned was that while the traditional Rom people (also called Roma or Romany) have a magical belief system, it applies within the culture. There was every indication in the materials available (and in discussion with a couple of people who had lived with Gypsies) that their "powers" don't work on others. The second sight a Gypsy might have in "reading" another Gypsy doesn't work in trying to "see" the future of the non-Gypsy (Gajo). The same goes for cursing another. What they believe may actually work on another Rom cannot do its magic on a Gajo.

However, many Gypsies were and are good readers of character and personality (the same applies of course for non-Gypsies). People on the outside have never really understood Gypsies (partly due to the difficulty in getting to know them and their culture; they keep very much to themselves). Therefore, their cultural practices looked rather alien and therefore suspect to outsiders. As nomads who wanted to stay on their own, this perception of the Gaje was a way for the Gypsies to keep apart.

The Rom have been tinkers, traders, and fix-it experts, among other things, over the centuries. But these things the Gaje could understand. It was other things such as their magical beliefs that contributed to both the awe and fear non-Gypsies felt toward the Rom.

Gypsy fortune-tellers, while they may personally not believe that their abilities could work with the Gaje, have been more than aware that the Gaje believe. Fortune-telling, in the history of the Rom nomads and their interactions with people in Europe and other parts of the world, became a mainstay in making money.

The Rom, by the way, were such good perceivers of others that they learned the best and easiest routes across even closed borders. As a historical note, this ease with which these nomads could travel may have been one reason Hitler targeted the Gypsies for extermination along with the Jews, causing the execution of hundreds of thousands of Rom during the reign of the Third Reich.

Besides the use of their "second sight" in influencing non-Gypsies (generally to give up their money), Rom fortune-tellers either created (or adapted) the idea of curses to both relieve others of their money or to cause great difficulties for others.

People who believe they have been "cursed" or negatively influenced by some kind of invisible force or enemy will often do much to avoid the perceived consequences. These curses that come up in contact with Gypsies are often not attributed to the Gypsies themselves, but instead uncovered by the fortune-teller. If the "client" being told he or she is cursed is perceived as believing it, the fortune-teller will generally ask for money (often thousands of dollars) to insure that the curse is gone.

This type of con, which has led some people to lose tends of thousands (and in a few cases in the U.S., over a hundred thousand dollars) works because people believe in the "power" of the fortune-teller who perceives the curse to begin with. The curse is usually attributed to an unknown human enemy or to some demonic force, and may, it is said, cause illness and death or simply bad luck in business or a relationship.

People who believe there is a "curse" will do much to overcome it (or spend a lot).

Unfortunately, this kind of con, called a "boojo" in Rom parlance, occurs all the time all over the world. NBC has included exposés of such cons on national news programs recently, and local shows have done such exposés in the past and will continue to do so. But this will continue because people are afraid of the unknown, are afraid of their perceptions that magic and psychic forces can affect their lives.

Instead of questioning the messenger (the fortune-teller) and asking for reasonable proof (rather than the proof that is supplied via sleight of hand) of the curse or questioning just how passing over

thousands of dollars can actually remove the curse (short of brib-
ing the person doing the cursing), people's fears and misconcep-
tions keep the con going. In fact, people rarely even question
whether the fortune-teller is really a Gypsy. Based on my experience, far from all fortune-tellers who do this kind of curse-con are
really Rom Gypsies, and far from all Gypsies are fortune-tellers.

In fact, Rom Gypsies are a minority in the population of the world
(and a very small minority in the U.S.). The majority of fortune-tellers
are *not* Rom Gypsies, though they often claim to be so. Whether
the majority of Rom women are fortune-tellers is difficult to say,
since the actual numbers of Rom in the U.S. is a number subject to
debate (the U.S. Census Bureau has a range of population numbers
for the Rom, somewhere around a million), partly because many
are still very mobile in this country. To say that the majority of Gypsies are con artists or still do fortune-telling or healing or curses is
undoubtedly not accurate (and would be a stereotype), though the
latter has become connected to Gypsies almost as much as the idea
of a "voodoo curse."

Many Rom gypsies have worked hard to overcome the stereotypes applied to their people, and some apparently hide their true
ethnic identity because of the negative stereotypes associated with
their past. Many Gypsies are "poorly educated, even illiterate" and
Gypsies often take their children out of school, according to Ian
Hancock, president of the International Roma Federation and representative at the United nations for Gypsies worldwide because
"put bluntly, the fear of cultural contamination." Gypsies do not
want their children influenced by a culture they believe promotes
drug use, low morals, and violence."[1]

Many educated Rom Gypsies may hide their ethnicity in order to
blend in. Others are fighting for a change in the way the world's
cultures perceive Gypsies. "Many Gypsies live a schizophrenic existence," says Hancock, who is also an English professor at the University of Texas in Austin. "You're a Rom when you're home. When
you're not, you try to pass." Some, including Hancock, have two
names."[2] Unfortunately, while many Gypsies live middle-class lives
and are no longer nomadic, while they attempt to blend in, the most

visible Rom then become the fortune-tellers and the con artists, those who "tend to be the least assimilated."[3]

So what of the "Gypsy curse," the one the Gypsy actually places on the individual? What of curses or psychic forces directed by psychics? Or voodoo practitioners? Or Satanic worshipers?

As far as the Gypsies go, it would appear that any cursing done that has any real effect is similar to the "second sight" abilities as far as their beliefs go. Gypsies have been aware of the perceptions of the Gaje when it comes to their supposed "powers," that fear and lack of understanding of their culture attributes much power to their "magic." Yet it would appear that their curses, from their perspective, can only have a magical effect on each other. The effect on the Gaje is psychological, and dependent on the "target's" belief.

What's a Gypsy curse like? The Rom call all forms of curses "armaya." These curses are typically verbal, simple, and straightforward. Author Jan Yoors, who lived for a time with Rom gypsies, gives examples of the armaya[4]. Such sayings as "May I die if . . ." or "May our favorite stallion die if . . ." and of course those directed at others were used in the past, with the "if" relating to something bad (or good) happening to the person who was "targeted." While the beliefs the Rom hold for their own magic may have changed as many have assimilated into society, the armaya themselves are undoubtably still used and are part of Western culture. Johnny Carson, while no Gypsy, often used armaya-type statements ("May the fleas of a thousand camels infest your armpits.").

People such as fortune-tellers have for centuries taken advantage of others' beliefs in evil forces, bilking them for money through cursing them ("pay me or else") or through charging them for counter-spells to remove a curse (which generally doesn't even exist). Of course, what you just read applies to con artists of all ethnic background (and, based on population statistics, the majority of con artists are not Gypsies). In fact, I was recently told by an individual with a possible ghost in his house that he and his wife visited a psychic (not a Gypsy) who, undoubtably after perceiving that the clients were both afraid and wealthy, quoted them a figure of 80 *thousand* dollars to rid their house of ghosts. Fortunately, these clients, though fearful, were not stupid and walked out.

Money was not (and is not) always involved. Sometimes the curses were and are directed at enemies in order to cause harm to them. A Gypsy who placed a curse on a Gajo knew that the fear the Gajo might have for the "evil eye" could, in itself, cause all sorts of complications for the victim.

Curses and spells are dependent on belief. The magic caster generally has a belief in the magic they use, as well as the "rules" of that magic (such as the Rom believing their "magic" would only truly work with other Gypsies). The victim has a belief in the power of the magic. The magic caster may be aware that there could be no real effect (as with the Rom) or may believe there is an effect (as, perhaps, with many voodoo or other magic-system practitioners). But it would appear that the belief of the victim is always a part of the equation.

The mind has an effect on the body. That is clear. The effects caused by the mind could be positive (a healing) or negative (causing oneself to get sick). From the outset, the mind-set of an individual causes good or harm. A positive outlook toward a situation may relieve stress, whereas a negative or fearful mind-set can cause intense stress, and that stress can cause problems in the body (as well as making one clumsy and accident-prone).

While "negative" effects generally mean some kind of openness to an illness (the increase in stress can upset the body enough to cause some breakdown of the body's defense mechanisms or might cause illnesses such as ulcers). A psychosomatic illness is a real one, with real physical symptoms, but with a psychological cause. And just as we can cause great healing in ourselves, we can do much damage.

So, people can affect themselves rather negatively. We can make ourselves very afraid, we can stress ourselves out with our mental and emotional states, and our beliefs in general and in a given situation can cause drastic stress-related problems (which may or may not go away when the stress is reduced or eliminated). In fact, there have been cases where people have died of fright and even seemingly just willed themselves to die.

Sometimes, "black magic" is said to be the cause. Or a curse or a spell.

All over the world, spells are cast, curses are laid, that may bring on illness or death. The "magic" has many names and takes place in the cultural context where there are both good and bad spells. The lifting of spells in many cultures requires some recompense given (maybe just an apology, maybe something of value) to the party who has asked for the spell (one would assume because of a wrong being done, but not always . . . sometimes it's like a "protection racket"). In most cultures, it requires some elaborate ceremony or exorcism.

In the root medicine traditions of people in the American Southeast, spells are placed on people by utilizing various substances (like clippings of the hair or fingernails or clothing of the victim) and herbs and roots, combined in a root bag and placed near the victim, usually on his or her property. To remove the spell may require visiting the local cemetery and asking the spirits of the dead to help.

Protective substances or symbols may be used to reverse a spell or like a "good luck charm," protect people from potential harm. By the way, do you have a rabbit's foot or a horseshoe hanging around for good luck?

In our culture, thanks greatly to the media, we often associate death by enchantment with belief systems like voodoo.

Voodoo is a religion that people often misunderstand. We see much in movies and on TV that show the voodoo practitioner as mysterious and evil. The same goes for Santeria and often for witchcraft (here I mean Wicca, the "Old Religion," and not anything associated with satanic worship). Wicca is based on a pagan tradition going back thousands of years. Voodoo and Santeria have their roots mostly in older religious traditions such as those of western Africa and the original religions of the slaves brought over to the New World in past centuries.

However, unlike witchcraft, voodoo and Santeria also borrow from Catholic traditions, with a mixing of spirits and saints, gods and demons. Satanism, as a counter to all, comes completely from Christian traditions, with the raising up of God's adversary, the devil, as the focal point of worship.

Voodoo and Santeria are religions in their own right today. However, while the media tends to focus on the zombies and curses and "evil" beliefs and practices within the religions, there is undoubtably more of the positive there.

Keep in mind that we, that is you and I and our contemporaries, have particular beliefs in how a religion is practiced that are different from what others believe. What we often get through the media about voodoo is that some animal has been killed in a ritual. How can that be? Why is it necessary?

God or the gods apparently have need of their worshipers proving their devotion and loyalty. The ancient Greeks and Romans as "civilized" as they were, sacrificed animals to their gods. Many belief systems around the world require some form of sacrifice, whether in the form of service, of money, or of life of plants and animals. So if a chicken (alive or dead) or some other animal is used in a ceremonial ritual, while we cannot necessarily relate to the need for that kind of sacrifice, it can be understood.

Unfortunately, because what one cannot relate to can often be seen as "evil" if there is no attempt to understand the purpose. In addition, there have been many ritual killings of human beings over the centuries. While some practitioner of voodoo or Santeria or some other nonmainstream religion may have done the killing, such sacrifice should not be the accepted general practice, any more than the occasional killing of an individual by another in "the name of God" or "in the name of Jesus Christ" should be an indication that human sacrifice is part of the mainstay of the Judeo-Christian tradition.

Voodoo practices, for example, do include the healing arts. Both from the perspective of faith healing and herbal medicine, voodoo priests and priestesses are the folk healers who help others. In general, voodoo is just a religion, not a magical pathway any more than praying to God for rain in a drought or to win the lottery (when those things happen) might be considered part of a magical pathway.

Of course, for all the positives out there in the world there are negatives. If you've read Wade Davis's *The Serpent and the Rainbow* (or seen the more fictionalized film version by horror film director Wes Craven), you learned about some of the negative aspects of voodoo in Haiti.

Voodoo curses include aspects of psychological terrorizing and occasional introduction of poisons and drugs into the victims. People have, in fact, died because of voodoo "curses." But not because the "magic" killed them.

All over the world, there are cultures in which the healing magic can be subverted for negative purposes, to cause illness or death. The same substances that cause healing can cause sickness. We all know that an overdose of sleeping pills will kill someone, as with an overdose of other drugs often prescribed for positive reasons. Even an overdose of some vitamins, such as vitamin A, can severely damage the body or even kill.

Some poisons, such as belladonna, can be taken in small amounts for healing purposes. For many substances, the amount causes very specific effects. One of the substances used by some voodoo practitioners, tetradotoxin, is a virulent poison. Yet in very small doses it can cause a deathlike paralysis rather than death. Zombies could not exist without this or a similar toxin to get the process started (a zombie being a person who has been declared dead, yet is later found up and walking around in a trancelike stupor, drug induced, of course).

Deaths caused by curses around the world may have a couple of possible explanations, neither of which is magical. The evil sorcerer who curses someone may see to it that the person is slowly poisoned. In this way, the victim of the "curse" sickens and dies, thereby proving the power of the sorcerer. Since autopsies in many cultures are not the next step for the dead, the cause of death might be labeled "natural causes" or "magical causes" for lack of understanding.

The other explanation for illness and death by enchantment has everything to do with the psychological mind-set of the victim. When someone is cursed in most magical belief systems, the victim is sent some kind of message that the curse is on. It might be a bloody animal body or a fresh chicken claw that shows up on the victim's doorstep. It might be some kind of symbol mysteriously painted on the victim's door. It could also be a matter of local gossip that gets back to the victim.

In any event, once the victim is aware of a "curse," he or she may simply dismiss it or begin to worry about it (or even seek help in getting a counterspell). But any slight belief that such a curse could cause harm will in fact cause stress at the very least. Depending on the reaction to that stress (and often fear), the body can begin to experience definite negative physical effects.

Can a person die because of this? Yes, apparently. It has been stated by a number of sources that since emotional reactions cause a surge of adrenaline, it is possible for the adrenal glands to be overloaded and drained by an intense reaction, such as the fear engendered by belief in a spell or curse. One can literally be scared to death.

In college, one of my anthropology professors told our class (which dealt with witchcraft and sorcery beliefs among primitive peoples) about a situation that had happened during his time in Papua New Guinea.

He had been staying with a tribe in the hills, living in a small shack for several months. At one point, he had to return to "civilization" for a short time, but he didn't want to pack up and carry everything with him. The "everything" included some steel tools and knives that the natives would likely steal from the hut while he was gone.

So, the head man of the village suggested that the local sorcerer place a spell of protection on the place. Instead, the professor decided to put his own "curse" on the contents of the shack. I recall his telling us how he made it known he was going to do this so that some of the villagers would become curious and watch.

When he had an audience, he launched into some impromptu dancing to rock and roll music on his tape player, drew tictack toe boards all over the walls with chalk, and sang a few songs (the Mickey Mouse Club song sticks in my mind as one of his examples) a few times (all, of course, sacred practices of Westerners).

He left.

When he returned weeks later, he learned the place had been broken in to just a couple of days after he left. The tools and knives had been stolen. But then he learned everything had been recovered. Apparently, the two youths in the village who had done the robbery died shortly after the theft. One dropped dead of unknown causes, the other apparently threw himself in front of the local constable's jeep.

Coincidence? Perhaps. Psychic or Magic? No.

Belief in a curse or negative psychic force can cause much damage. Psychological mind-set is often directly related to the belief system of the individual. So, if you believe, even a little, that a curse can hurt you, that little belief can grow to create fear and general nervousness and stress. That can lead to physiological effects that can cause illness or lower our guard against diseases. Or, it can cause us to worry so much that we become accident prone (and any accident that occurs because of our clumsiness only adds to the "power" of the curse).

Of course, this is all saying that the "sorcerer" doesn't use poison or drugs to help things along.

But what about a more direct influence? Can mental forces harm people and even kill them? The answer to that is yes, of course. As I mentioned, people can die because of an intense belief (coupled, one would assume, with other factors such as that belief or the situation causing such physiological reactions that the body "gives out"). While curses may lead to negative reactions, sickness, and even death, depending on the interpretation of the situation, an illness or physiological reaction may also lead one to assume there is someone or something causing it, that one must have an evil force as an enemy.

Deeply hidden psychological causes such as a repressed memory of a negative event or trauma can bring forth physical effects, and then a misinterpretation of the cause, which can go on to reinforce the negative effects.

In fact, these can even be rather dramatic effects. Let me tell you a little ghost story with a twist.

The Choking Ghost or Monsters From the ID

It started with a woman I'll call Diane coming in to see Sharon Franquemont and myself at John F. Kennedy University in Orinda, California (in 1985, back when there was a graduate parapsychology program and office space at the university). Sharon and I were on faculty together, and were two of a few who handled reports of ghosts and poltergeists and other psychic events.

When she first visited us at the university, she came with a security guard buddy of hers who, she said, had witnessed an attack by some invisible force, or so she told us. Diane herself came in with a scarf around her neck that covered (she showed us) bruising, and told us of the most recent attack, the first of which had occurred six months before when she had moved back to California after living in Alaska for a few years.

In the witnessed attack, Diane and several coworkers were at their supervisor's house. Diane had gone down the hall (presumably to use the bathroom, though she never actually said why). She had stopped in the hall when she saw a shadowy figure suddenly appear. It approached her and grabbed her by the throat, shoved her hard against the wall in the hallway, and began lifting her by the throat off the floor (still against the wall).

Her coworkers heard her cry out, rushed down the hall, and saw her levitating off the floor, the marks appearing on her throat (she did not claim they could also see the shadow since it only apparently appeared to her). They pulled her down and began seeing to her condition. Diane said that the figure vanished as soon as the others touched her.

According to her friend (let's call him Steve), whom I interviewed once Diane was out of the room with my colleague, he and the others heard Diane cry out and as they entered the hallway, saw her essentially bang back against the wall (he couldn't really say whether it looked more like she was thrown or pushed or threw herself against the wall. They did not see her levitate at all. Once she hit the wall, she slid down to the floor (they didn't pull her down). They did, however, see the marks manifesting themselves on her throat with no apparent cause.

So, Diane's perception of the events was not as the witnesses experienced. But the marks on her throat were very real.

She had invited us out to her mother's place, a one-bedroom apartment on the coast south of San Francisco, where she was living at the time.

I sat in the comfortable chair in the living room of the apartment, my back to the view of the ocean one could see out the balcony doors. Across the room to my right sat Diane, a blond-haired woman in her late thirties. Across from me was my colleague, Sharon Franquemont, seated next to Diane's mother.

Diane was telling us more about the attacks she had experienced, attacks on her person by a shadowy figure that liked to choke her. The shadowy figure Diane had seen was a little over six feet tall and very human in form. She said all his features and even clothing were in deep shadow, so she couldn't identify any characteristics of the individual or what he might have been wearing. Of course, she wasn't convinced it was a "ghost" at all, since she thought it might be some evil force or demon. She was fairly certain it was a "he."

She got up and walked into the open kitchen, opened the refrigerator, and got herself a glass of water. She drank it rapidly and put down the glass. In the meantime, Diane's mother was speaking of her reactions to the attacks on her daughter.

Diane began to walk back into the living room, then stopped with a puzzled look on her face. She turned and walked back to the hallway by the kitchen, looked down toward the front door, then turned back. She whirled a moment later, as if she heard something again, shook her head, and walked back into the kitchen.

This was all in my view, though Sharon had her back to the kitchen. Diane stopped in the kitchen, looked toward the hallway, and a frightened look appeared on her face. She threw her hands up in front of her face and began to collapse. As I was watching this occur, I was out of my chair and by her side just as she slumped to the floor, Sharon and Diane's mom just behind me.

We all watched as her face turned red, her throat bulged out, and what looked like depressions of fingers appeared in the soft tissue of her throat. "Get it off," she was able to squeak out.

It was a scene right out of the movies, one I never expected to encounter in real life. So, as in the movies I reacted in kind. I grabbed her hands tightly and shouted "LEAVE HER ALONE."

The attack immediately subsided, her throat went back to normal (though with bruising appearing on the skin), and she began to breathe more evenly. I then told her the thing would not bother

her again, as far as I was concerned. Diane agreed that it "felt" like I had scared it off. We promised to continue with her until all was definitely over, but I reassured her again that I had chased it away.

As Sharon and I left and began to discuss what we had learned, we both agreed that it was a truly weird scenario. Sharon, an intuitive herself ("intuitive" is another, perhaps less charged, word for "psychic"), said she sensed no outside presence. In my mind, I couldn't logically think of why an entity would scare off just because I yelled at it (although I did consider myself a pretty powerful guy in those days).

So, we reviewed what else we had learned from Diane and her mother.

Diane had a rough childhood. Her father was apparently physically abusive and her mother unwilling to "see" that had gone on, though she much later recognized the signs of that abuse. Her father was dead a number of years, and only after his death did she discuss the abuse with her mother. Unfortunately, Diane had repressed memories of the extent of the abuse, memories that showed her father as sexually abusive as well. These memories came up to her consciousness through nightmares that she began having just after coming back from a several-year stint as a cop in Alaska.

After the nightmares started, she began seeing a therapist who was helping her deal with the rising memories. However, the therapist had been kept in the dark about the attacks by the shadowy entity (Diane wore scarves to cover the bruising of her neck).

We also learned Diane was divorced, her sixteen-year-old son living with his father in a nearby community. Although she didn't see him much while she was out of state, he was coming to visit her at her mother's one or two weekends a month.

As Sharon and I discussed things, more and more began to click into place. We had asked about the timing of the first attacks, and piecing things together after we left we figured out that the nightmares had started just after her son's first weekend visit, and the attacks had begun just after that. We also discussed another connection.

Diane's mother had a small one-bedroom apartment and Diane

slept on the queen-size sofa bed. When her son came to visit, he, too, slept in the large sofa bed.

Based on the timing of the events, the sexual abuse by her father when she was young, and the presence, no matter how innocent, of her son in the same bed, it was clear there was a connection between the nightmares and the attacks.

When we spoke again to Diane, I asked her whether the shadow-figure could be her father. This hit her like a revelation, and she was both happy she "knew" who it was, and even more terrified that her father was back from the dead to "get her." She also expressed feeling as if his motive was "to punish" her "for telling what he did" when she was a child and teenager.

The next step was to connect with the therapist. With Diane's permission, the therapist was contacted and a discussion of our investigation ensued. The therapist was amazed that Diane had so skillfully avoided any discussion of or signs of the attacks. In addition, what may have been the stimulus for the rise of the repressed memories, the weekend same-bed visits of her son, had not been told to the therapist. What was provided to the therapist was a missing piece that was keeping Diane from progressing.

Was this the spirit of her father? If so, why did this apparition listen to me when I shouted him down during the attack on Diane? No, it wasn't that "simple."

Armed with what we learned from the therapist (and the therapist armed with what we had learned), a "solution" was arrived at.

Diane's shadow-entity, an amorphous representation of her abusive father, was there to punish her, possibly for the guilt feelings she was expressing, even though the abuse was not her fault at all, but her father's. Lots of abused kids grow up thinking they did something wrong, not the person who did the abuse. And Diane was undoubtably right about the punishment being related to her finally talking about the abuse with her therapist.

But, we concluded, this was no outside entity. The very idea of her son sleeping in the same bed, followed by the action itself, was undoubtably too reminiscent of her father "sleeping" with her. This created a massive inner conflict that triggered the nightmares and the attacks.

The inner conflict bore what Dr. Morbius, a character in the film *Forbidden Planet* (played by Walter Pigeon), might have called a "monster from the id," a creature from the subconscious. As you'll read in Chapter Eight, as in many other cases where someone is suffering from such emotional tension and stress, such inner conflict can cause a poltergeist, a subconsciously directed force. An effect was triggered by the stress and tension, but unlike most poltergeist cases, this poltergeist was directed at the person who caused it, rather than at furniture and appliances.

Diane had conjured up a representation of her father, one only she could see. The force of her mind was so set on her being "punished" for her guilt feelings that she, in effect, punished herself.

But is what I witnessed possible? How could she have caused herself to have marks and even deep bruises appear on her throat without touching it? Think back to the discussion of stigmata. People, through their faith, bring to the surface of the body effects that can be interpreted as positive or negative.

As mentioned earlier, you may have heard of experiments or demonstrations where people in altered states, such as might be brought on through hypnosis, being told to believe a pencil was red hot, only to have the touch of a pencil raise a blister.

We are capable of self-healing. We are therefore capable of self-harming. This was a rather dramatic example of a psychosomatic effect, but real nonetheless. And, it did not involve any sort of "outside" force, just the mind acting on its own body.

I have found it interesting that some people who believe in PK and poltergeists have actually had a hard time with that story. They believe that it would have to have been an outside force, that such effects are not "as likely" as a "ghost." If one can accept that the mind can affect matter at a distance, as in poltergeist cases, why should it be more difficult to accept we can damage our own bodies, even as dramatically and visually as Diane did? In fact, more people would accept Diane's situation over any claimed psychokinetic event where objects seemingly moved by themselves, because it was Diane's mind affecting her own body.

In investigating such a case, I learned much about accepting a reported "entity" as such up front. Just a little digging brings a real solution.

Oh, and Diane never did have another attack. Apparently, thanks to the work we did, and mostly to her therapist, she was able to deal with her memories and feelings left from what her father did to her.

*

Okay, so our own minds, given different stimuli, can cause all sorts of bad things to happen to us. There is still the question of whether someone can use whatever force might be used in healing another to harm another. Can psychokinesis be used to hurt people, to negatively influence them?

I believe the answer is both No and Yes (with the heavier emphasis on the "No").

As with distance healing or psychic healing, the effect of one person's mind on another would naturally have a flip side to the positive effects of healing. Where one instance is the stimulation or speeding up of the healing process, the other side of that is the slowing or maybe even stopping of natural processes, or causing degeneration of body tissue, or causing reactions in the body that might have negative results.

The reverse of healing body tissue is degenerating body tissues.

However, if one makes the argument for psychic harm being similar to healing and the process working the same way (with different intention and results), one must also expect that the same rules that apply to healing apply to harm.

If I do not have the will to live and I am very sick, I may worsen and even die. If a healer comes in to do his or her stuff, my lack of the will to live, to get better (couple, perhaps with an expectation that I will get worse and die), the healer will undoubtably have little or no positive effect. And of course, the lack of positive effect may even strengthen those negative expectations I have.

If, on the other hand, I want to live and get better, the healer has a willing participant, one whose body processes will cooperate because the mind of the patient wants to cooperate.

If I don't believe in the power of the healer, there may still be a positive effect because my desire to get healthy matches the purpose of the healer's visit, to help me get healthy. While I am skeptical about the healer having any unusual ability to help me get better, my desire to get better may allow the healer to have a real effect.

And, keep in mind the prayer/healing studies Larry Dossey has written about, that the patients did not need to know they were being prayed for, that there was still a difference between the group being prayed for and the group who wasn't in their healing.

But the desire to be healed was there in both groups.

The expectations and desires of the "patient" also applies to psychic harm or attack.

If I *believe* that someone has cast some sort of spell on me that can have a real effect, there is likely to be some kind of negative effect on my health, *whether there is a curse on me or not.* If someone truly tries to use their mental "magic" or psychic abilities to harm me, and I feel bad or guilty about something I did to that person, I may convince myself that somehow I need to be "punished," and there may be a negative effect on my health, whether I do accept such "power" as real or not. And of course, if that "attack" or "curse" comes at a time when I am physically or psychologically vulnerable, when my body image is more negative, that "attack" or "curse" isn't going to help my health any.

In other words, whether or not there is a real "power" behind the psychic or magic attacker, a great deal depends on my state of mind and my current health. For my health to be affected negatively, the same rules apply as for my health to be affected positively. I would have to either *want* to get ill (and possibly die) or create in myself a sense that something bad or negative is affecting my health.

And of course, this can happen at a subconscious level, as with healing.

What it all means is that there has to be some kind of acceptance, either conscious or unconscious, of the psychic harm or attack for my own defenses for the attack to have a real effect. Or, my own psychology, believing in the negative, in something bad happening to me (or in fear creating stress on the body), may cause the damage to my own body (as with the case of the choking ghost).

Over the years, I've handled calls from a variety of people who believe there is a curse or spell on them, or that someone (or a group) is using their psychic powers to harm them, or perhaps even using some kind of technology (everything from hard radiation to microwaves to technology that simulates psychokinesis or telepathy) to control their minds or make them sick.

For the last kind of report, I refer them to the police, to the various utilities companies (who can check for various electrically related problems), to the FCC (if the attackers are using radio waves), and even to environmental agencies (if there may be a problem with radiation or energy or even chemical pollution causing their health problems).

Most of the people who report such attacks by others are fearful, and stressed out. Some have serious psychological problems, some are in their perfectly right mind, though often with beliefs that could lead them to conclude that they are the target of some psychic attack. Most I refer to counseling, if only because they are afraid and the fear needs to be dealt with.

However, for all of the people who report this, I ask the questions: "Who is doing this?" and "Why would they want to harm you?" The "who" is often a neighbor or acquaintance. If so, the "why" is generally answered with "I have no idea." Being able to come up with a motive for the attack on them indicates a few possibilities for concluding why the "attackers" have done so. Perhaps the "victim" has noticed strange behavior on the part of the "attackers" (strange only in that the "victim" does not understand the reason for the behavior, which may be anything from different religious beliefs and practices, to stereotypes to the neighbors just being "odd"). Perhaps the proximity of the "attackers" is the reason for the conclusion (just because they live next door). Perhaps it's because the "victim" has done something that has upset the "attackers" and the "victim" expects some kind of retribution.

In any event, the reason why the "victim" perceives the attackers as that has more to do with the "victim's" beliefs and physical and mental state at the time than the behavior and beliefs of the perceived "attackers" (most of the time, that is).

If I believe I am sick or upset because of some outside force, I may look for something or someone to identify as that force, to blame for my status.

Over the centuries, millions of people have been jailed or tortured, injured or killed, simply because of being "different," the differences leading to being blamed for everything from bad health to bad luck, from crime to war, from bad weather and failed crops to natural disasters.

Today, in the "new" South Africa, people are being executed for being witches and sorcerers. Not by the government, but by the people who apparently are afraid of their current situation. The same is happening in other countries in Africa.

In other parts of the world, people are still being jailed and even executed due to accusations of witchcraft, magic, or sorcery.

In some of these instances, the people receiving punishment may actually be shamans or witch doctors or self-professed psychics. In others, there is little evidence of such beliefs or practices.

How can this be going on in the late twentieth century? Fear and a lack of taking responsibility. People want explanations for everything that happens. People, in general, do not take well to the idea that some things happen because they bring them down on themselves, or because they just happen (why did your house get struck by lightning? why didn't you win the lottery? Because. No reason. Just "because.").

Negative events in our lives, and that includes illness, happen for a variety of reasons. Some things happen because we are in the wrong place at the right time. Others happen because we are exposed to forces of nature, which are neither positive nor negative (a rain storm that brings just enough water is a good thing, but too much is a bad thing; a virus just is, it's not "good" or "evil"). And much happens to us that we bring on ourselves.

So, most of what people believe is "psychic attack" is a reaction to something negative in our lives happening and our desire to look for someone or something to blame for our situation. What is perceived as an "attack" is really a mislabeled natural illness, or stress reaction, or toxic leak in the environment, or an event we lead ourselves into, or perhaps even just a bit of bad luck.

Also realize that we are naturally, and unconsciously, affected by the thoughts, emotions, and behavior of those around us, though not necessarily in a psychic way. There is a great amount of non-verbal communication that goes on between people, most of it received on an unconscious level, and people (and animals, especially our pets) often react to our state of being without realizing what they're receiving from us or how they are reacting.

Add to this a psychic dimension, an additional level of awareness, and you may actually be affecting people around you even more (both positively and negatively) than you might normally expect. If you are in a bad mood, but effectively acting out as though you are not, others may not consciously know this about you, or react accordingly, but they may unconsciously be receiving cues, both physically (say, with your body language) and mentally.

And we may react to someone else's "bad" state in a way that makes us believe this negativity is actually directed at us, just because we're picking up this negative feeling nonverbally, without explanation.

But what if there really is a person out there with psychic powers who doesn't like us?

Assuming that person even decides to do harm to you, I again remind you the rules of healing also apply to the rules of harm. To be healed by your own mind or the mind of another, some part of you needs to want to be healed, or expect to be healed, or at least be open to being healed.

To be harmed by your own mind or the mind of another, some part of you needs to want to be harmed, or expect to be harmed, or at least be open to being harmed.

How do you protect yourself from such an attack?

Keep a positive attitude about your physical and mental state. Accept that you can't be harmed (psychically) unless you allow it. Believe that you can fend off an attack of this nature, for many psychics and parapsychologists believe this is the case.

Here are some words of advice from Kathy Reardon. who is a channeler and psychic I have worked with for a few years who has a good handle on things. The following is written by Kathy, taken from one of the information sheets the Office of Paranormal Investigations offers, on "Psychic Self-Defense."

If religion gives you strength, use the images and prayers learned in that religion to strengthen your belief that you deserve to feel safe. If you are not feeling religious, use any calming image. If you were once on a vacation and found the surroundings to be very soothing, remember that image and use it to calm you. If you are not very good at visualizing, just think about it and believe it is there. It is not necessary to see it in your mind for it to work. If your memory is usually of sounds, then play soothing music to fill the room with your own safe sounds. If you are at work, hum a tune to yourself that is calming. If your memory is usually of smells, wear a scent that is soothing to you, or fill your home with a scent that feels pleasant. (Example: the smell of burning sage "clears" a room for me.)

If mentally filling the room with a particular color makes you feel protected, then try wearing that color to help remind you that you are always able to protect yourself. Some images to choose from: Think of yourself as a tree connected to the deepest part of the earth. Let your branches fill the area and make it your own. Think of yourself as a beam of light. Let that light fill the room with your bright, safe energy. Stand in the middle of a large mirrored ball and have all the negative energy reflect off of the ball without harming you or anyone else. Try standing in the middle of a huge brightly colored rubber beach ball with all the negativity bouncing off of the ball. If you are not visual, hear the sound of things bouncing off the ball. If you feel things, feel the vibration of the ball as the negativity bounces off. If you have a religious figure that helps to protect you, imagine them putting their arm around you or talking to you. If you believe in spirit guides, conjure up your own sights, sounds, feelings, smells of a protective guide that is taking care of you every minute of the day.

The very act of mentally taking control of the situation will help to calm you. All of these protective thoughts are coming from you. Let them fill the area around you, forcing out any unsettling thoughts. Paying lots of attention to the physical world around you can also give you a feeling of accomplishment. Physically cleaning the house, doing chores around the home can help you to feel powerful and in control of your space. If all these psychic distractions have caused you to temporarily forget the physical side of your life, then these chores may be a bit overdue.

If you have tried these things and are still feeling vulnerable to the emotions and energy of others, consider a few sessions with a professional counselor. It is possible that you were feeling responsible for the happiness of others before you opened up psychically. Dealing with your own emotions through counseling can help you to recognize when you are asking others to depend on you without realizing it. This is like leaving the screen door open and wondering where all the flies came from.

If you believe that it is a spirit bothering you, talk to it like a live person. Realize that they are very limited. They may just be so happy that someone can see or hear them, that they are stubborn about leaving. They may be able to scare you briefly. Keep in mind that you are able to move in the physical world all the time. They are not. All they can do is send images to your mind. If you block them or ignore them, they will get tired of you.

When you believe that someone is very powerful and therefore you cannot block them out, you are on one level giving them permission to bother you. You can always seek the help of a counselor, professional psychic, or clergyman. My point is, you are not alone. There are many services to help someone feeling alone and vulnerable.

Seeking help should not exceed your budget, whether it is a counselor or a psychic. If you have never been religious, it is not likely that you will suddenly have enough faith to protect you. Consider the other choices already mentioned. If you are religious, lean on your faith. If you do not feel close to the leaders of your church, seek another branch of that same faith.

The important thing is to find something that makes you feel safe. Take charge of protecting your life and your living space. if you do not feel comfortable doing this alone, seek help. You have a right to mental, emotional and psychic well being.

In addition, there have been studies that indicate that people can block telepathy through simply visualizing a shield or brick wall.

And, of course, let's keep in mind the lessons of the martial arts. The energy in the body and mind is quite capable of shielding from physical attack, and by extension, from psychic attack. But the way to do so is mental attitude.

So, for those of you who believe that someone can psychically hurt you, can hurt you with the mind, or with some kind of magic or voodoo or witchcraft, here's a summary:

1. One's own belief is more potentially damaging to oneself than any magical or psychic force from someone else.

2. One's own psychic self-defense mechanisms (that's your mind, by the way), is capable of fending off an attack by the mind of another.

3. Your defenses will be down if you fear psychic or occult attack, because the very fact that you are afraid of such power indicates you believe in its ability to harm you. This belief, whether unconscious or not, may *allow* the perceived attack to have an effect.

4. If you believe there is a curse or attack on you, and you're in a bad physical or mental state to begin with, your belief can have a negative effect on you (whether there's really an "enemy" out there or not).

5. Fear of or belief in an unreal enemy or attack can cause real damage to your mind and body (though it's really you creating the physical problems in your own body).

6. "Protecting" yourself is generally as simple as wanting to stay healthy (or get healthy if you're already ill) and believing you will be that way.

7. If you ever get mixed up with true practitioners of any religion or belief system that incorporates the use of herbs or roots or drugs as part of their rituals, keep in mind that any real "attack" might have nothing to do with sorcery or psychic powers. Don't call a parapsychologist or psychic, but have yourself physically checked out by a physician for any substances that could have been given to you to make you ill. Remember that the substances are physical in nature, not magical or psychic, but your reaction could be partly a mental one (it's that belief that the

"magic" will hurt you, and so it does). Any belief to the contrary could actually add to your troubles.

8. The moral of the story is that we hurt ourselves far more than others hurt us. Healing doesn't happen as well if there is any internal block to it. Harming works the same way.

✳

As a final issue, let's deal with the idea that a ghost or spirit, not a living being, is responsible for an attack.

First of all, I need to define our terms here. I will use ghost and apparition (the preferred term in parapsychology) interchangeably, and meaning the personality, the mind or consciousness, of a living individual that has somehow stayed among us after his or her body has died. That apparition, that consciousness, still is capable of somehow communicating with those of us who are alive.

The mode of communication would almost certainly have to be mind-to-mind communication, or telepathy. A ghost, being without a physical body, has no vocal cords with which to speak, and no ears with which to hear. No body to be seen, either.

Keep in mind that when we see or hear something, while there is raw data going into our physical senses, our brains and minds then make some sense of the data being received and create *perception*. In other words, everything you see around you is only as real as you perceive it to be, and not everyone perceives the world in the same way.

Our eyes, for example, have a physical blind spot (back of the eyes where the optic nerve connects). Do you see a blank spot floating in front of you? Of course not, because your brain/mind fills in the blank with what it "knows" must be in the "picture" (which is actually received upside-down by the eyes, and reversed by the perceptual processes in the brain/mind).

An apparition, which is not seen by everyone, is undoubtably not a visible, physical thing, or everyone would see it. Instead, the one witness to the apparition is somehow receiving information directly into the perceptual processes in the brain/mind, so that the apparition is combined with the "real" input, like an image superimposed on another in television.

Because our perceptions involve all our "normal" sense, some people may see a ghost, others may hear the apparition, still others may smell his cologne or her perfume. Another witness may feel as though the apparition is touching him or her. (No, I haven't heard of any apparitions or ghosts being "tasted)."

For many people who report a ghost touching them, there may be no physical touching going on, just a sense of being touched.

Try an experiment with a friend standing close to you. Close your eyes and ask your friend to slowly (and at a random time) bring his or her hand close to part of your body without actually touching even your clothing. You may not only be able to "sense" where the hand is, but actually "feel" like you are being touched there.

So, for some people claiming that a ghost is touching them, there is really only a sensation, meaning it's literally all in their minds (even though it may have been "sent" by the mind of the ghost).

Some people have reported being pushed against a wall, or down stairs. What I usually find is that there was no physical force pushing them, but rather either a sense of being touched (and a fear reaction causing them to be clumsy) or simply a reaction to the ghost being there that causes them to trip over their own feet.

However, if a ghost is mind, can't that ghost also work things via psychokinesis, through Mind over Matter?

Interestingly, the motion picture *Ghost* (with Patrick Swayze, Whoopi Goldberg, and Demi Moore), dealt with that issue in a very creative (and maybe even realistic) manner.

Swayze's ghost character was unable to move anything physical. Then, he had a run-in in the New York subway with another ghost (played by Vincent Schiavelli), who was capable of knocking people's newspapers and affecting other material things. He told Sam (Swayze) that one moved objects with one's mind, since ghosts really didn't have bodies. Sam learned the lesson after much concentrating.

Most apparition cases I investigate do not involve physical object movement. Most ghosts apparently have not learned the Mind over Matter lesson (my biggest fear after seeing *Ghost* was that *real* apparitions might also see the movie and take the Schiavelli's advice).

The ghost cases I know of (including the one's I have investigated) where physical object movement goes on are few and far between, and seem to typically involve very friendly or simply mischievous (though dead) people.

Those cases you hear or read about where people are raped or attacked physically by ghosts typically turn out to be cases similar to the choking ghost in this chapter, caused by the victim herself or himself.

I do need to say that some of the cases are not cut and dried. In some cases where people report being "attacked" by some outside force, it has not been possible to exclude some sort of external intelligence or "negative energy." Some of these "attacks" may cause physical illness or bruising or even small cuts and bleeding. Traditional means of ridding people of spirits (such as an exorcism) may or may not work, and sometimes have even escalated the phenomena (usually if the individual's subconscious is involved as opposed to an outside entity). But, what's interesting is that *belief* is again a major factor.

I have been amazed by the number of people who seek out a Catholic priest for aid *even though they are not Catholic*. Others seek out help of other religions or mystical traditions or psychic practitioners (watch for the last . . . the "boojo" also applies to getting rid of demons and ghosts, not just curses). Ultimately, whatever the ritual that is finally used may have absolutely no effect unless the "victim" believes in it (and, if there is a real ghost, undoubtably whether the entity believes in the ritual . . . ever wonder if a Catholic exorcist can affect a Jewish ghost?).

The key is often to try to find out a motivation for the attacking force. Often, there is none, and the investigator must look to the victim's psychology (as with the Choking Ghost). Sometimes, it would appear that there's no intelligence at work, no reason for the attack, and the whole thing almost seems like an allergic reaction to some kind of "energy" in the environment, and it may be that fixing things is as simple as changing the environment (new furniture, new paint on the walls, or at the extreme end of things, new place to live).

In general, what goes for protecting oneself against psychic attack from the living also works for psychic attack from the ostensibly dead or from unseen "forces." You, with your living mind, have as much or more "power" than a ghost does. Shielding yourself is a matter of taking the responsibility for doing so, and looking into yourself to see if there's anything there that could allow in some attacking force, whether the attack comes from outside, or from inside yourself.

Know yourself and believe in yourself and little, on the psychic level at least, can harm you.

Oh, and don't forget to duck if you see a flying glass or picture (more on that in the discussion of the poltergeist, Chapter Eight).

∗ **7** ∗

Manipulating Nature:
The Occult Perspective

Over the centuries, people who believe in and practice various magical arts such as those related to witchcraft, voodoo, the Kabala, demonology, and the sorceries of other, more primitive cultures have set out to manipulate the natural world around them. From weather control to changing the migration patterns of wild animals to add to the food supply, using magic to effect physical change has stayed with us.

Here we are at the dawning of the twenty-first century, a time of high technology all over the world, and yet people are seeking "New Age" answers to age-old questions, looking for inner strengths and higher powers that can make their lives better. At the same time as computer users are also seeking spiritual guidance, occult and supernatural beliefs flourish all over the world and even have political impact.

According to news reports, in South Africa, ritual murder and witchcraft cases are on the rise in both urban and rural areas. Witch hunts are conducted for the culprits who are murdering others in bizarre rituals, stealing organs and other body parts for magical rites, while innocents are often jailed or beaten to death or killed in other manners as witches. Social unrest coupled with a deep, traditional belief in magic has led people to accuse others of witchcraft, sometimes because they are truly afraid of a sudden turn of bad luck, sometimes because that person may stand in their way politically, socially, or in business.

In India, news reports tell of people accused of and killed for practicing witchcraft and sorcery.

In Indonesia, people are jailed for such "crimes."

All over the world, there is a cry for explanations for social unrest. The explanation is often "bad" magic and sorcery.

In the U.S., things are a bit different. Or so one would think. However, I get dozens of phone calls every year from people who believe someone has cast a curse on them, or is psychically attacking them. One recent call came from a woman who is a practicing psychic in the Southwest and has had an adoptive child taken away from her because she has been accused of practicing witchcraft (which, if that is the only reason, is clearly a violation of her constitutional right to freedom of religion, given that even if she was a witch, that is more or less a religious choice).

In addition, with the rise of fundamentalism in religion here in the U.S., there has been a rise in claims of satanic groups committing ritual crimes, and a rise in the cry for the government to censor certain avenues of occult information dissemination. Every once in a while, you can pick up a news item on another religious group attempting to censor certain books and magazines, getting them ousted from local libraries and schools because of their sexual or violence or occult content.

What I find very telling about our culture is that just as more and more people cry out against sex and violence and the occult, the TV shows and news pieces that always seem to grab the attention and get the ratings are those three topical categories. It would seem that Americans are fascinated with the things we can't face up to.

Belief in *magic* is universal. Since before recorded time, humans have had a need to have explanations for all natural forces and occurrences, as well as a need to attempt to control those forces and occurrences. When one takes both an historical and an anthropological perspective of the *occult* (which merely means "hidden"), several interesting themes come to light.

In the field of anthropology, the study of magic, witchcraft, and sorcery beliefs typically falls under the heading of the "Anthropology of Religion." In the anthropological world, while anthropologists themselves hold their own personal religious beliefs that may or may not fall into traditional religions, man created God(s) in his own image (the same idea has been well put in many of Michael Moorcock's fantasy novels involving incarnations of the "Eternal Champion"; read them!). Religions, according to Sir James Frazer (author of *The Golden Bough*), grew out of what was essentially early man's science: magic.

One might describe magic as that which gives order to the universe. Understanding magic meant one understood how the universe worked. Controlling magic meant the ability to control nature. Magic (and there are as different perspectives on magic as there are cultures) came together as attempts to create techniques that would allow people to accomplish specific aims and goals through mastery of the natural world.

In many respects, magic is the science of the nontechnological. Magic plays by very specific rules of the universe, though those rules may vary slightly or dramatically from culture to culture. In the past, magic was the way to gain answers from natural forces, to learn how the world worked, and why certain things happened to people. It was (and is, with many) the way people gain insight about people and the world around them. As science is the search for how things work and technology the resulting methods by which we sometimes bend the natural world to our wills, magic is both knowledge and method, insight and tools.

However, magic on the part of the human magic-wielders was insufficient to control all one could see as nature. So, if there were forces humans couldn't control, it would make sense that there were "higher" beings who could control these forces. Religion was born out of the discovery that magic was an ineffective method of controlling nature, and that supplication to the "higher" beings who did control things was the next step.

Magic is essentially control of the supernatural, while religion is subservience to the supernatural (that term including all inexplicable forces, including God(s)).

Magic denotes actions that are validated by a belief that occult (hidden) processes cause visible events. Magic can change existing conditions in the physical, natural world, in the social environment, and in the various spiritual realsm. The occult is a term applied to the hidden forces and beings of the universe, the hidden "laws" that are behind them, and organized attempts to explain or manipulate these forces, beings, and laws. A technique or process may be considered "occult" when its explanation by a believer, no matter how logical it may seem within the cultural context of the believer, contradicts scientific knowledge of cause-and-effect relationships.

Basically, many ideas have been considered "occult" or "magical" over the centuries, yet become absorbed into scientific thought when the explanation shifts to one that fits with current knowledge. One might consider ball lightning magical, a sign of a ghost or will-o'-the-wisp, and science denied its existence until it was demonstrated with an explanation of just what it is. Quantum physics may seem magical in its thinking, yet because one can utilize mathematics to describe it, and at least partially come to terms with the Newtonian and Einsteinian views of the universe, it is accepted (though several ideas in quantum physics are still not accepted or believed by many; they're just too theoretical at present).

Religion evolved out of that need we all have to give explanations for everything. Humans have an apparent need to at least believe we understand the universe around us. We also have a driving need to somehow learn to control our environment, both socially and physically.

The supernatural describes powers beyond the understood natural forces. As science understands more and more of the universe and its nature, what is considered "supernatural" or "occult" is absorbed into the body of science. The supernatural, in this way, deals with many *impersonal power* sources; invisible forces that allow things to work in inexplicable ways (such as things disappearing and reappearing, inanimate objects moving on their own, situations developing without apparent cause or source). The supernatural deals also with *personified power,* that which belongs to supernatural intelligences, beings such as gods and angels and demons.

Magic is an attempt at utilizing impersonal power, though the goal may often be to influence or control the personified power of supernatural beings. Magic consists of ideas and acts that imply control by man over the supernatural, while religion implies control over man by the supernatural. Religion is more an organization of individuals into a group or institution, and any connection with the supernatural happens through that institution. Magic is the work of individuals, or the combining of power of individuals.

The main point is that while individuals may connect with their deities and perhaps influence them (typically through prayer or supplication), it is the power of the God(s) that people must contend with. In the occult, individuals achieve power of *their own* and utilize that to effect changes around them.

Psychic abilities are typically thought of as inherent in every individual, though some individuals may tap into these abilities with greater ease, and some may actually have more to tap into. Throughout history, psychic abilities such as Mind over Matter have branded individuals as outcasts and priests, sinners and saints. It has all depended on the individual's place in society and the cultural context in which his or her psychic abilities have been utilized.

For example, a healer might be labeled as "evil" if he or she failed to heal a particular powerful (socially, economically, or politically powerful) individual or member of such a person's family. A thief displaying any form of ability to move objects is already starting on the wrong foot, whereas a priest who does such things and gives forgiveness for God providing him with such a wonderful gift may be accepted as a new saintly being.

All over the world, the context in which a person's talents and abilities, whether psychic or artistic or athletic, display themselves can be seen as "acceptable" or "unacceptable," as "good" or "evil." In addition, if such "special" people are different enough from others, they may generate fear and reprisal. Throughout history, people seen as "different," because of physical appearance or abilities, because of intelligence, because of beliefs they may hold, are a threat to the status quo of the society in which they find themselves. They may be ostracized, discriminated against, run out of town, or imprisoned and even killed. Humans have a tendency to fear what's different instead of looking as differences as chances to learn, to grow.

People (mostly women) burned in Europe or hung in the colonies in North America as witches were often simply those people who didn't "fit" into the local culture, for one reason or another, or were people who got in the way of someone else in power (a common reason for accusations), or perhaps had seen or done something to threaten the accuser's standing (say, had an affair with the married man who now claims the woman is a witch and a succubus because his wife found out).

It seems that misfortune is never our own fault, nor is stupidity, and so we must seek out other people or other forces to blame for it.

Magic practitioners around the world include priests of various religions and shamans and witch doctors of varying belief systems. Any attempt to tap into and control the natural unseen forces of the universe, the impersonal supernatural power out there, makes one a magic user.

Alchemy was an excellent example of an "occult science" as attempts were made to control or alter physical substances and events using both physical reactions between various substances and a release of spiritual or supernatural forces. There was a touch of animism, that all things have some kind of spirit or spiritual forces in them, from trees to animals, from minerals to the wind. Metals and other substances were considered "living things" that could get fatigued or old (through rust or other breakdowns), so working with such substances required control of life forces (that of the metals and the other substances combined with them).

In many respects, alchemy, through its attempts to do things like change base metals into gold, utilized procedures that evolved into empirical scientific experimentation. In fact, alchemy, though disdained by modern science, is the direct parent of chemistry.

Astrology, the "science" of understanding the forces of the heavens that influence all our lives required both a bit of psychology in understanding personalities of individuals for whom horoscopes were being cast, and more importantly the positions and movements of the stars and planets. From there, we come to astronomy.

Various occult practices led to some understanding of the structure and processes of the human body. After all, much of modern medicine has evolved from other healing traditions.

So, the occult, or magic, is often the precursor to understanding how the world *really* works.

Magical rites and practices generally involve the desires of either the shaman or magic-maker or some other individual who has asked (or hired) the magic-maker to achieve some goal. Such goals may be influencing decisions, affecting the health of individuals (for good or for ill), locating game, achieving power to defeat an enemy, affecting the growth of crops, or altering the weather (to name just a few things).

Using the power of magic for any of these is using impersonal power. On the other hand, these are some of the same goals that people pray to God(s) for. The difference is that for the magic-believers, the power is within themselves (or their learned representative, the sorcerer or shaman), and for the religious, the power is with God(s). The magic-believers must *use* the power, while the religious must *ask* for the being(s) above to work his/her/their power for the benefit of those who ask.

Mind over Matter comes in here throughout. If there is any power as a result of the *intent* of the magic-users, it reacts to the direction of the mind of the shaman or sorcerer. While one can never rule out that God(s) is reacting to the requests of the worshipers and following through, it is the *intent* of the worshipers that initiates any effects in the physical world.

From the perspective of parapsychology, magical rites and beliefs may be methods by which individuals can tap into their own psychic abilities. Many psychics have their own particular meditations or mentors or other mental or physical rituals they go through to achieve better control of their abilities. Many of them may do these things unconsciously (as some people might have unconscious habits associated with good performance in athletics or music). People often say a particular thing or do a particular action just before another action (such as crossing one's fingers, or a crossing oneself, or knocking on wood) that may be related to cultural superstitions, or may be personal habits developed over time.

Any ritual behavior can help an individual remember a particular physical or psychological state. That memory may then help spur on a particular action.

For the magic-maker, rituals, coupled with the belief that such-and-such will happen as a result of the particular ritual can possibly bring on a state of consciousness allowing the goal to be achieved. As with psychic healing, a magic-maker may believe he or she can heal someone else, but only if a particular ritual is first performed. While the ability may always rest within the individual, the ritual may be required for the person to give permission to use the ability.

The evidence is clear that we can affect our own bodies, whether in relation to health or physical achievement. The evidence is there that people can influence the health and well-being of others (with conscious or unconscious permission of the others, of course). There is also much evidence that people can affect objects and processes outside the body, as you will read about in the following chapters.

However, there are many natural forces that people, using magic or prayer, claim they can influence. Some are easier to accept than others. The growth of crops, for instance, might be only a broader use of the same psychic healing abilities that people such as Oskar Estebany have demonstrated on plants, bacteria, and fungi.

But some claim to cause or avert natural disasters or to be able to influence the weather.

While some people do believe they may *cause* natural disasters (or avert them; though how can you possibly prove you stopped an earthquake that no one ended up feeling because you stopped it?), it's more likely that the individual somehow *knows* the disaster is about to happen (precognition), and gets confused about the need for a cause-and-effect relationship (let's face it, it's hard for most people to imagine the effect, the prediction, coming before the cause, the disaster). So, some people who are aware in advance of certain happenings may mistakenly assume that they must be the cause of those happenings.

With the exception perhaps of prophets like Moses, who called on the power of God to part the Red Sea, the age of really *BIG* miracles is long gone. Either there is no need for such power, or such

things never really happened as written. In addition, for every individual who *wants* to cause a natural disaster there are millions of
people out there whose subconscious minds want to *avert* such a
happening. Unfortunately, the big forces of Mother Nature, such as
earthquakes, seem to be beyond the scope of any psychic abilities
as we know them today.

Then again, are we past the age of big miracles? Perhaps not.
Science and Technology have replaced magic and often religion as
the miracle-makers in our world. Think about the miracles we have
seen just in the last half of the twentieth century. We've landed men
on the moon. We're beginning to see to the ends of time and the
universe with the Hubble Space Telescope. We've allowed people
to talk to one another worldwide instantaneously (or nearly), both
with the spoken word and the written word (through the Internet).
We've discovered a new form of life (the organisms in the deep
oceans that live by ingesting materials that would be toxic to other
organisms through chemosynthesis). We've gained mastery of many
diseases. And, unfortunately, we've devised new ways to destroy
life from a distance.

Of course, we have much more to learn. We try to predict the
weather (and can, with some accuracy) and we try to predict or at
least gain warning of earthquakes and other natural disasters. But
we still have limited or no control over those things. That's still out
of the range of science and technology.

As for weather control, this has been a mainstay of magic-users
and religious figures alike since the dawn of time. Can people affect the weather? Science has tried, and succeeded in this, though
the result may not be what we wanted. Seeding some clouds with
chemicals has had some success in creating rain. However, through
our pouring of pollutants into the atmosphere and the oceans, we
have had some effect on the weather patterns around the world.
We can affect the weather, and have done so, in this way.

On an individual (or small group level), some rituals of various
peoples around the world may revolve around the goal of altering
the weather: creating rain in a drought, stopping rain during a
flood, making it warmer or colder, etc. Mind over Matter abilities
displayed by individuals don't quite seem to be powerful enough

to affect weather patterns, especially since such patterns all over the world are so interconnected.

However, there are anecdotal accounts from all over the world, from a wide spectrum of cultures and religions, that are very coincidental in the way a shift of local weather follows on the finish of a ritual or prayer for that particular change.

Several years ago, I was told by a sports personality one such story. Just before a professional golf tournament in South Africa some years ago, the tournament folks hired a "witch doctor" to affect the storm that was, for all intents and purposes, almost on top of the location of the tournament. After the magic practitioner finished his ritual, the storm suddenly veered off, leaving the tournament in good weather. Coincidence? Or mind magic? The answer may depend on what you believe is possible.

What about the "evil" powers that are out there? Can rituals that purport to harm people really allow demons and devils to do so?

First of all, what is considered "good" and what is considered "evil" is a very cultural thing. Belief in an evil entity such as the devil or Satan or whatever you want to call him is often a matter of belief in some force that must be behind the bad things that happen to people, because obviously God or good gods can't be. Satanism would not really exist without Christianity, since it is the antithesis of that religion. Worshipers of Satan are those who wish to put their own personal wants and desires above those of others, and, seeing no help forthcoming from God, they worship his opposite.

But people are people. We do sometimes wish ill of others. We do sometimes want bad things to happen, often because of anger or fear. Sometimes bad things will happen because of our own action or inaction. Is this an evil power manifesting itself, or is it our own "power" influencing things around us?

I believe it's the latter. Magic, both impersonal and personified, might be likened to the Force in the *Star Wars* films, or any other energy or force of nature. One can be good to others (the "Light side of the Force") just as one can make positive uses of nuclear energy. One can also be bad or think bad of others (the "Dark side of the Force") just as one can use nuclear energy to destroy. Nature is neutral; it is humanity that frames the context of what is good and what is evil, out of understanding and acceptance, or out of fear and dismissal.

It is important to remember that what has been seen as an "occult practice" or as magic in the past might have been something that lead to a scientific discovery or invention. To paraphrase science fiction and science writer Arthur C. Clarke, any technology or science sufficiently advanced will seem as magic to the observers.

Think about how some "primitive" or native peoples around the world have reacted to encounters with technology over the past century. Think about the fact that most people may have no concept how television actually converts pictures and sound into energy, transmits them through the air, then reconverts them in a TV set (or VCR). To many, that may be magic (although it's the "magic of science").

For the people who use magic, who attempt to use occult forces to manipulate the physical world around them, their minds, their *intent,* seems to have a real effect. When a ritual is witnessed by people who are the targets of the magic, their belief that something is happening, something magical, will often cause them to view the world differently, as though there was a real change.

For example, let's say that in the course of a ritual, a person who is ill is given a potion to drink. The potion may be made up of quite innocent substances, such as sugar, water, fruit juice, and other plant matter, or it may have ingredients that might otherwise make most of us sick to our stomachs (you know, the old "eye of newt and bat's blood" recipe). On the one hand, we know that many natural substances, as in Chinese herbal medicine, have both positive and negative effects on the body and mind. On the other hand, many substances, as with the sugar pill (placebo) that may be prescribed by a doctor, have a purely psychological effect caused by the belief of the patient.

If the person drinking the potion reports an effect, a change in his or her body, mind or life situation (many rituals are for good luck or romance or power), there may have been a physical change or there might have been a *perceived* change, one based on the belief that the magic worked. Whether the change was physically *caused* by the potion or not, if the person believes there was a change, then that person now relates differently to people and the environment. He or she may feel more self-assured, imbued with more personal "power," and Clark Kent has become Superman (or Dr. Jeckyl has become Mr. Hyde). The way people might now react to the magic recipient will be affected by how that person interacts with them. Since the interaction is now based on a new self-image, it's bound to change.

Magic!

One example of this I can share comes not from my personal experience as a parapsychologist, but from past experience as a bartender.

In 1979, I was working at a blues and rock club in Chappaqua, New York. I had gotten to know more than a few of the regulars, and in fact became friends with some (a couple of whom I am still in contact with today). One evening, a couple I had become friendly with came in and sat at the bar.

Mark was in a pretty down mood that night and made comment that he wanted to get drunk. His girlfriend, Donna, had given me signs that I needed to help her avoid that. I figured I could always cut him off after a couple, but had another idea that night.

Mark drank Bloody Mary's, a drink that often masks its alcohol content. After three drinks made in the normal fashion, I began giving Mark Virgin Mary's (without the shot of vodka), though with a drop or two of the liquor on top so he'd have some taste of it. (I was keeping a tab for them that night and began charging for the Virgin Mary's). Donna was sticking with nonalcoholic beverages.

Over the course of the four or five hours that they were there drinking, Mark had a total of ten drinks. After that amount of time, with only three real Bloody Mary's in him, his blood alcohol would have dropped to show that he had metabolized all the drinks. In other words, biologically speaking, he was stone cold sober. However, his behavior showed otherwise.

I, the bartender (and wielder of the magic of creating an altered state of consciousness through providing the potion called liquor), had fulfilled a ritual function. Mark got drunker and drunker, or at least, so he thought. His behavior, as far as others around him could tell, was that of someone who had had ten Bloody Mary's (except to Donna; I had let her in on what I was doing early on). Mark was drunk, through magic.

As they got up to leave, Donna paid the bill and Mark got up, stumbled, and asked for the keys to the car, insisting he was going to drive. Donna looked at me as if asking for my opinion as to whether he should drive or not. I nodded, and she handed the keys to Mark. He seemed surprised that she was going to let him drive in that "condition." I decided to work "magic" again.

I got Mark's attention and told him that he'd been drinking Virgin Mary's for a few hours, and that he couldn't possibly be drunk. He looked at Donna for confirmation. She nodded.

He looked back at me. I never saw anyone sober up so fast in my life. Fortunately for me, he saw the humor in the situation, thanked me, said good night, and off they went. I'm still friends with them, by the way.

In that instance, the ritual I performed, the pouring of the drinks, had no long-term effect from a physical standpoint. From the standpoint of Mark's perception of the situation, I was giving him the "potion" that would allow him to get drunk. He believed it. He got drunk. He believed me when I revealed the truth. He got un-drunk.

Magic can work in much the same way. The effect may be due to a change in perception, that they and others around them, believing that there has to be a change, perceive one (whether it's there or not).

In the idea of what's called "death by enchantment" or "hex-death" discussed in the last chapter, the physical change in the "victim" can be caused by the victim's own belief in the magic of the person putting on the curse.

With psychic healing, self-healing may be initiated by the intense belief on the part of the patient that the healer has real powers. The magic-wielder in most cultures is called on as a healer, and whereas some would call the process a psychic one, others use terms like *magic* or *witchcraft* or *sorcery* to cover the cause/effect relationship.

Magic can also be believed to have an effect on the natural world when a magic-wielder can cause some change in the environment that can be witnessed by others. For example, a ritual to bring rain for crops, followed not long after by a storm can be linked to the magic of the shaman, or to the power of the gods answering the priest's cry for help. In either case, *magic* is the thing causing the rain.

It may be that the magic-wielder is able to judge by atmospheric conditions or by other natural signs that rain is coming (maybe his joints hurt from a change in the barometric pressure), giving him or her the opportunity to do the ritual at a time when it is nearly certain that it will look as if there is a real effect. We certainly don't believe the meteorologists on TV *cause* the weather (they have a hard enough time with accurate predictions). But in cultures where magic holds sway, rather than any scientific understanding of the way the world works, the apparent cause of the rain, the magician, may get the credit.

As a performing magician and mentalist who often does magic effects that look to be psychic, I have learned the importance of being opportunistic. Several years ago, I began taking "credit" for odd happenings around me. A light might flicker, something might fall off a shelf, there might be a loud noise from outside at a particularly coincidental time (apparently emphasizing something I'm saying). I learned to immediately say something like "See, just like that" if the happening relates to what I was saying or, more often "I did that."

In fact, it's gotten so that I may respond in this manner almost automatically. People often look at me funny after a while. . . .

Magic, both the "real" kind and the kind that stage performers do, has always relied on the perceptions and beliefs of the magician and the witnesses or audience. Magic, in the entertainment sense, relies on making events appear to have only a magical cause-and-effect relationship.

In the "real" sense, magic relies on some of that on the part of the magic wielder, but more importantly on a connection drawn between the magic wielder and a real shift in the physical world, whether that be the environment or people. The effect may only work or be perceived as magical if there is belief that this is so. Perception, affected by belief, allows the analysis of the situation to yield the inevitable conclusion that it must be magic, not coincidence, and not some other "normal" explanation.

Then again, the effect may be due to the magic user and the witnesses or participants tapping into their own pool of psychokinetic power, giving permission for the unseen powers of their minds to affect the matter around them.

Rituals that allow such power to appear can truly reinforce the subconscious desires for a goal to occur. The mind, given permission by the role it has taken on as magic-maker, affects matter around it, all responsibility and/or blame for what comes next falling on the magic itself (and sometimes on the shaman for using correctly or incorrectly the power around him/her).

As we get into a discussion of psychokinesis, you will see that often our own abilities to affect matter with our minds often requires some degree of letting go of personal responsibility.

An anthropologist once related a situation with the Huichol tribe of Mexico. She was observing the tribal shaman doing some hands-on healing. Before the healing ritual happened, he gathered many people around himself and the patient. He did what was described to me as a bit of sleight of hand, producing small objects and making others disappear. Then he began the healing ritual.

Apparently, the ritual as described to me relied on the "power" of the witnesses as well as the shaman. As people started getting into it, participating in the ritual, the anthropologist noticed not only a shift in the feeling of the place, but also watched in amazement as stones, pieces of wood, even soda and beer bottles that were littering the area rose up into the air and began flying around. She described it as "like that scene in the movie *Poltergeist*" when the researchers go into the room where all the toys are whipping around.

The anthropologist firmly held the belief that what she observed was psychokinesis, probably caused by the group's expectations that something quite magical was going to happen (and undoubtably aware through past experience and tradition that the events would include floating or flying objects).

Notice, though, that she pegged the shaman as doing a bit of sleight of hand first. Anthropologists have observed shamans and other magic wielders around the world often doing some trickery to help get people in the mood for magic, or to convince them that what was being done was real magic.

This still happens today. A number of psychics I've spoken to or read about have said that they only use Tarot cards and crystal balls and the like as window dressing. In other words, their abilities don't rely on the occult trappings, but their clients may wish to use them or may have a belief or expectation that the psychic needs to read cards or palms for anything to happen.

A psychic I knew in New York City years ago told me that she almost never uses such window dressing. But every once in a while, she gets a client that has a hard time accepting that all the psychic needs to do is look at the client, rather than use crystals or rune-stones. So, there may be a comment from the client like "aren't you going to read my cards" (or "use a crystal ball," or "check my aura" or something like that).

Sometimes, the proper atmosphere is important if one expects the client or patient to accept what happens.

Shamans may also use such sleight of hand to get themselves and everyone else in a receptive state of mind so that real magic can happen. In effect, by reinforcing the belief through trickery (provided the witnesses don't perceive it as trickery), one can remove doubts about the validity of what will come, and help increase the *sense of wonder* about witnessing such magical happenings.

Throughout this chapter, I have used the term magic in a more traditional sense, rather than in the Harry Houdini, magic-entertainer sense. Magic *performers,* more correctly called *conjurors* (by historians of this brand of magic, anyway), also utilize natural principles and forces, though their goal is to influence the perception of the observer for the purpose of amazement and entertainment.

To conclude this chapter, I just wanted to mention that as a performing conjuror or magician myself, I have met and discussed psychic phenomena with many other professionals and amateurs. What has been most interesting to me has been the fact that most conjurors do not disbelieve in psychic abilities, and that some have actually had psychic experiences of their own, often *while performing their acts,* which are in and of themselves "magic rituals."

Some of the experiences have involved apparent flashes of telepathy and precognition while pretending to do those very things on stage. Others have involved occurrences of apparent psychokinesis aiding particular effects that may not be working right for the performer.

Marvin Kaye, a mystery writer and mentalist, discusses the benefits of a mentalist (who essentially fakes psychic powers) practicing real ESP experiments as an aid in understanding how and why people believe it's real in his book *The Handbook of Mental Magic.* In the course of this practice, though, other things may happen:

> Practice with genuine ESP also provides valuable insights into the telepathic function, and these may also be worked into shows. For example, I once tried to receive unspoken words from a friend. Suddenly, the word "Albany" flashed into my mind. It literally blinked on inside my head like a neon sign. It was the very word my friend was trying to send to me. . . .
>
> When the usual trick methods fail, real telepathy might come to the rescue, though it's certainly nothing to be depended on. Once, when I was in an agent's office, I asked him to put a word on a pad of paper, and offered my pencil. He ignored it and used his own felt-tip pen. Unfortunately, the pad of paper I'd given him was supposed to deliver a carbon impression of his writing—but the felt-tip marker wrote too softly to disturb the carbon. I might have switched to another method at that point, but suddenly the word "dog" flashed into my mind—again, like a neon sign. Taking a chance, I slowly and dramatically revealed it, letter by letter.
>
> It was indeed the word he had been thinking of. Needless to say, he was properly amazed—though not half so much as I was.[1]

Over the years since I got into magic, which was just shortly after I got into graduate school, I've encountered conjurors like Marvin Kaye who have told me a number of stories similar to his. The most common occurrence is, like Kaye's experience with the agent, something that may pop into the performer's head.

Stage magicians are in the position of doing effects that pretty much have to work again and again. Magic apparatus should be nearly foolproof, as should sleight of hand. While things can go wrong, the stage magician has to be prepared with something to cover up a mistake or failure, since the audience is often unforgiving of a miracle-maker who fails.

Not so with mentalism. The mentalist, pretending to utilize psychology and psychic abilities, has a natural "out" in that ESP and psychokinesis *don't always work*. So, if something goes wrong in the course of several demonstrations and experiments in psychic powers, it's okay (and may even make the effects that do work seem stronger; some slight failure certainly makes the performer appear that much more human, and perhaps even more clearly psychic).

So, as various mentalists have told me over the years, when the performer is in front of an audience doing some form of telepathy or prediction effects, and a word or name or series of numbers flashes into the mind of the performer, he or she will state the mental messages out loud looking for a response from the audience. One performer told me when that happens, he is almost always pulling something specific from an audience member, sometimes a relative's name or sometimes a driver's license number. Another mentioned that he occasionally got flashes from his volunteers of additional tidbits outside the range of the effect.

If the mental flash was incorrect, no big deal. ESP doesn't always work. But when it does, it's extremely powerful . . . even magical.

It may be that in the pretending to be psychic, the performer's subconscious more or less helps the presentation along with *real* magic.

With psychokinesis, there are times when an effect might fail, from a mechanical perspective, yet still function.

I read an account by another stage magician in which he reported doing a rising card effect, where a card chosen by an audience member would rise out of the deck by itself (or by what the magician would call "sheer mental force" or "force of will" or even "psychokinesis" or "mind over matter"). The methods for doing this vary from manipulation directly by the hands of the performer to mechanical methods where the deck pretty much has a mechanism that pushes the card out (if you want to know more, head to your local magic shop and be prepared to spend money on books and effects).

In the anecdote, the performer thought he had set the method up properly, but as he was motioning to get the card to rise, he noticed that the mechanism was clearly not connected. He continued to motion with his hands as his mind whirled to come up with a way to cover for the failure. Suddenly, the selected card began to rise out of the deck, apparently on its own. The performer was a bit nonplussed, but being a consummate professional, recovered his reaction and took the applause as he normally would. However, he mentioned that he thought twice about doing the effect again.

Mentalists who appeared on a panel at the 1983 convention of the Parapsychological Association in New Jersey, stated that they had had experiences while performing that convinced them that psi was real (though such comments did not come from the skeptical magicians on the panel).

In my own experience as a performing magician and mentalist, I have often used humor to recover from a failure of an effect (since some of the venues I perform in bring me in as a comedy magician). I have, though, had a few experiences while performing mentalism when, like Marvin Kaye, something flashed into my mind from a volunteer and I used it, to the amazement of the volunteer and the audience (and myself).

I and others have also experienced effects screwing up when they really should have worked, simply because the performer was in a bad mood or perhaps simply not into performing that night. Then again, there may be outside forces at work.

In one performance where I and my mentalist partner Larry Loebig were performing at a reputed haunted restaurant called the Moss Beach Distillery (in Moss Beach, California; read all about it in Chapter Eight), I was finishing with the stated hope that the ghost, the Blue Lady, would honor us with a message placed in an empty, locked box.

The box, seen as empty by the audience, was of course rigged, and as I placed it down in front of the audience on a spectator's table, I slipped a message into the box. At the end of the show, I asked that spectator to unlock it. He picked the empty box up, shook it, and showed his surprise by stating that it sounded like something was in it (several people heard a slight rattling sound as the paper inside bounced around). Yet when he opened it, there was nothing there!

Did the *real* Blue Lady play a trick on me? I have no idea. Of course, I told the audience that the Blue Lady was playing a trick on us (or on me, specifically). But neither Larry nor I could explain where that message vanished to. Thankfully, one can say that where ghosts are concerned, where *magic* (the real kind) is involved, things are often unpredictable.

I firmly believe that being in a situation where one is performing *magic* of any sort, whether stage or close-up sleight of hand or illusion, or mentalism or ritual magic and sorcery, the setting and the even temporary belief shifting of the performer/magic wielder and the audience/witnesses can create an environment in which real psychic phenomena can occur and be encouraged.

For now, let us finish here by saying that rituals that ostensibly tap into impersonal or personified powers of the supernatural often allow the subconscious and conscious desires of the magic-user (or religious personage) a bit of latitude in making something happen, without directly putting the power in the individual. The magic-user learns to manipulate the power. The religious personages learns to ask for another power to do for them.

But for some, neither magic nor religion is required for the mind to affect matter. Sometimes it is just enough for the subconscious to want it to happen. And to "Make It So!" (in the words of the immortal Captain Jean-Luc Picard or *Star Trek* fame).

* **8** *

Poltergeists and Ghosts: Is It Mind or Spirit?

It is a quiet evening in a typical family home in the suburbs of San Francisco. The mother and father are watching television in the living room with the younger son. The older son, just turning thirteen, comes in the room and tries to get his parents attention; he has something he wants to talk about with them.

His father tells him they'll talk as soon as the show is over. The boy scowls and turns to leave.

Suddenly, they all hear a popping sound above their heads, immediately followed by the sound of water splattering the ceiling. While they are almost directly underneath the splattered water, only a few drops hit their heads, as though the water has spread out on the ceiling in a way it would if it had hit the floor.

A moment later, there are sounds of several other pop/splat combinations from the living room down the hallway toward the kitchen.

*

The elderly woman was now alone in her home. Her husband had died of cancer, a long and protracted illness during which she had to care for him. It was hard to be alone, especially since she had been with him most of her adult life.

As she sat in the house thinking over her life, she also experienced much regret, especially with regard to her husband. Not as much regret that he was gone, more that there were things, too many things, in their relationship left ignored and unresolved. She felt anger at him rising, for leaving her with so much unsaid. Then she felt guilty for the anger.

Suddenly, the painting of her husband dropped off the wall with a loud crash. This was immediately followed by several small crashes around the house, the sounds of glassware bursting or falling on the floor.

Yet again, she apologized to the "spirit" of her husband for her anger and asked him to stop throwing things around.

✳

The investigator sat in the couple's living room, listening to them describe the flights of objects, books, and knickknacks, as they seemingly moved around the house of their own accord.

He asked them if there was anything happening, any point or points of stress that they can say began about the same time the objects started their movements.

The couple began arguing about the husband being laid off and not really looking for a job, as well as the wife taking up smoking again because of the stress. The investigator sat quietly as the argument progressed, waiting for an opportune time to step in and stop it. The couple, however, appeared to have forgotten he was there.

Suddenly, a large ashtray on the coffee table slid across its surface and fell to the floor.

The investigator got on his hands and knees and checked the ashtray, then the table, for any form of rigging, just on the odd chance that the couple was trying to fake him out.

The couple stopped arguing when they noticed him under the coffee table.

"Do things move around a lot when you two are arguing?" he asked them as he climbed back to his feet and sat on the chair again.

"Almost every time," said the wife with a scowl. "Do you think there's a connection?"

The investigator suppressed a smile as he began to explain the nature of the poltergeist. . . .

*

Ever been stressed out? Well, of course you have. Who hasn't.

Have you ever noticed odd things happening when you are stressed out? Like objects out of place and unfindable (generally until you calm down)? Or your computer or car (or even your toaster) acting oddly, not working properly (though things work just fine later, once you've calmed down)?

Yes, often these things are happening because in your agitated state, you may not be thinking "right" and simply not looking in the right places for your keys, or using the equipment the way it should be used.

But there is plenty of evidence to indicate that sometimes the misbehavior of the machines and technology, the location of the keys or book you put down in a certain place, are affected by your stress level. Somehow, your mental/emotional stresses are affecting things around you. This makes the effect Mind over Matter.

In a general way, one might consider these events "mini-poltergeists" based on the current model parapsychologists have for the unexplained and recurring movements of objects in a home or office.

In Chapter Ten, I will more directly address the way our minds appear to interact with technology. Now, let's deal with what one might call the ultimate uncontrolled act of Mind over Matter, the poltergeist.

Poltergeist is a German word meaning, literally, *noisy ghost.* The term was applied to cases of unusual object movements, odd rapping or crashing noises, materializations and dematerializations of objects, smells with no apparent cause, movement or rearrangement of furniture, and situations in which water or fire would mysteriously appear in a home, or the house would be bombarded by stones with no apparent source. Reports of poltergeist phenomena go back many centuries in the historical record, so there is nothing "new" about this.

Today, it would seem that there's lots that a poltergeist can do besides simply tossing objects around or knocking pictures off the wall. With homes wired with electricity, with so much technology around, reported poltergeist effects also include odd electrical effects, appliances starting and stopping (or working oddly) on their own (including times when they're not even plugged in), TVs going on and off or changing stations without the use of a remote (even TVs that have no remote control), computers doing things outside the range of their software, phones dialing up numbers on their own, and much more.

Naturally, people first thought that some discarnate spirit was responsible for the typically destructive (always annoying) phenomena. While there are some cases in which the "agent" of the phenomena would appear to be a ghost (like the case of the ghost of the Banta Inn, who you'll read about in a few pages), many of these reported situations of unusual physical phenomena seemed more closely attached to one or more people *living* in the house or working in the office. The three examples at the beginning of this chapter are illustrations of events centered around, and *caused* by living people.

Over the years of study of the phenomena by people in the field of psychical research/parapsychology, a model of the typical poltergeist case emerged that had little to do with the dead and had everything to do with the living.

Preeminent parapsychologist and field investigator William George Roll best summarized the current model of the poltergeist when he coined the phrase *Recurrent Spontaneous PsychoKinesis (RSPK)*. In a poltergeist case, the phenomena, while it generally has a pattern, is spontaneous, it happens again and again, and it is caused by someone's unconscious mind.

The poltergeist is truly an extreme example of Mind over Matter gone haywire. Fortunately, it is also a fairly rare occurrence in its full blown, furniture tossing state (except as what I like to call the mini-poltergeist, which may occur many times a week for an individual). In addition, people rarely get injured in poltergeist cases, except where the poltergeist is directed at oneself by one's own mind (like the choking ghost case I discussed in Chapter Six), or perhaps if one ducks *into* the path of a flying object.

The general stereotype of the poltergeist "agent" (the person whose PK is causing the disturbances) has been popularized by the press as a teenage girl. In reality, the poltergeist scenario can occur with people of either sex and of all ages (though little children, while they may be the focus of the activity, are very rarely even considered the agent, the cause). One of the reasons why teenagers have been pegged for more of this type of activity is the inherent stress on both body and mind that adolescence places on the growing human. But keep in mind that adolescence actually goes into one's early twenties (it's not like turning twenty or twenty-one turns off the body and emotional stresses and changes). Also keep in mind that the start of puberty doesn't necessarily begin when one turns thirteen. For some children it's earlier, for others, later.

For most people experiencing what may end up being described as a poltergeist case, the very idea of seeking or needing help may not occur to anyone in the household until and unless the phenomena gets either extremely annoying or scary.

It's generally when people get annoyed, or more likely frightened, that they might call in a paranormal investigator such as myself. I and my "ghostbuster" colleagues occasionally get phone calls directly, because of a direct referral from another parapsychologist (who is often tracked down through a college or university psychology or anthropology department familiar with that individual) or sometimes from a writer or reporter. Often the referral goes from one university to JFK University or to Duke University, because of past associations with the field of parapsychology.

The group I established, the Office of Paranormal Investigations, gets referrals from universities, from police, from psychologists, from the media, and often simply because it is listed in the phone book and Yellow Pages in a couple of places in the San Francisco Bay Area. Referrals to me or to OPI come frequently from the various parapsychological institutions such as the American Society for Psychical Research and the Parapsychology Foundation in New York and from the Institute for Parapsychology at the Rhine Research Center in Durham, North Carolina.

If there's just a couple of things falling or getting misplaced every once in a while, or occasional problems with appliances or one's car, nothing frequent or even obviously moving without cause, the average person will just shrug it off and not think about it too much. This is probably wise, since it is more likely that the explanation for these occasional things is perfectly "normal."

For example, for a few weeks after the 1989 earthquake in San Francisco, I received more than a few calls from people who believed that they had a ghost or poltergeist. Why? Odd noises in the home. Pictures would shake on the wall or things would fall off shelves. And these were things that the people swore had never happened before.

The explanations tended to be rather mundane, though not necessarily that obvious (or maybe they were *too* obvious). Because of the earthquake, many buildings were settling back into their "normal" states, and noises never heard before occurred. Objects in the home vibrated or fell sometimes because of an aftershock, but generally because of the rerouting of traffic through San Francisco due to the collapse of part of the Bay Bridge and sections of freeways (a large truck rumbling down a city block can cause lots of vibration).

Why did the people even think the happenings could have been paranormal?

The earthquake occurred on October 17th, just at the real start of the Halloween season, when every bit of media, from print to broadcast, likes to do stories on ghosties and other "things that go bump in the night" (and on the "ghostbusters" who investigate them). I believe that if the earthquake had happened in February, such an explanation would not have ever occurred to most people.

People tend to look for a poltergeist-buster when they *believe* or *interpret* or *perceive* events to be out of the ordinary, to be paranormal. They may come to that belief or interpretation because of media they are exposed to at the time (maybe they just saw one of the "based on a true story" movies about a family in peril because of a supernatural force, or because they are avid watchers of TV shows like *Sightings* or because they read, and believe, everything in the tabloids), because of set beliefs they already hold about the way the world works (perhaps they have a spiritual belief system in which unusual occurrences are always caused by positive or negative "energies" or "thought forms" or spirits, as with some who follow certain New Age philosophies), because of their religious beliefs (their priest or pastor has taught them of the power of the Devil and how his evil may cause unusual happenings), and because a friend they told about the "weird stuff happening" made the paranormal connection (the friend possibly falling into any of the categories above).

If the situation is occurring with people who are very much on edge, their stress may cause them to react in such a way as there is an immediate realization that help is needed. In fact, even if the object movement is imagined (due to being stressed out), the belief that something paranormal is happening will (hopefully) cause an individual or family to seek help.

Of course, since the poltergeist is connected by investigators with people who are indeed under stress, the belief that something paranormal may happen, or the misinterpretation that something paranormal is already happening may actually spur on a true psychokinetic reaction. As with healing, athletic performance, and other mind-telling-the-body circumstances, the unconscious mind of the stressed-out individual may cause the belief in paranormal object movement to be acted out, and *real* poltergeist phenomena may result.

This is not to say that things don't start out the other way around. In fact, one major thing I've learned from investigating all forms of paranormal phenomena is that the initial phenomena, especially when real, can reinforce one's beliefs and fears and therefore the stresses in the situation, and cause both more real phenomena as well as a lot of additional misinterpretation. If the phenomena seems to be very much out of the ordinary or potentially harmful, such as bursts of water or a glass flying across a room, people are more likely to come to the "paranormal conclusion."

Unfortunately, once they believe something paranormal is happening, any normal sound they may not have noticed before, any coincidental knocking over or falling of breakables, any problems with appliances, no matter how normally explainable, are often included as "proof" that there's a poltergeist.

So, what happens in a "typical" poltergeist case?

Firewalking at the Firewalking Institute of Research and Education, Box 584, Twain Harte, CA 95383.   (*Courtesy Loyd Auerbach*)

Firewalking with no pain.   (*Courtesy Loyd Auerbach*)

Psycho-Kinesis (PK): the ability to interact with objects and events using the mind alone.   (*Artwork by Francis Mao*)

Aiko Gibo of Yokohama, Japan detects a "ghost" in a house in Archer, FL, while investigators Barbara Gallagher and Loyd Auerbach look on. (*Courtesy Jude Prest*)

Investigators at work. Central area set up in haunted house in Archer, FL, for receiving data from environmental equipment. (Left to right) Russell McCarty, James Bosworth, Barbara Gallagher, psychic Aiko Gibo, Loyd Auerbach, and Andrew Nichols. (*Courtesy Jude Prest*)

The Banta Inn, Banta, CA (in the San Francisco Bay area). A restaurant and bar where many physical paranormal events have been witnessed. (*Courtesy Loyd Auerbach*)

The bar at the Banta Inn, the center point of much of the physical phenomena. The apparition of a former owner/bartender has been seen and is pointed at as the cause of the antic disturbances. (*Courtesy Loyd Auerbach*)

The Moss Beach Distillery in Moss Beach, CA (just south of San Francisco), an exceptional restaurant due to great food, great atmosphere, and a ghost known as "The Blue Lady."
(*Courtesy Loyd Auerbach*)

The main dining area of the Moss Beach Distillery, with view of Pacific Ocean. A spot where people often "sense" the ghost.
(*Courtesy Loyd Auerbach*)

Author and aviation/aerospace expert Martin Caidin, with a variety of his telekinesis targets. (*Courtesy Loyd Auerbach*)

Making a Target.
(Illustrations by Loyd Auerbach)

Start with a *square* piece of paper or foil,
approx. 3" on a side is best.

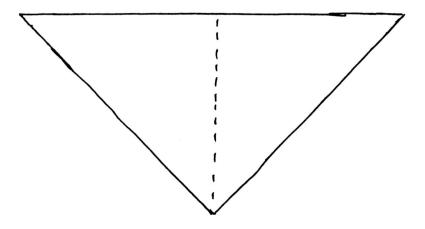

Fold diagonally, corner to corner.
Unfold, then refold with other two corners.

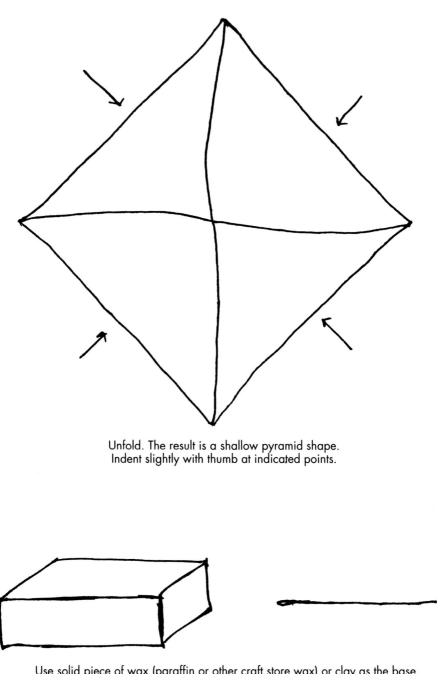

Unfold. The result is a shallow pyramid shape.
Indent slightly with thumb at indicated points.

Use solid piece of wax (paraffin or other craft store wax) or clay as the base.
Stick long sewing needle or pin up from center of the bottom of the base. Make sure
it is long enough to go through and support the Target.

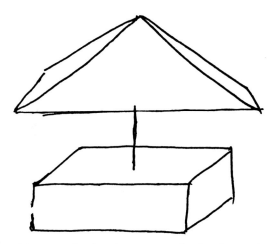

The Target must be able to turn freely. (Blow on it to check.) The inside of the tip might need to be lined with good quality tape to prevent the point of the needle from pushing through. Martin Caidin decorates the Target so he can clearly tell how many turns it has made.

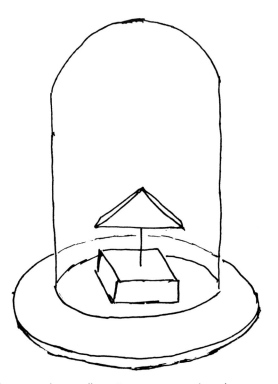

The Target can be put under a collector's jar or some other glass cover to prevent air-flow induced movement.

The author tries has hand at turning a target (commercially available model). (*Courtesy Chris Stier*)

A Target. (*Courtesy Chris Stier*)

Keybending made simple.
(Photos courtesy Gerry Griffin)

1) Borrow a set of keys or use your own.

2) Remove a good, strong key from the keyring.

3) Hold the key in one hand and focus your attention on it.

4) As the key begins to bend, stroke it with a finger (or fingers) of the other hand. Display intense concentration on your face.

5) Continue stroking the key and watch as it continues to increase the angle of the bend.

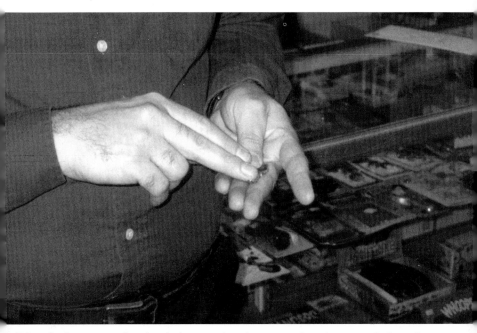

6) Lay the key in your hand with the point bending up and stroke upward along the bend to coax it to bend further. Move your fingers away from the bend to accentuate the angle as you stroke the key.

7) Pick up the bent key and display it for all to see.

8) Do *not* reveal that you started with a key that was already bent. They won't think you're psychic if you tell them.

Gerry Griffin, owner of California Magic and Novelty, Pleasant Hill, CA, displays some of the wares one can purchase from a magic dealer to simulate Mind over Matter, and other things.
(Courtesy Loyd Auerbach)

Gerry Griffin causing a pen to levitate via pseudo-pk (in other words, it's a trick!!)
(Courtesy Loyd Auerbach)

The author struggling with a "sleight" pain in the neck.   (*Courtesy Gerry Griffin*)

To begin with, an individual (sometimes more than one) in the family or work environment is undergoing some emotional or mental stresses (which often have negative physical effects on the body, of course). For whatever reason, the stress (and the cause of it) is not being dealt with or relieved. Many of us do things to help relieve stress, tension, and frustration. Perhaps we run or lift weights, maybe we do a little martial arts, or paint or play computer games. Maybe we even feel it's okay to hit a punching bag or our pillows or even just let out a primal scream (and unfortunately, some feel it's okay to lash out against a spouse or a child to relieve stress . . . poltergeists are much preferable to such unacceptable activities).

But for some, the energy of the stress and frustration gets bottled up for some reason. The individual doesn't have some manner to relieve the tension building up. Some of these people end up being ill, the stresses from the mind directly affecting the body. But for a few, the mind "lets off steam" from the body itself, in an explosion of energy that affects physical things around them.

The events in a poltergeist scenario may happen at random times, but more likely happen when there is an argument or crisis in which the agent is involved, or when whatever causes the stress to build up continues (at least in the agent's mind).

In the examples cited at the beginning of this chapter, I was the investigator. I did witness movements of objects as a couple began arguing about the husband's job status. In further questioning them, it was clear that the movements (and destruction) of objects in their home coincided with their arguments, and that the pent-up emotions that they both had were connected to what objects moved and broke.

Another case involved a woman who resented having to stay at home with her several months' old infant rather than get back to work. There was no resentment aimed at the baby, only at the husband, who insisted she stay at home rather than hire daycare (and money was not an issue). Whenever she thought about her husband's attitude, appliances in the kitchen would go on and off by themselves (sometimes without being plugged in), the TV would run through the channels (especially when her husband was watching), the stereo and VCR would go on and off, and even small objects would move (though not more than one or two of these incidents would happen at one time).

The stress of the nonworking status, coupled with a lack of understanding of why the objects were moving, somehow caused the phenomena to escalate, until she reached the conclusion (without my help, mind you) that she was somehow responsible for the phenomena. It scaled back almost immediately in intensity, and my advice that she and her husband should talk things out (perhaps in counseling) and work out a nonstress compromise was followed. The phenomena stopped.

The events may come to a (temporary) halt when the argument is over (or when the movements caused pull the attention of the people involved away from the argument), or perhaps when the energy the agent has built up at that moment is spent (when enough things have broken and the subconscious feels like it's done enough). Ending the events permanently may require finding out what's causing the stress and dealing with that directly (after, of course, identifying who the agent is).

The late D. Scott Rogo brought out the idea that the matter of poltergeist *agency* may not be limited to one person in the home or work environment, but may actually be a matter of bringing the same people together, their being together somehow creating a situation that may be stressful, whereby the reaction is a run of poltergeist effects. In that situation, it's effectively a group gestalt that causes things to happen, rather than a single individual.

Based on the PK theories of British researcher Kenneth Batcheldor, a group in Canada created their own "noisy ghost." Batcheldor had suggested that in a group environment, expectations, both conscious and unconscious, could bring on a variety of Mind over Matter effects that individuals couldn't. Part of that was the anonymity that the group provided the source(s) of the PK (no way to figure out whether it was a particular individual or several who caused the PK), and part of it was that in a group, where there are other witnesses also expecting something to happen, there's less of the normal inhibitions that people have to witnessing PK.

This group sat down and made up a person who "lived" centuries ago, and then had a seance to contact this fictitious person.

After a time, physical phenomena began manifesting itself, from table raps to apparent levitation of the table and other apparent instances of PK. While the results of the Philip Experiment remain somewhat controversial, this idea of creating one's own poltergeist is very interesting nonetheless. (See *Conjuring Up Philip: An Adventure in Psychokinesis* by Iris M. Owen with Margaret Sparrow. New York: Harper & Row, 1976).

Most poltergeists are person-centered, the events following a single individual from place to place (although the events are more likely to happen in one particular place where the stress and tension come to a head). It is the job of the poltergeist investigator to play detective, to learn who the agent might be through interview, through observation, and by analyzing the reported poltergeist events.

What things move, or what kinds of smells, or what additional phenomena (like small fires or bursts of water) are quite telling when trying to determine both who the agent is and what the keys are behind the stress the agent is building. While some poltergeist cases have just random acts of paranormal unkindness, there is often consistency. The events may focus on a particular location or area, they may center in on a specific object (like a picture on the wall and nothing else) or on a type of object (ashtrays or appliances or simply breakables). Or they may create something "new" to the environment, such as small fires or water bursts.

Such a consistency can help determine who the agent could be. If only the husbands "stuff" is being affected, one must look at whether the wife (or one of the kids) is somehow directing her tensions at the husband, or whether the husband, for some reason, is blaming himself for some problems and directing things at himself. Fortunately, there are some signs in the behavior of the individuals in the situation that help determine this.

You can also try to analyze the situation as though the objects being affected or the phenomena happening are symbols as in a dream. Water may symbolize grief (as in a case I dealt with where an individual hadn't dealt with her grief over th eloss of a relative . . . she hadn't cried at all . . . and water was drenching her and her furniture . . . it stopped when she began dealing with her grief, and began to cry). Fire may symbolize anger (as in a case investigated by researcher Dr. Julian Isaacs, in which a woman resenting a difficult new living and job situation was releasing her pent-up anger in the form of small flames putting burn marks on furniture and other possessions).

I've learned over the years that the phenomenon of the poltergeist is one in which the subconscious mind "plays" like a petulant child, throwing things, affecting things in very annoying ways, without fear of reprisal since it's not as though the people in the situation can immediately point a finger at the agent and punish him or her. So, like a child, the poltergeist may actually stop its influence when the agent is identified (more or less fading away because he or she "has been caught").

In the case of the water-throwing poltergeist mentioned at the chapter opening, it was learned that the older son was frustrated with his parents, though not made at them. He was essentially an active, though noncompetitive kid, and had been taking martial arts lessons. He dropped those when it came time for the students to get into a sparring competition, though he never told his parents why he wanted to drop out.

The parents, thinking he needed something extracurricular to get involved with, and knowing that he liked to swim, pushed him toward the school's swim team. He went along with that, even though he resented the competitive nature of the activity. Shortly after his first practice meets, the bursts of water began appearing in the house.

It took a few weeks for the parents to begin to suspect that the son was the "agent" of the phenomena, and only because several "attacks" happened while the boy was at his grandmother's house, at a piano teacher's home, and at a neighbor's. The water bursts continued, though, even after identification of him as the common denominator, probably because the cause was not directly connected to him.

Once I got involved, and through simple interviewing ("so, what's been bothering you lately?") identified the connection (that he hated the swim team because of the competitive nature), and brought the parents in on it all, they were able to work out the stress-inducing situation that apparently brought on the psychokinetic water bursts. The phenomena stopped.

In another case, electrical devices in a home were malfunctioning and going haywire every time a young woman witnessed her parents arguing. They at first thought she was physically doing something, but after witnessing phenomena while she was across the room, they realized something "else" was going on. But the pattern was clear once the interviewing revealed when and where the phenomena happened, and who was around. The phenomena stopped once the agent was identified and the cause of her stress was revealed (as to the parents arguing, I'm afraid I never continued follow-up long enough to see if the parents stopped that behavior, or if they separated; one follows up just once or twice to see if phenomena is still halted).

In some instances, the phenomena may not be "real." I and most of my colleagues have been involved, for example, in cases where one family member was causing things to break or move through purely physical means, while playing on the other family member(s) fears of the paranormal (I'll discuss some of these methods in Chapter Twelve). In some cases, the agent or another family member may add to the problem by faking some events, consciously figuring that everyone else will think that whatever "bad" things happen in the house can be blamed on the poltergeist.

In one case related to me by a colleague, a young girl was at the center of what appeared to be genuine phenomena. However, some fraud was identified on the part of the girl (she claimed to start doing some damage to her parents' belongings after seeing that the "ghost" would catch the blame). Later, though, the investigator also witnessed genuine phenomena. Understanding that both was going on, and that the girl was at the center of both the fraud and the PK led to an identification of her stress points and why the phenomena (both paranormal and fraudulent) were happening.

So, catching the agent responsible sometimes means sorting the normal from the paranormal. In either case, exposing the agent responsible generally helps alleviate the problem. The phenomena generally stops.

But if this is a real poltergeist case, the phenomena may reoccur unless the point of stress, the real underlying cause of the PK in the first place, is dealt with. If there is fraud, this is also a good plan, since there's generally *some* reason why one family member may try to fake out and even terrify another.

Another interesting way to handle the poltergeist, especially when there's no easy-to-identify agent, appears to be to have everyone involved *try* to move objects with their minds. Since the process seems to be an unconscious one, bringing the conscious mind into the action tends to somehow curtail the excessive PK that's going on. In addition, this requires taking responsibility for the actions of the poltergeist. The unconscious "temper-tantrum" nature of the poltergeist seems to relate to a lack of taking responsibility for dealing with one's stresses and tensions. Adding in the personal responsibility for one's actions, whether conscious or unconscious, seems to generally help curtail the phenomena.

Of course, there are exceptions to this, as Julian Isaacs and others have worked with individuals who had some degree of control after taking responsibility and accepting that they are poltergeist agents. In Chapter Eleven, you'll learn a method to try a little PK on your own from Martin Caidin, who certainly takes responsibility for his own PK (even though it can be misdirected from time to time).

For all of this so far, I have been discussing the poltergeist scenario as a result of stresses and tensions. Are there other explanations?

One of the more interesting theories about PK and poltergeists is that PK may happen (as with other psi experiences) because of something odd happening in the brain. A percentage of poltergeist agents over the past years who were given neurological examinations showed some signs of epilepsy or epileptic-like activity in the brain. The PK bursts in the poltergeist case may be a form of release of energy that happens during a kind of seizure or massive misfiring of neurons in the brain. Rather than the body acting out the seizure as in most epileptics, the energy (whatever that energy is) gets directed outward and things happen.

Other forms of psychic experiences have been tentatively tied to activity in the temporal lobes of the brain, and to influence of the magnetic fields of the earth, which do shift throughout the day and night. Certain shifts may be responsible for some (or maybe all) psychic experiences, causing activity in the brain that leads to everything from a precognitive dream to a poltergeist outbreak. The hypothesized relationship of the geomagnetic field to PK and ESP experiences will be discussed in the next couple of chapters.

The actual mechanism by which objects outside the body of the poltergeist agent can be affected, the mechanism of PK itself, is not understood. How the mind can utilize some form of energy to direct the levitation or movement of objects, or change the temperature of a part of a room, or make water appear apparently from nowhere has no more an acceptable explanation than how my thoughts get the right neurons in the brain to fire up and direct my fingers to type the right letters on my keyboard.

Because there is no sufficient evidence of what form of energy may be utilized to cause the psychokinetic movements, there is no equipment that allows investigators to point the finger instantly at a particular individual and say "you're the agent!" It is a detective game that sometimes, though rarely, ends up with the most likely suspect being outside the range of possibilities.

While most poltergeist cases, situations in which things in the environment are being moved or affected physically, revolve around living individuals, some are what have been called "place-centered" poltergeists. In these types of cases, the anomalous physical phenomena happens in a particular building or part of a building, no matter who visits or lives there. There is often also a pattern of the events, the same sorts of things happening at the same time during the day or night, or the same time every month or year, or under certain conditions (like a full moon, a thunderstorm, during sunspot activity, etc.). Sometimes the events happen because of remodeling or rebuilding, as though the attempts to cause any change to the structure "disturbs" something.

In addition, the events that happen, the objects that move or appear or disappear, may relate to some point or points in the actual history of the location.

One hypothesis about such place-centered poltergeists is that there is an actual spirit (or more than one) that is somehow locked into the location, and, like the old-fashioned ghost stories "doomed to repeat the events of the past forever." Because of this direct link to the past, the ghost repeats the events he or she was involved in at some past time. Even the object movements that occur may be tied into the spirit's past, an attempt to simulate, to re-create, past activities. One would suppose that the ghost conducts his or her repeats whether there are any witnesses there or not. Of course, this repeating pattern makes for a very boring ghost, and one that displays none of the signs of consciousness or intent.

Another hypothesis that is more directly related to PK is that the place-centered poltergeist relies on living witnesses for anything to happen.

In the investigation of paranormal occurrences, we run across what has been termed a "haunting" quite often. This is the idea that the environment may somehow record the events of the past, and under certain conditions, can replay them back to the minds of witnesses.

In other words, certain emotion-laden events that have happened throughout the past of an old house may have been locked into the environment of the house (undoubtably some kind of energy field that has yet to be identified). People in the house occasionally receive the mental "images" or "sounds" of these past events, which get merged with real perceptions of the surroundings (like the explanation for an apparition from Chapter Six).

Of course, as with apparitions, people may experience the haunting as sights, sounds, smells, or feelings (again, I've heard no reports of taste being involved).

In one haunting case conducted in Alameda, California, the family reported strange sensations in particular spots in the house, and visions of an old woman (whom they all described the same way) walking into and out of a particular bedroom in a repetitive pattern. Also the impression of particular articles of furniture (which were not physically there) was reported.

Through the process of interviewing the family and their landlord (they were renting the house), it became evident that the old woman doing the repetitive movements was a recording of the landlord's deceased mother, who lived in that house until her death just a few months before the new family rented it. There was no sense of "intelligence" or "communication" as one would expect in an apparition case.

However, myself and the three others with me all felt strange sensations in the same spots in the house the famly reported them (we asked them not to tell us where these points were until we were through checking things for ourselves). In addition, we were using a hand-held magnetometer (which detects magnetic fields), which gave much higher than background readings in all the spots noted, yet nowhere else in the house (once the appliances were disconnected—we learned that day that a coffeemaker sends out a very large spike of magnetic radiation when it goes on).

Because of extensive contact with these cases, I believe I have gained some higher degree of sensitivity in some cases. In December of 1993, the Office of Paranormal Investigations received a call to help a woman living in an apartment in San Francisco. The woman, who we'll call Wendy, had sensed a "presence" in her apartment for the entire two years she lived there. However, since November, she began to see a shadowy figure come into her bedroom, moving closer and closer. One night, she was awakened to see the figure leaning over her.

Upon turning on the lights, the figure vanished. She received some corroboration from a friend of hers who had stayed over and asked about a "presence" she sensed as well.

Wendy was frightened, and ended up at her boyfriend's place every night after nine. She asked us to come in and check things out.

I brought with me two other OPI team members, Gary Storm and Dean Pardee. Kathy Reardon, one of the intuitives we work with and our prime team "psychic" was to meet us a bit later.

Wendy took us through the fourth-floor apartment, explaining just where things had happened. We also took readings with our Tri-Field meters, measuring the local magnetic fields. Of course, near active appliances and sources of electrical current in the walls, we got high readings. We also got higher than background readings in a couple of other places.

As Wendy took us into her bedroom, I felt a strange sensation.

I stood in the doorway in a position that felt "right" and asked her if "this is how the figure appears."

She nodded, although a bit apprehensively. I began to move into the room slowly, stopping at the end of the bed, then around the bed to the right, finally stopping again near the headrest. Wendy was nodding as I was moving, her eyes widening more and more.

To me, I was just moving in a way that, again, "felt right," whatever that means. At the final position, I bent over the pillow, feeling as though there was someone there, I'd be attempting to tell the person in bed something. "Wendy, when he bent over you, could it be as though he was leaning over to wake you up and tell you something? As though he was even trying to kiss you first, gently?"

She thought about it a moment. "Yes, now that you put it that way, I think you're right." This calmed her down a bit, though she had many questions for me (so did I).

Just before we went back into the living room, I got a fleeting impression of the man wearing a trenchcoat and hat, and of him falling or being pushed out the window by the bed. Apparently Wendy also had an impression of the hat and coat, but not the window.

A few minutes later, Kathy Reardon arrived. After talking with Wendy for a bit, we were able to talk over a speakerphone with her friend who also had "sensed" the "presence." Following that, Kathy, Wendy, and I moved back to the bedroom. Up to then, I hadn't discussed my impressions with Kathy, just that I had "gotten something."

Kathy began to describe a similar movement of the man through the room, also coming up with the reason behind him leaning over the bed. She felt the man had been going through those motions in the late 1940s or early 1950s, which "felt" right to Wendy and myself.

But I suddenly got the idea that the person in bed was supposed to be the trenchcoat's girlfriend or wife, but wasn't. Instead, it was a man waiting to do the trenchcoated man harm. I said this aloud and Kathy agreed. Kathy added that the trenchcoated man either fell because of surprise or was pushed out the window right behind him, and fell to his death. I felt he was pushed.

Kathy asked Wendy if she was getting anything herself. Wendy said she got a name: Paul. I immediately understood that that was the trenchcoated man's name, and that the woman he was expecting to find in bed was named Jesse. Kathy added the first name of the man in the bed, Frank.

Kathy (and I) felt there was less of an actual "spirit" in the place than leftover impressions of the event. She tried "clearing" the place, and it did feel better. Wendy had little problem there for a time, but has begun to suspect that the phenomena is continuing.

With hauntings, one deals with *recordings* of some kind, which may be as hard to get rid of as the sounds of a nearby highway.

Have you ever gone into a place and felt that it was a "good" or "bad" place to be? This may be because of a) expectations based on what you already may know about the place, b) sensory cues in the physical environment that you may not consciously notice, and/or c) information your mind is picking up directly from the environment, information about the history of the place "recorded" by the place itself.

Okay, so here you are walking into a supposedly haunted place with its history somehow locked in. How does that information only come out at certain times?

The best guess right now is that there are environmental factors that allow for the release of the information. It may be anything from magnetic field changes in the place (which have been noticed as relating to hauntings, as was noted in the Alameda case) to tidal forces to weather changes (which can cause changes in air ionization, air pressure, etc.).

Where the PK comes in is in those cases where, during the haunting, physical objects are seen to move or be affected (not just perceptions). The PK, under this hypothesis, comes from the witnesses. In some case where images are "seen" or unusual sounds are "heard," physical objects are sometimes directly observed to move or be affected in other ways.

One case I had involved people living in a house where they were frightened because of the footsteps they heard every night. Soon after they began noting the footsteps, they saw a figure walk down one hallway. Both events were repetitive and happened in a pattern (every few days at the same time of night). But after a few weeks of the footsteps and the figure (which never broke from the pattern), they noticed objects falling or breaking, furniture being moved, and their TV and VCR acting oddly.

The footsteps and figure stayed within the repetitive pattern. The only thing that really changed was the couple's reaction to the phenomena, which involved a growing fear and stress. We dealt with the PK events through explaining to the couple what they were experiencing was something akin to a recording, and so quite neutral (if annoying), and that the other phenomena was likely due to the stress and fear they were experiencing *because* of the haunting.

They understood and accepted the "diagnosis" and advice. The movements halted and the footsteps and apparition were soon ignored.

What happens is that the mind of the witness receives the information and begins to "play" it back, with some enhancements. To add to the realism of the "playback," the subconscious helps it along with some psychokinetic special effects.

Is this fact?

No, only supposition at this point. Yet in most cases where there's a regular pattern, it tends to make the most sense. So, when you go to a haunted house and things move around, you might try telling yourself that "I am doing this. It's my responsibility" as with a poltergeist case, and even try to consciously affect things with your mind. If nothing else, your fear will dissipate even if the phenomena keeps on going.

Where there's no regular pattern, where there is both the sense or sight of an apparition and physical phenomena apparently directed by the apparition, it may be that the ghost has learned to use his or her PK. After all, the ghost, being a mind, ought to be able to use PK like a living person's mind (or one would assume this if one believed in ghosts).

Most apparitional cases I have investigated, where the apparent ghost seems to be intelligent and conscious, have little or no physical events going on. I have, however, investigated a few cases that fit the idea of the PK-mischevous spirit.

The Banta Inn, in the small town of Banta next to Tracy, California, has apparently been haunted by the ghost of Tony Gukan, since his death of a heart attack behind the bar in 1968. The husband of the owner at the time, Tony began occasionally showing himself to a couple of regulars and bartenders shortly after that. While he is "felt" more than seen, what he most likes to do is move things around.

Bottles, glassware, and ashtrays have been seen to skid across the bar or tables, or even pop up into the air or across the room. I witnessed an ashtray on the bar pop up into the air, flip over, and land flat on the bar rail without breaking. I've also witnessed unusual (and fairly lengthy) movements of a chandelier, a glass sliding across the bar, and some weird goings-on with the CD jukebox (it played without being plugged in). The jukebox often flips its pages of CDs without anyone touching it (it's not built to do this).

One witness who works as a physicist reported being amazed as a bottle picked itself up off the back bar and floated across the room (the man was there for lunch and had not had anything to drink, in case you're wondering). Others witnessed this. When he was asked what he, as a physicist, thought about what he witnessed he replied "I think I have to rethink physics." He's since become a regular restaurant customer there.

The most common physical occurrences seem to revolve around the cash register and with bar patrons who scoff at Tony's ghost. While he was alive, Tony had the habit of stacking the change in the change compartments in the register. Today, even with the register drawer being opened and closed regularly and often quite hard, the coins will be mixed on closing the drawer, yet stacked neatly a couple of minutes later.

Skeptics have watched, mystified, as their coins on the bar moves around just after pooh-poohing the idea of a ghost being there. (Joan Borland, the owner, told me of one time when two guys watched in disbelief as the coins in front of them stood up on end. They left in a hurry and haven't been back since.)

One other interesting things is that when TV crews have gone into the Banta Inn, if something happens, it often happens *behind* the camera. If that's not the act of an intelligence, I don't know what is. On my first trip to the Banta Inn with *Hard Copy,* I was facing the bar with the camera facing me (the crew had their backs to the bar). As I was being interviewed, I watched as an ashtray popped up about four feet off the bar, flipped over, and landed, without breaking, on the bar rail. The crew heard the ashtray land, and turned to see "what was that." The three guys and the bartender and I got a good laugh at the reaction of the TV crew, realizing that they had missed something that we all saw clearly.

A second place is a wonderful restaurant on the northern California coast called the Moss Beach Distillery. This prohibition-era-built restaurant in Moss Beach, south of San Francisco, has for decades been haunted by the ghost of a young woman killed on the beach. Called the "Blue Lady" because of the dress she typically wears when she has been seen (and because the records of the time are lost and her real name is not known), she has rarely appeared to people in the restaurant as an apparition (like the Banta Inn's ghost), but has more been heard (her voice) or he presence felt.

In addition, there have been physical object movements, most often reported by the owner, John Barbour, and his employees (and the previous owners as well). Tampering with the locked thermostat, objects floating across the office, spatulas in an otherwise empty kitchen slapping repair people on the rear end, a locked side door opening by itself, and furniture being moved have all been reported. All, according to the witnesses, have been quite purposeful in their movements.

One of the more interesting physical phenomenon often associated with ghosts is the stopping of clocks and/or the breaking of objects at the moment of someone's death. One of the most common forms of apparitional sightings happens just at (or shortly after) the death of a relative or loved one or close friend, whereupon the experiencer may see and/or hear an apparition of that person (who is often there to say goodbye) or have a dream that the person died or simply get a feeling or *know* that the person has passed away.

Sometimes, it has been reported that a clock (at times more than one clock) either belonging to the deceased or to the person seeing the apparition of the deceased will stop at the moment of death, often never working again. Sometimes an object may fall or shatter at that moment.

It has been suggested that whatever allows the person dying to reach out and be seen by others at the moment of death (kind of like a final burst of energy) also contains the energy to affect physical objects. As Scott Rogo and others have suggested, a clock may be the most common object because of its symbology to our lives ("his *time* has run out").

Is this PK of a ghost or a just dying (not quite dead) person? That's impossible to say for sure. In addition, there is the added complication to the explanation that it may be the experiencer causing the physical effect, not the dying/deceased.

It has been suggested that these deathbed apparitions are not ghosts at all, but part of the process of the experiencer using his or her ESP to become *aware that the person has just died.* If this is the case, it would be the PK of the *experiencer* that further sets in his/her mind the idea of the death of the loved one by causing a physical effect that cannot be denied (as opposed to an apparition that can be dismissed as an hallucination).

Attributing the source of the PK is often difficult, and those of us who do investigations do the best we can with the current information we have. The important thing to remember is that there are alternate explanations, and that, as Scott Rogo has said in many of his writings on PK, psychokinesis is just a word, a label for phenomena, *not an explanation* of the phenomena.

So, do ghosts exist? We can't prove it, any more than we can prove the existence of the human mind on a physical level. As apparitions, by their very definition are mind's without bodies, it'd be kind of hard to imagine a ghost detector that would detect the consciousness of a ghost without being able to detect the consciousness of a living person.

And yet the media is always asking investigators like myself about equipment for ghost and poltergeist detecting. In reality, rather than showing up at a place in complete ghostbuster jumpsuits and gear, paranormal investigators work more like investigative reporters than those guys with the backpacks. The scope of a typical investigation involves a lot of interviewing of witnesses (we don't even like to check places reputed to be haunted if there are no witnesses), checking out the premises for other possible explanations for the events reported, checking on the past history of the place (where applicable), and using some form of detection devices if the investigation warrants it.

First, let me say that *human beings* are the best detection devices (since they are the "devices" that reported the phenomena in the first place). To help keep track of what witnesses perceive, we use tape recorders and video cameras, notepads and still cameras.

If a ghost were to appear on a photo, yet not be seen by the eyes of the people in the picture or taking the picture, something else besides straight picture-taking must be going on. That something else may be psychokinesis. In the next chapter, I'll discuss unusual effects people have been able to produce with apparent Mind over Matter abilities, including that of Ted Serios, who displayed the ability to affect film, to "put" images on a photographic plate.

So, most of the basic equipment is used for record keeping. Of course, in a poltergeist case, as long as the camera is pointed in the right direction, one should be able to get the movement of physical objects on tape or on film (and yes, this has apparently happened more than a few times).

We have gotten unusual energy streaks and other effects on Polaroid film, often in conjunction with other detection devices used in cases.

Researchers have used detectors that work in the infrared, microwave, electrostatic, and even ultraviolet ranges of the electromagnetic spectrum. Geiger counters have sometimes registered something unusual. Infrared thermalvision cameras, which translate heat patterns into color images (as in the movie *Predator*) have been used to look for cold spots and unusual heat displacements.

Our most frequently used device is a magnetometer, which picks up magnetic fields, as mentioned in the Alameda case, where we tied higher magnetic fields to the spots where people were having their experiences.

Keep in mind that all of these detection devices pick up environmental factors, real physical things. That means one must always be careful about sources of contamination. Could the unusual read-

ings have another, normal, cause (say a high magnetic reading because of unshielded wiring or a powerful appliance in the area or
hot spots on the thermalvision that look like footprints because one
of the investigators walked on the floor a few seconds before,
changing the temperature where he walked). In fact, one of our
cases involved a family that smelled strange smells, the heating
didn't seem to cover the whole place, and there were strange
sensations walking through it. With our gear and some structural
checking, as well as some checking of the vicinity, it became a non-
paranormal case as the house was shoddily built, had several code
violations, was close enough to a landfill for methane to be seep-
ing up from the ground, and was directly under some power lines
(which, besides giving off high magnetic fields, also gave off a low
frequency hum that caused headaches and "strange sensations").

"Ghostbusting" equipment often tells us more about the physical environment we are investigating than about the phenomena itself, since we have no idea at this time just what kind of energy a
ghost or PK might be, and even if we knew that some form of magnetic field was responsible, it would take quite a bit of work to pin
down exactly what the frequencies and field strengths were.

We use the equipment to corroborate what the witnesses report.
Sometimes, we find that unusual readings may show an environmental cause for a cold spot or an unusual feeling, rather than a
paranormal one. So, the equipment, while looking pretty fancy on
television, may not provide any useful or insightful information to
the investigator unless it can be correlated to the witness reports
responsible for the investigation in the first place.

In addition, the equipment is fairly expensive. There has never
been funding for investigations of ghosts and poltergeists on a consistent basis. So, the equipment is often out of reach on most investigations. On occasion, TV companies may come up with the
money or equipment for a ghost hunt in hopes of capturing something worthwhile for their ratings (they care less about whether the
researcher actually learns anything). With exception of some basic
gear, investigators deal mainly with the witnesses and their own wits
to determine what's happening in a case.

One more word about equipment: REG. This stands for Random

Event Generator, a device used in laboratory research on psychokinesis. The REG is a machine that has some form of random process going on inside, which may be a computer program or a tiny radioactive source element that decays at a truly random rate. Used in the lab (more in Chapter Ten), the device shows whether an individual might be able to cause the device to become temporarily less random.

Used on field investigations, as shown by the work researcher George Hansen is undertaking, the REG may show whether there is PK of some sort going on, and even help test individuals for being poltergeist agents.

For the time being, poltergeist and ghost investigators play detective, using deduction to figure out "what" or "who done it."

The common thread in all cases where physical things are moving or being affected is Mind over Matter; someone's mind (or more than one person's) is affecting the physical environment directly, through some unknown, and generally unconscious process.

But what about the more conscious forms of PK?

9

The Force Is With You

The phenomenon of the poltergeist speaks to an individual able to cast the energy of the mind outside the body and affect matter in a direct manner. Psychic Healing also has an implication that the mind can potentially affect the body of another in a direct fashion (assuming, based on evidence, that all such healing is not an extension of the placebo effect). The reported abilities of saints, physical mediums, and shamans, from healing to levitation, and the implications of some occult practices that the natural world can be affected by ritual magic again suggests the direct effect of the mind on matter.

So, here we are in the last part of the twentieth century. Parapsychology has been around in one form or another for over 100 years, beginning with studies of physical and mental mediums, although the experimental research in the laboratory really didn't get underway until the 1930s. A wide range of reported PK abilities have been reported and examined (to some extent).

The disbelievers (who often, wrongly, call themselves "skeptics") continue to claim that nothing has been learned about PK and ESP, that there is no real evidence for either, and that perhaps parapsychologists should just give up and move on to something else. The fact that PK is not repeatable on demand under any conditions and that it can often be easily faked are parts of their arguments that support theses statements.

Is this true? It all depends on what you believe and how you look at the research evidence (much of which the so-called skeptics never look at personally; they often rely on other skeptics to tell them whether there is evidence or not).

There are a wide range of PK abilities that have been reported, perhaps as numerous as athletic or artistic skills. They include (but are not limited to):

1. Healing
2. Psychic surgery
3. Psychic harm
4. Self-levitation
5. Levitation or movement of objects
6. Placing images on film
7. Affecting video- and audiotape
8. Affecting the weather
9. Affecting local temperature
10. Causing/creating fire
11. Condensing local moisture into water
12. Dematerialization/rematerialization of objects
13. Materializing objects or substances from nowhere (i.e. bursts of water, food)
14. Teleportation of objects (and people?)
15. Creating sounds
16. Creating light effects
17. Affecting magnetic fields
18. Affecting electrical fields
19. Affecting the atomic or molecular structure (such as the minute piece of radioactive material that may be used in Random Event Generators; making it less random in its decay)
20. Affecting the body's performance
21. Shielding the body from harm
22. Bending metal (like spoons and keys)

While the first few and the last one are probably the most widely "known" PK applications, there are an amazing number of ways science fiction, fantasy, and comic book writers have thought of in connection to the "powers of the mind." One need only look through "The Official Dungeon Master Decks: Deck of Psionic Powers," published by TSR, Inc., for an idea of the dozens of "powers" one may have (if one exists in a more fantastic universe than our own, of course). Later in this chapter I will take a brief look at the more fantastic applications of Mind over Matter in popular culture.

In "real life," the range of mental effects on matter is incredibly broad, especially if one takes into account the thesis of this book, that the mind affecting even the performance and operation of the body is Mind over Matter or psychokinesis. Unfortunately, like extraordinary athletic performance, sometimes it's difficult, if not impossible, to get the subject to perform on command.

The study of Mind over Matter began in the nineteenth century with the physical mediums. Of course, given the spiritualist bent of the seances of those days, the mediums attributed the happenings to outside spirits rather than their own innate capabilities. One of the consequences of such a belief was that the medium might feel quite uncomfortable doing anything that could constrain the spirits from "coming through," and therefore scientific controls in the seance room were quite difficult, if not impossible, to set up. That rationale also prevented controls set up that could prevent or expose the fraud that was more likely the norm rather than the exception with self-styled physical mediums.

The researchers who studied the mediumistic displays of object movements, materializations, and dematerializations, and unusual energy displays, were limited in being able to get a handle on what was really happening (except when they uncovered fraud, of course). The problem with uncontrolled demonstrations, is that there is no way to eliminate other possibilities (fraud, misperception, "normal" happenings such as those caused by the physical environment, and even coincidence).

So, after much uncovering of fraud (and more left uncovered), some researchers turned away from the study of the medium in the seance room. The reported evidence of physical effects from the seance room and the more widespread reports of unusual physical effects in everyday life seemed to indicate that people, not spirits, were likely to be responsible for or connected to at least much of the phenomena. Some mediums came to believe that they, themselves, not the spirits, had the "power." Researchers arose who wanted to study this ability to affect matter, but under controlled laboratory conditions so as to prove that psychokinesis was a reality (not merely good magic tricks).

In the early part of the century, William McDougall, a psychologist from Oxford, came over to the U.S. to teach at Harvard, and to act as president for the American Society for Psychical Research. McDougall brought in the term "parapsychology" to help distance the laboratory studies he was beginning to conduct from the work of the psychical researchers with mediums and spiritualistic phenomena, at a time when much of the field was embroiled in controversy over a physical medium known as "Margery" (accused of fraud by many, "verified" as genuine by others; even Harry Houdini was involved in this one).

His original use of the term related to experimental and quantitative studies of psi (ESP and PK), more or less a subset of the original psychical research. Today, we tend to use the terms parapsychology and psychical research interchangeably, although "psi research" is a more proper, and current, term.

Two young researchers, Joseph Banks Rhine and his wife Louisa followed McDougall to Duke University in 1927 for their postdoctoral studies. The three were interested in making studies of psychic phenomena acceptable to the academic world through bringing the studies into the controlled experimental situation of the laboratory. While their work was first directed at trying to observe both ESP and PK at work (what's called "proof research"), they had an interest in seeking out some pattern or explanation for the phenomena, for the process that was responsible for psi ("process research").

While there was some interest in the early research studies in working with so-called "gifted" subjects, the Rhines were very interested in demonstrating the universal nature of psi abilities, that everyone had some degree of ability, that the "gifted" subjects were not all that unusual, just that they were perhaps better performers (or in some cases, better frauds).

According to Louisa Rhine:

> Systematic research in PK can be said to have had its beginning one day in early 1934 when a young instructor in the psychology department of Duke University in North Carolina, J. B. Rhine, had a caller in his office who seated himself on the corner of the instructor's desk and said, "Hey, doc, I've got something to tell you I think you ought to know."[1]

Rhine, at the time, was concentrating his efforts on telepathy. Students had often been subjects in his research, guessing at symbols on cards (often at a rate higher than chance would indicate was coincidence), and some were regular visitors to Rhine's office "either as subjects in further tests or as student assistants to help in the experiments."[2]

> The young caller, however, was not a Duke student. Although he was still in college at a neighboring institution, he announced his main occupation: gambling. And it was in the course of pursuing his "profession" that he had learned the something he thought the instructor should know. It was a discovery, he said, that he was certain ought to be studied scientifically. . . .
>
> The discovery was this. He had found that he could control the fall of dice—*by willpower*. At times, he said earnestly, when throwing dice in gambling, he could get the faces of the dice to come up as he wanted them to. He was certain of it. He said he could not do it all the time, but only when in a special highly confident mental state and desperately needing to have specific faces of the die come up. The instructor asked if he could demonstrate the claim. With only a bit of hesitation because, he said, he had never done it for a professor, he agreed to try.
>
> In a matter of minutes, the gambler and the instructor were hunched down in a corner of the office, the gambler throwing his dice on the floor. His actual success is not on record, but it was great enough to impress the observer and to arrest his interest and atten-

tion so much that it lead him to start a new line of inquiry immediately.[3]

Early researches in psychokinesis at Duke and other locations mainly dealt with the statistics of certain faces of dice coming up. With subjects concentrating on specific numbers, the dice would be thrown (for a time by hand, then by machine to eliminate any issue of control of the throw by the thrower). Statistically significant results were achieved, yet there has never been any great consistency in the results. As the "gambler" who apparently initiated the research said, it couldn't be done all the time.

Over the decades that followed, PK research has taken many forms and has been conducted by a number of researchers. Rhine continued his research on ESP and PK until his death in 1980. He helped establish the Parapsychology Laboratory at Duke in 1935, with publication of the *Journal of Parapsychology,* a scientific publication, starting in 1937. Initial emphasis of the lab was on strictly controlled experiments. While this was not the first time controlled laboratory experiments in psi were conducted (most notable were early experiments at Stanford University published in a massive monograph in 1917), it was the first time an organization or laboratory was set up for the stated purpose of continued statistical analysis of psi effects.

The first few years of the work of McDougall and the Rhines produced little in the way of knowledge of how psi functions, and the statistical evidence, though piling up, was not overly impressive (although there were clusters of high scores by certain subjects in the early days). After a while, a few consistent effects did begin to rear their heads in the scores of the tests.

These included the idea of "psi missing" or significant scoring *below* chance. If the odds are 50/50 for each flip of a coin, for example, getting tails consistently when one is focusing on getting heads means you are wrong, but the system has still become nonrandom. *Something* has moved the performance of the task away from chance. That something may be PK, though in this case the subconscious, for some reason, makes the target behave in a way opposite to what the subject's conscious mind desires.

Another effect noted by Rhine was a "decline effect," which indicated that a subject's scores would decline toward chance over a number of trials. In other words, even if the subject started out doing well, the apparent PK or ESP would disappear over the course of many trials.

If PK is really tied into performance, once can easily understand why the decline effect happens. Whatever the mechanism that causes a physical effect is in the mind/brain, it may have a limit to how much it can do at a given sitting. Just like the body has a limit to how much it can do over a period of time. Sooner or later, your arms get fatigued if you're lifting weights or bowling, your legs get tired if you're running or walking, your jaw gets tired if you're chewing gum, and your mind/brain gets tired if you're trying to affect the throw of dice, or move objects, or affect an REG.

Most research until the 1960s was aimed at trying to prove the existence of psi abilities, and what was learned along the way about the processes behind it, like psi missing and the decline effect, helped herald in the switch to "process research." While researchers argued for psi's existence, a few really looked closer at the phenomena to isolate characteristics of subjects and states of consciousness in which psi might be brought out.

In 1946, Dr. Gertrude Schmeidler, a psychologist, was appointed research director of the American Society for Psychical Research (ASPR), an organization pursuing the same controlled situations as the Rhines, shifting away from its history of mediumistic investigations. Dr. Schmeidler is one of the pioneers of research into *how* psi works, with studies on the subjects' beliefs and attitudes leading to what she termed the "Sheep-Goat" effect.

This effect, which has again and again been replicated, predicts that people who *believe* or tend to believe in ESP and PK (sheep) will score *above* chance (though not necessarily significantly so) and those who *disbelieve* in psi or in the possibilities (goats) will tend to score *below* chance (again, not necessarily with any significance).

If psi does exist, it would appear that as you've read throughout this book, *belief* is a (if not *the*) major factor in its performance. If psi does not exist, as the debunkers state, then there is some other psychological effect that must allow people to have scores in their experimental results that are tied to belief.

The dice experiments at the Duke lab, where certain faces were focused on to come up, were followed by what were called "placement" tests in the early 1950s. The goal of such tests was to influence falling or rolling objects so they would come to rest in a certain designated place (such as one side or the other of a dice table). The late W.E. Cox worked at the lab in setting up placement tests with dice, as well as with other objects such as spheres and coins. Placement studies were also conducted by Louisa Rhine and Haakon G. Forwald in Sweden.

Over the years that followed, there have been a number of targets used in PK research, from attempts at affecting living organisms like paramecium, blood cells, and even small animals, fish, reptiles, and humans (especially in healing studies) to attempts to affect magnetic fields and temperature.

The research in the effect of moving objects such as falling or rolling dice appeared to have greater (or more frequent) positive results than experiments on moving stationary objects (which hardly worked at all in the lab, no matter how often reported outside the controlled environment). As affecting a moving system is based on affecting a random process, these studies led to trying to find more random systems that could be even better controlled.

In the early 1960s, Dr. John Beloff of the University of Edinburgh conducted research using a radioactive source element and a Geiger counter. The object of the experiment was to see if the subjects could affect the rate at which the particles would be released by the source (a random decay) and make it less random. This form of study was conducted later in France, and was the basis for the work of Dr. Helmut Schmidt, a physicist who refined the idea into a device capable of even providing feedback to the subjects, letting them know whether they get a "hit" or not (the Random Event Generator).

Such a device allows for consistent testing without the need to worry about fraud. The REG's results can be analyzed statistically for variance from chance, and can be used (and has been used) as the target device at the center of studies designed to learn more about what kinds of subjects do better/worse at PK. The REG (which today has many variations, including various computer programs one can use for PK testing) is at the heart of micro-PK research.

Parapsychological research into the area of Mind over Matter has been divided into two categories of research, based on how one observes and analyzes the phenomena. The categories are basically effects you can see (Macro-PK) and events too small to see with the naked eye (Micro-PK) that must be detected by the machine or computer that controls the experiment.

Micro-PK research, the most prevalent and easiest to control, researches mental effects on microscopic processes or targets, such as the random event generator (trying to make a random process nonrandom). As mentioned above, the REG basically flips a coin at any given moment, and the subject simply has to try to make the machine have more "heads" than "tails."

This kind of target, since it exists in an electronic device, is not subject to tampering in the way that targets that can be handled are. However, the effects are so small and generally so subject to the rules of chance, that thousands of trials must be conducted before getting to the "there is PK here!" stage. In other words, a few tosses of the coin that yield heads may be due to chance or coincidence. Hundreds, or better still, thousands gives better and better evidence that some influence is really affecting the mechanism.

Macro-PK research, which tends to be much more popular with psychics and the general public (and a target of the debunkers) revolves around targets and effects one can observe directly (macro = big). Metal bending, moving objects, projecting images on film, and other more visible effects fall into this category. Unfortunately, the visible effects are the ones that are harder (or sometimes nearly impossible) to control against fraud and manipulation and "normal" physical influences. If the subject has to have his/her hands on the target to cause something to happen, it may be difficult if not impossible to eliminate the possibility of manipulation by the subject's hands (instead of his/her mind).

Consequently, most parapsychologists have tended to shy away from macro-PK research, even though they may be personally interested in the phenomena. However, over the years, there have been more than a few "gifted" subjects apparently capable of PK under controlled conditions, some of it in the macro-PK category.

Of course, in the early sixties, the American public was gaining its knowledge of psychic phenomena from continuing sources such as *Fate* magazine, and from new sources on television. *The Twilight Zone* had some psychic-related episodes, but it was John Newland's show *One Step Beyond* (which today runs occasionally on the SCI FI Channel, and can be found on video), which dramatized reported psychic experiences that really portrayed psi as something quite real. Of course, the experiences chosen for dramatization were more exciting, more sensational psychic experiences, yet they introduced many concepts from reincarnation to psychic healing to the viewing audience.

In 1962, with the retirement of J.B. Rhine from Duke University, formal ties between the university and the Parapsychology Laboratory were severed. The Rhines then set up the Foundation for Research on the Nature of Man, and its Institute for Parapsychology. Still in operation today in Durham, North Carolina, the foundation was recently renamed the Rhine Research Center in honor of its founders, and Dr. Sally Rhine Feather, a daughter of J.B. and Louisa, has returned as executive director of the center, with Dr. Richard Broughton as director of the institute. The Institute has continued publication of the *Journal of Parapsychology*.

While Rhine was setting up his new institute a stone's throw from Duke (which probably is the reason that to this day people still think Duke University has a parapsychology department), there was a rise in interest in occult, supernatural, and psychic topics. In fact, during the mid to late '60s through the mid '70s, there was what more than a couple of authors called an "occult explosion." During this time period, publishers watched their sales of occult-related books and magazines skyrocket, television provided shows like *The Sixth Sense* and *Dark Shadows* (with many other shows having some occult or psychic themed episodes).

The Sixth Sense was particularly interesting for blossoming parapsychologists like myself because the researcher, Dr. Michael Rhodes (Gary Collins), was often shown working in a parapsychology lab conducting research much like what was really happening in the field. On the other hand, the unreality of the show, that the parapsychologist was also a highly sensitive psychic, probably helped along the idea that all psi researchers are psychics.

Other science fiction-oriented shows of the '60s and '70s included psychic episodes, from *The Six Million Dollar Man* to *Star Trek*. Cartoons and comic books often had main characters (as they do today) with extraordinary psychic superpowers.

Authors like "white witch" Sybil Leek and investigator Hans Holzer had many well-selling titles between them, and they were joined by dozens of other authors who found that the occult and the paranormal had a real, money-spending market out there. Unfortunately, little or none of the money from the buying public actually reached the researchers (a trend that continues to this day).

The public heard much about "new" experiments in parapsychology, both in the U.S. and the Soviet Union. For the first time in decades, "gifted" subjects such as Uri Geller, Ingo Swann, Ted Serios, and the late Russian psychic Nina Kulagina were invading the public consciousness again.

While most parapsychologists did mainly concern themselves with the performance of "normal" folks like you and me in the lab, some were interested in these self-professed psychics, enough to bring them into laboratory situations and begin to study them.

However, as with the spiritualist days, the appearance of these so-called "superpsychics" also brought with them the reemergence of the true debunkers, some of them scientists, some magicians. Because of the media's focus on the superpsychics (and, some would argue that the controversy brought up by the skeptics did nothing more than *increase* media coverage and public interest), much of the genuine work in psi research was overlooked by the public and ignored by the media (as it was too mundane . . . who cares about statistics and replications when you have a psychic bending a spoon or moving an object in front of your face and camera).

Some of the "gifted" subjects resisted accusations of fraud merely because they really spent no time at all promoting themselves to the general public. In fact, it was often the researchers working with them that had anything really public to say about them.

Nina Kulagina (also known by her maiden name Nelya Mikhailova) became known in this country when films of her PK performance came to note by several scientists (and the media). She was apparently able to affect both metallic and nonmetallic (even organic) objects, causing them to move, rotate, lift up, roll, sometimes erratically, sometimes with deliberate direction. Controls, such as placing a glass cover on top of the objects, did nothing to stop their movements, and other controls were included in studies of her to eliminate the possibility of fraud.

As someone who has seen films of Kulagina's demonstrations, I can say that much of what she did could have been easily faked if certain conditions were right for fraud. Depending on the actual lab setup and conditions (whether someone was with her at all times, whether she had access to the targets before starting to "PK" them, etc.), a magician skilled in the duplication of PK effects might or might not have been able to duplicate such demonstrations as Kulagina did.

However, given the descriptions of the controls that have both come from the Russian scientists working with her, and from American researchers including J.G. Pratt and Montague Ullman, who went to see her work, it would appear that Kulagina had some genuine PK abilities.

One more thing about this: Kulagina's vital signs were monitored throughout several of the tests. The results of checking her physiology showed a number of curious things. According to the late D. Scott Rogo "When the experiments were completed, it was clear she had lost weight; her heart was beating erratically; her blood sugar had increased; and her muscles ached."[4]

It was clear she was under great physical stress, and that her body reacted to this. Not exactly something easy for a magician to duplicate (on top of the PK effects, that is).

Nina Kulagina died a few years ago.

Another controversial figure in the '60s was Ted Serios. A former bellhop who was both a chain smoker and an alcoholic, Serios was able to do what has been called "thoughtography," the ability to use thought to impress film (photographic) with images. While not the first person to do this, nor the last, Serios was studied under well-controlled laboratory conditions by psychiatrist Dr. Jule Eisenbud.

Serios was apparently able to focus his attention on a camera (provided by the experimenters/investigators) and, without handling the camera, was able to cause an image to appear on the film. This could be done with a variety of films and cameras, including Polaroids, and hundreds of psychic photos were taken. The images were often out of focus, but recognizable. There was no consistency of types of images that appeared, the sheer variety testimony to Serios's abilities.

However, there was one "glitch" in the experiments that skeptics have grabbed onto. Serios used what he called a "gizmo" in most of his work. This was basically a tube of some kind, sometimes paper, sometimes plastic, that he placed on the lens.

> Ted claimed that this device, which he held between his thumb and index finger, or between his thumb or index finger and third finger, and placed more or less flat against the lens, was originally adopted to keep his fingers away from the lens (this didn't make too much sense to me, but I didn't argue the point) and at the same time limit the amount of light and surrounding imagery (this I could see).[5]

Skeptics Charles Reynolds and David Eisendrath were able to construct their own gizmo, which used a lens and a piece of transparent film (with an image) to create similar looking images on film. They, and others, accused Serios of fraud (and by association, Eisenbud of being taken in by Serios).

Eisenbud challenged the skeptics back, with his own statements that the gizmos Serios used were fully examined and never once in the hundreds of trials over the years was a piece of film that could have been used ever found. In addition, there were other controls levied on Serios, including experimental runs in which he was asked to duplicate targets in sealed envelopes (the target not to be revealed until after the "thoughtograph" was taken) and runs in which Serios stood well away from the camera (and would have been unable to manipulate the fraud that was claimed in the manner suggested).

Eisenbud has challenged skeptics, including the skeptical magicians, to undertake duplicating Serios's effects *under the same controlled conditions.* So far, there have been no takers. Pro-Serios researchers state that this is because, given the conditions Eisenbud and others imposed, no magician could duplicate the effects. The debunkers claim that the controls proposed by Eisenbud are different, stricter, than what was imposed on Serios, and that the researcher's memory of the events and controls put on Serios cannot be complete enough to reconstruct the exact same conditions. This latter point is interesting in that it supports an argument that there can be no *exact replication* of any scientific study where humans are directly involved in setting up the conditions.

Today, many accept Serios as genuine, while other, more skeptical voices cry out "fraud." The argument that because an effect *can* be faked it *must have been* faked is a specious one. In fact, I have been able to put an image on Polaroid film (with some preparation of course). Does this mean I can't accept the possibility that PK is at work? No. I'll deal with this duplication argument in Chapter 12.

But if Serios was truly genuine, how could the images have gotten on the film in the first place? How could Mind over Matter do that?

Film is covered with chemicals. Exposure to light changes those chemicals in different ways, depending on the amount of light exposure and the color of the light. Therefore, for someone to create an image on film *without the use of some device* one would have to be affecting the chemical emulsion on the film, changing it in ways similar to how light changes it. Such changes would occur at the microscopic level.

Psychokinesis, therefore, even when labeled "macro-PK" may actually be "micro-PK. Affecting a healing means affecting the body at the cellular level (or smaller). What's interesting is that for psychokinesis to work at the microscopic (or smaller) level, somehow the mind must be aware of, or able to understand, the physical and biological processes on those levels, even though the individual may have no conscious factual background in those processes.

Mind over Matter would appear to be goal-directed, therefore. Like an athlete who needs to draw on *something* to achieve his or her goal, with that *something* perhaps being extra stamina, extra energy, additional strength, etc. generally being unknown even after the fact, when a task is laid before the mind to affect some outside object or event, the mind draws on *something* to give it enough know-how to affect the appropriate changes.

What the conscious mind observes about all this is that *something* enabled the athlete to outperform the norm, and *something* allowed the mind to affect processes the individual may have no comprehension of. It was the end result that was observed, not the process.

Metal bending may be the most widely seen PK application (outside of the special effects arena where movement and levitation of objects is more common). One can trace the popularity of this form of PK demonstration to Uri Geller, the Israeli entertainer/psychic who became so famous and controversial in the early 1970s (more on Uri in a moment).

During the early to mid 1980s, while John F. Kennedy University in the San Francisco Bay Area was still offering master's degrees in parapsychology, an aerospace engineer from southern California by the name of Jack Houck often ran "metal-bending parties."

The skeptics have long made fun of these events, but I don't know of any members of the "official" skeptics groups who came to any of the "parties" that were run at JFKU (or by JFKU faculty) during that time (please write and correct me if I am wrong). These "parties" were done, not to prove anything, but to allow people to have a new experience, to have fun, and to study whether people could bend metal paranormally, or whether people were simply fooling themselves (and each other) and were bending with strength only.

Houck actually did learn from those sessions, as did many of us. His prep work for the audience actually seemed to induce some sort of mild-altered state of consciousness, giving each of us sort of a detached feeling, like we were watching ourselves without being involved. In such a state, it would be easy for a person to be unaware of the physical pressure one was putting on the spoon or fork, which led to bending it. In fact, most of the bending that I observed was caused by physical exertion. Even thick metal bars would bend in the participants' hands, though it appeared that there was a great deal of muscle put into the bending. However, some of the metal bars would have required a strength beyond what one is normally capable of. Mind over Matter (increasing physical performance) was at work, though not in the way that Houck and others hoped for.

On the other hand, I and others observed metal essentially flopping over with little or no prodding or pulling. In addition, I saw people twisting thick metal bars into various odd shapes (metal thick and solid enough to resist conscious efforts to do so). "Brittle" metal strips, such as hacksaw blades that would snap if bent too far or too quickly, were tied into knots, very quickly. I myself bent more than a few objects.

As an amusing aside, people who knew I was also a magician accused me of "faking it" almost immediately . . . I can honestly say that I faked nothing, that things appeared to bend by themselves or with little or no pressure. Of course, I was also in that light altered state that Houck had suggested to us.

Houck had a metallurgist analyze samples from the sessions, and it was reported that there appeared to be a difference in the molecular structure of pieces of metal bent by pressure or force and those that were apparently "paranormally" bent. The boundaries in the structure where the grains of metal touched were fractured and torn in the normal sample, yet somehow melted or even vaporized in the paranormal sample.

The metallurgical analyses indicate that when PK does occur, it affects the microscopic structure of the metal. But by the working definition of Mind over Matter, when the mind somehow enhances the body in a way that a piece of metal, too strong to be bent by the individual normally, can be bent, *something* on the order of PK is going on, as with exceptional performance by athletes and martial artists. People in that light altered state were able to bend such too-strong bars of metal because they *believed* the metal would bend for them.

During one of the sessions, a staff member of JFKU brought along a friend who was highly skeptical and was a professional magician. During the session he participated in, I observed him twisting a thick solid aluminum rod (I recall it to be at least one inch thick) after Houck got through with is induction piece (relaxing us and getting us into the right frame of mind).

When I discussed this with him later (after he unsuccessfully tried with all his regular conscious strength to bend it more or unbend it), I asked him how he thought the rod bent, if not by PK. He remarked that while he was rubbing the rod, the friction must have caused it to heat up, soften, and allow for him to easily bend it. When I pointed out to him that the melting point of aluminum was over 1000 degrees (actually around 1200 degrees Fahrenheit) and that his hands had no blisters, he had no explanation, but "it wasn't psychokinesis, I know that much."

On the other hand, the skeptics have a point when they say metal-bending can be easily faked. It can be, of that there is no question. For that reason, Chapter Twelve deals with "Faking It" and how and why metal-bending is an easy piece of fraud to accomplish. Doing a metallurgical analysis of the bent metal may be the only way to determine if something out of the ordinary did in fact go on, since there really is no way to measure a person's strength under all conditions.

As I mentioned, metal-bending became popular with the spoon and key bending of Israeli psychic and entertainer Uri Geller. Geller, it can be argued, is a very controversial figure whose stated abilities allowed many skeptics and debunkers to come to the vocal forefront. When he first appeared on the scene in the early '70s with his claims of being able to bend metal, getting stopped watches to start, affecting compass needles, and duplicating drawings kept secret from him (all of which he could demonstrate), Geller made himself the center of much worldwide attention.

His primary focus appeared to be performing before (and entertaining) audiences, both live and through television. However, his demonstrations and claims also brought him to the attention of researchers and debunkers alike. He was studied, with some controversy, at Stanford Research Institute (now SRI International) by Hal Puthoff and Russell Targ in 1972, and while his PK demonstrations at the lab overall were interesting, his performance under tight controls brought back a less than enthusiastic response from the researchers.

His ESP demonstrations were a bit better under controlled conditions, yet other subjects in the history of the field have also done well at duplicating pictures (and many of those were not self-professed psychics).

Along with Geller's rise to fame was the rise of the professional debunkers, including the magician James "The Amazing" Randi, who seemed, to the general public, to come out of nowhere to duplicate and challenge Geller's abilities. The controversy spawned by Randi's (and others) accusations of fraud is arguably a major reason why the media coverage of Geller was so intense (controversy breeds coverage in the media).

There have been many reliable witnesses over the years who have watched as Geller did things that they felt were quite genuine PK. In addition, one of the more interesting developments around the Geller phenomenon has been termed "the Geller Effect." Uri has, since the beginning, stated that everyone has PK and ESP abilities. On many of his TV appearances (even recent ones), he asks that people at home pull out their stopped watches and pieces of cutlery, and that they try, along with him, to bend the utensils and focus on starting the watches.

TV shows that do this are typically flooded with phone calls attesting to the success of the tasks. Skeptics claim that the restarted watches do so for a short time because they are handled, shaken even, and that silverware is bent by sheer hand pressure or already had bends in it that were just noticed by the owners who really look closely at it for the first time.

While this type of audience involvement does not support Geller's own claims of being psychic, the numbers of people reporting positive results after Geller basically revs them up to be psychic themselves indicates that, again, changing one's mind-set, one's beliefs even for a short time can somehow allow for extraordinary performance. In the case of "the Geller Effect," the extraordinary performance seems to relate to Mind over Matter.

Is Uri Geller a skilled magician/fraud or does he have genuine psychic abilities? I have heard reports from observers of Uri Geller, both believers and disbelievers, many of whom were skilled observers. I have seen videotapes of some demonstrations on TV talk shows. I watched him do an ESP task on a local talk show in San Francisco several years ago (after which I got to meet him for the first time). I spent some time with him at his estate in England in 1991 where I got to know him better. I have had lengthy discussions with people who know him very well, as well as with debunkers who take the opportunity to disdain his abilities at every mention of his name.

The best answer I can give to the above question is that Uri Geller is a wonderful entertainer who sometimes displays psychic abilities. Keep in mind that I don't think anyone can be psychic, whether using PK or ESP, all the time. Keep in mind that an entertainer *has* to perform every time he or she is in front of an audience. Keep in mind that everyone has some degree of psi ability (as even Uri has said). In fact, I have spoken to a number of magicians and mentalists who believe that they have had PK and ESP experiences in their personal lives, and even on stage during their performances. I believe that Uri has often provided a stimulus for others to have a psychic experience.

So, you may make of my statement what you will. As Uri and many others have stated, we all have psi. We can all, to some degree, better on some days than others, make use of our innate abilities of Mind over Matter in such a way as the mind reaches beyond the body.

Other "super" psychics have been less well known that Geller, yet have demonstrated great abilities even in certain scientific studies. One who is still doing some psychic work is artist and author Ingo Swann. Possibly best known for his out-of-body experience (OBEs) and remote perception work, in which he was able to describe distant locations with some degree of accuracy (including situations where he was merely given coded map coordinates), Swann also has been capable of influencing physical objects and processes in the laboratory.

Working with Dr. Gertrude Schmeidler in the early 1970s, Swann was able to change the temperature of objects attached to sensors with great proficiency, making them either hotter or colder as the researchers requested.

In other PK experiments, he was able to affect electromagnetic sensors with a high degree of success. He also worked as a subject in experiments at the ASPR (in OBE research) and at Stanford Research Institute (remote perception research).

While he is not directly involved with psi research today, Swann has written a number of books on psychic functioning that have aided in the public's understanding of the phenomena, what it's like to "be psychic" (though he, like other psi functionaries dislike the term and what it brings with it), and how the average individual can learn to use his/her own psi abilities.

Another individual who made his mark on the field of parapsychology was Dr. Alex Tanous. A holder of several degrees, including an M.A. in philosophy and a doctorate in divinity, and an educator in the state of Maine (with a wonderful book still in print telling parents how to work with the psychic experiences of their children; see Appendix A), he became the main subject for the research conducted on out-of-body experiences at the ASPR for a number of years, though he was also involved in psychic healing studies.

I was fortunate to be working at the ASPR during some of the research he was doing. The main experiment both involved the OBE state and some PK.

While Alex would relax and go into an altered state in an isolation room (hooked up to an electroencephalograph to chart his brain waves), he would project what he considered "part" of his consciousness out of himself, an out-of-body alter-ego he called "Alex 2." Alex 2 was to go to the other side of the floor of the ASPR and try a couple of tasks.

One involved Alex 2 looking in on a special apparatus Osis and McCormick had set up. In a special box, there was a slide projector and a color wheel, as well as a construction utilizing mirrors and lenses. The slide projector was connected to a device that would randomly select and project a slide of a line drawing. The color wheel would spin and stop randomly. The projector would randomly aim the slide at a particular quadrant of the four-part color wheel. So, looking through the front lens of the big box, one would see the color wheel with the line drawing appearing on one of the colored quadrants.

The way the device was actually constructed, though, the image was not actually projected on the wheel directly. Instead, it was the system of mirrors and lenses that combined the slide's image with the color wheel. In this way, the only view that would allow Alex 2 (or any real person) to see the combined image was through the front lens of the box.

Alex was conscious and able to talk while undergoing the experiment, and would describe the drawing and color and quadrant, while his brain waves were being observed. His success rate was not dramatic, though it was very significant.

The second component of the experiment was, perhaps, more impressive.

Hanging from bungee cords in front of the viewing window was a box containing strain gauges that would sense physical activity (the box was hung from the ceiling and checked constantly for other influences that could cause it to shake or vibrate). Alex 2 would be asked to move about in or affect the box and the gauges it contained. There were signs, especially in the trials where Alex 2 "hit" the correct answers in the image box, that there was direct physical influence on the strain gauges.

The experiment was designed to see if there was a physical component of out-of-body experience, and the conclusion was, based on the results of the experiments with Alex Tanous, that yes, there was a physical effect.

Whether there is some "astral body" that Alex projected out of himself as Alex 2, or whether the strain gauges registered a direct impact of his mind, both scenarios suggest psychokinetic activity.

By the way, while Alex believed that "some part of his consciousness would split off," he never considered Alex 2 to be his "spirit" or "soul." "If my soul left my body," he once told me "I'd be dead."

Alex was never one to shy away from an interesting challenge: he conducted some healing work in an unusual setting (a New York hospital working with cancer patients under the supervision of doctors) and he worked on a number of police cases with law enforcement officers up and down the East Coast for years, always keeping publicly quiet about his involvement (this was a request of the officers). In addition, he often involved himself, along with Dr. Osis and Donna McCormick, in ghost and poltergeist investigations. In fact, along with Dr. Osis to check out the infamous Amityville Horror house at the time it was reported, Alex used his psi to learn much about the case, though undoubtedly not what the Lutz family (the family reporting the "evil" in the home) expected.

Alex perceived the past of the house, which was the site of several murders (the murders were done by Ronald DeFeo, who killed other family members). He sensed no active phenomena, however, and couldn't quite come to terms that the Lutz family had, either. Alex had been shown something by the Lutzes: A sample of DeFeo's handwriting that he deduced was on a contract for a book and movie.

Alex Tanous had a direct impact on my own psychic development, in that working with him during the time I was at the ASPR (1982–83), I felt somehow excited and stimulated both by watching him in the experiments and in other settings, and by hearing some of the stories he told about his own experiences, which involved psychokinesis (mainly healing), time slips, OBEs, and precognition.

In fact, I had a number of psi experiences, including a couple of out-of-body experiences and some PK experiences (most notably moving a heavy crystal ashtray while bored at a family dinner).

Alex Tanous died in 1991, but he affected enough people directly that he shall be a superpsychic for a long time to come.

Today, the majority of the well-known psychics seem to be best known for their extended perception abilities, rather than their psychokinetic ones. With the exception of healers, psychics may find doing psychokinetic effects makes them easy targets for the debunking magicians (and often suspect by parapsychologists' standards; see Chapter Twelve for the uncovering of psychokinetic fraud).

Psychics, sometimes calling themselves "intuitives," tend to work as "consultants," whether that means they give advice to businesspeople or to the police and other law enforcement agencies. Or they may show up in the media as purveyors of doom and gloom in the coming turn of the millennium (the actual change of date being hotly debated in some quarters as the start of the year 2000 or the year 2001, or even 1996 according to some biblical scholars).

The "super-psychics" seem more made to order by their media exposure than by what they can apparently achieve. Some psychics who gain much exposure for their apparent abilities on talk shows seem to me to be doing nothing more than cold reading (essentially using observational skills and general statements). Others gain some exposure for their practical accomplishments, as with Noreen Renier, Kathlyn Rhea, Nancy Myer-Czetli, Greta Alexander, and Riley G, who work with law enforcement and provide helpful information—psychics rarely *solve* crimes, though their information can be quite useful.[67]

Most of these people are quite content in the way they utilize their abilities in practical matters, and have little interest in proving their talents through laboratory research. In fact, when it comes right down to it, because lab research is mainly statistically based, a single series of experiments hardly "proves" any more abilities than those of the average person. In other words, psychics have learned that there is little personal gain in being part of a laboratory series since the parameters of the experiment may not allow for the kind of obvious performance they do in a practical setting.

The researchers have stayed away from such people for another reason. Over the past twenty years since Uri Geller and other "superpsychics" hit the scene, the rise in the skeptical movement has made many parapsychological researchers really shy away from working with any self-professed "gifted" subject who could bring the debunkers down on their heads. It is safer, it has been reasoned, to work with the abilities as they occur in "normal" people, although healing has been an exception.

Mind over Matter research in the lab has focused primarily on micro-PK. Organizations utilizing random event generators in their work have come and gone, and the statistical data has grown. Research on PK has been conducted at places like the Mind-Science Foundation (no longer doing such research), the American Society for Psychical Research, the Psychophysical Research Laboratories (closed), the Institute for Parapsychology, and the Princeton Engineering Anomalies Research program (PEAR).

The PEAR program, established by Dr. Robert Jahn, the former dean of the School of Engineering at Princeton, is still conducting research on PK and remote viewing, with a huge database of micro-PK results having been compiled.

Research on PK today has cropped up quite strongly at the the the Consciousness Research Laboratory at the Harry Reid Center, University of Nevada at Las Vegas, and at the University of Edinburgh. In addition, Physicist Edwin May, formerly associated with psi research at SRI International, established a psi research program at the Cognitive Sciences Laboratory of Science Applications International Corporation in Palo Alto, California.

Again, with little exception, most of the work revolves around the effects of the mind on variations of the random event device, which can both give feedback to the subject and keep close track of what actually goes on for statistical analyses. Physiological monitoring devices and brain scanning technologies have also been incorporated to attempt to find correlations to parts of the brain and processes in the body that may be active while psi is active.

Other strategies have included what has been called "bio-PK" or more commonly today "Direct Mental Interactions with Living Systems" (DMILS). Such experiments as those conducted by Bernard Grad on plant growth (Chapter Five) or experiments on single celled organisms to try to affect their behavior, as well as some of the other healing experiments on enzymes and blood hemoglobin fall under this category.

More recently, successful studies have been conducted in one of the most commonly reported experiences that may be considered "psychic," the feeling that one is being stared at. In the current version of the experiment, the subject doesn't "guess" when he or she is being stared at, but rather the "sender" is both staring (and ostensibly influencing) the subject while watching him/her on a video monitor. Physiological measuring devices check to see if there is any change in the target subject's nervous system at the random times the starer is focusing on him/her. Results have been very promising.

While this is considered to be a PK experiment, one must also consider the category as possibly some form of unconscious telepathy, that the unconscious mind of the "staree" is aware of the moments he/she is being stared at, and his/her nervous system reacts accordingly. Separating out ESP from PK is often difficult.

Analyses of the data of the micro-PK experiments has yielded more than enough evidence that there is some kind of effect happening, yet not enough information to determine just how the devices are affected or enough evidence to convince skeptics.

I have found that skeptics seem to want demonstrations of macro-PK in a repeatable fashion. Yet macro-PK can typically be duplicated (though often not under the exact same controls) well enough that these same skeptics may decide "if you can duplicate it, it isn't so." Therefore, in many respects it's a waste of time to try to convince self-declared skeptics (who are often disbelievers from the start, not true, "I'll decide when all the evidence is in" skeptics).

From other fields of study come a variety of PK-related reports that add to the evidence. Anthropologists have reported a variety of unusual healing/harm-related effects that testify to the mind affecting its own body. The literature of a variety of cultures, such as studies of the Kung bushmen of Africa, includes much in the way of description of unusual, though effective healing techniques.[8] Studies of hex death, such as that in voodoo practices, clearly demonstrate that we heal/harm ourselves or others using our beliefs and perhaps psychic abilities.

In addition, over the years, I have read and heard accounts from anthropologists and from grad students out in the field of poltergeist phenomena and directed Mind over Matter effects happening in a variety of cultures, both "primitive" and "modern," as with my description of the example an anthropologist told me of stones, wood, and bottles floating during a ceremony of the Huichol Indians of Mexico (Chapter Seven).

Two of my professors at Northwestern University told tales of inexplicable and dramatic movement of objects through the air or along the ground in both ritual settings and in family dwellings. In his book, *Faces in the Smoke*, documentary producer/director Douchan Gersi gives extensive eyewitness accounts (his own) of paranormal phenomena in a variety of cultures, such as levitation at a monastery in India and during a ceremony at a small village in Zaire, as well as during a number of voodoo ceremonies in Haiti.[9]

Things move without apparent physical cause. Sometimes the movements are associated with some kind of ritual, other times they're associated with the cultural norms, as with the Australian Aborigines.

I have had an interest in Aboriginal culture for some time, since I first read some of their myths about the Dreamtime (also called the Dreaming). The reported experiences and abilities of the Aborigines runs the gamut of PK and ESP abilities including extraordinary healing and moving distances in little or no time (as though they are teleporting, though this has been described as "walking through the Dreaming"). Just read Marlo Morgan's bestseller *Mutant Message Downunder* and you'll get some idea of the range of the Aboriginal experiences and abilities (Note: Morgan's book is listed as fiction, but to my mind and based on my reading of anthropology books on the native peoples of Australia, and my brief experience in Arnhem Land in 1994, it is an excellent story in which real Aboriginal abilities are explored).[10]

Physicists have expressed a growing interest in consciousness. Quantum physicists such as Nick Herbert, Fred Alan Wolf, Jack Safardi, and Nobel prize-winner Brian Josephson are among those who have begun exploring the physics of consciousness, a physics that includes the mind's influence on the physical world.

To my mind, the evidence of the mind affecting matter at a distance is overwhelming. When one considers the enormity of number of eyewitness reports of PK-type experiences, when one looks at the evidence from some well-controlled experiments with macro-PK, when you add in all the statistical evidence from micro-PK research, and if you even in passing consider examples of extraordinary human performance, you either accept this ability as real and as one we all have or you don't.

As my friend Martin Caidin has said about flying planes, "It either flies or it don't!"

Martin Caidin has, since 1987, been playing at moving objects himself. As a science journalist and aviator, he is an excellent observer, aware of environmental influences and physical anomalies, and yet he believes he can do telekinesis, and that most anyone else can, too. His story, his method, of learning to move targets is told in Chapter Eleven.

Marty has made some excellent points about performance and belief that apply not only to what he has been able to do in healing himself in the past, and to utilizing Mind over Matter (he prefers to use the term telekinesis or TK), but also the performance of any physical or mental feat in general. Most important may be his statement that I've used at the beginning of this book: *"What someone can do or cannot do is absolutely not proportional in any way to anyone else's belief or disbelief."*

So, rather than letting someone tell you what's impossible, how about exploring what's possible? As you may have gathered throughout this book, the experiences and abilities demonstrated by people that illustrate both the mind's influence on its own body and the mind's influence on the environment around the body are diverse and numerous. From healing to harm, from pushing the body well past its limits to pushing objects around the body with unseen forces, people have demonstrated what today are extraordinary abilities, yet which tomorrow may be as acceptable as running a marathon.

In real life, such abilities as those that may be psychokinetic in nature don't happen frequently in a way that we notice. In the next chapter, I'll discuss some very common mind/matter interactions.

In the entertainment media we see lots of examples and displays of PK and related extraordinary abilities. Television, film, books, and comic books all have provided us with much to wonder at and much to be afraid of when it comes to "psychic powers." Science fiction literature has spent much attention on psychic abilities, especially psychokinesis and telepathy. (For a lengthy discussion of psi in literature and the mass media, see the chapter entitled "Psi Fi: Psionics and Wild Talents: Psychic Phenomena in Fiction" in my book *Esp, Hauntings and Poltergeists: A Parapsychologist's Handbook*. New York: Warner Books, 1986).

The *Star Trek* family of shows, from the original to the new series *Voyager,* have shown us aliens and humans with exotic abilities to do everything from contact telepathy (the Vulcan Mindmeld) and "straight" telepathy to empathic reception (as with Counselor Troi's abilities on *The Next Generation*), from psychokinetic abilities (as in the classic Trek episode "Plato's Stepchildren") to reality shaping abilities (like those of "Q" in *The Next Generation* and *Deep Space Nine*).

Babylon Five has also demonstrated people with psychic abilities, and even has a featured group called the "PSI Corps" in the Earth Alliance (although they're not so nice folks).

In *Kung Fu: The Legend Continues,* we see Kwai Chang Caine utilizing his *Chi* in ways that are psychokinetic almost every week (as discussed in Chapter Two).

Episodes of other science fiction and adventure shows over the decades that have shown psychic characters (sometimes recurring or even main characters) include *Lost in Space, My Favorite Martian, The Powers of Matthew Star, The Six Million Dollar Man, the Bionic Woman, Fantastic Journey, The Time Tunnel, Space Precinct, Kolchak: The Night Stalker, Superboy, Seaquest DSV, The Greatest American Hero, Tucker's Witch, Misfits of Science, Something is Out There,* and of course, *The X-Files,* just to name a few.

What's interesting is the way such characters are handled. In the context of many of the shows, the abilities displayed are accepted as normal and nonthreatening. Very often, there is a "good" character who displays the psychokinetic abilities who is either a "hero" of the show (a regular character) or is a guest character brought in as a plot device to help solve some disaster. On the other hand, often when there is a "good" character who can manipulate Mind over Matter, there is an "evil" counterpart, the villain of the piece that has to be stopped.

In comic books, one finds superheroes, both male and female, human and alien, that show a variety of psychic abilities. Psychokinetic powers show up usually with some kind of limitation. In other words, where one character can generate heat, another can generate cold. One hero might be able to levitate objects, another only him or herself. The new Superboy uses his power of "tactile telekinesis" to change or blow apart inorganic objects he touches, while the current Supergirl has psychokinetic abilities that allow her to do a variety of things, including sending out "blasts" of power.

The range of applications of mind "powers" truly reaches its imaginative peak in comic books, if only because it is the mission of comic books, it seems, to try more and more heroes and villains with new powers in order to keep its current readers and find new readers. That comic books have no special effects budget, only the imaginative limitations of the writers and artists, allows the characters to do literally anything in the stories that can be dreamed up and shown visually (or hinted at through the dialogue and narration).

Science fiction literature has brought forth many, many novels and short stories in which psychokinesis plays a role. As with comic books, there's no special effects budget, and the authors are only limited by their imaginations (and what they think the readers will accept in the context of the stories). PK is used for good and for bad, with occasional novels focusing on the "superpsychic" rather than the more common situations in which PK is part of the normal society portrayed in the book. In science fiction, PK and other psi abilities are used in contexts where they help the stories along, but may not be the main factor in the plot.

This is important in that science fiction allows the reader to accept PK as a *normal* thing, if only for the length of the book. It is when we consider such an ability, which would appear to be part of all of us (as creativity is part of all of us) as *special* or *unique* or something to be revered or feared that we (both the people displaying the abilities and all of us "normals") may create problems for us all.

Horror fiction, by its very nature, uses PK as a tool to create fear amongst the many characters in the book/film. PK is usually *special* or shown to be a power for evil, which is not how it works in real life. Unfortunately, because horror tends to create a more emotional reaction in its audience than science fiction, people connect with such images in a more direct fashion, and any suggestion that the story has any basis in fact (even if such a suggestion is, itself, fiction) causes the audience to see such "powers" as *unique* and *evil* or *dangerous*.

Movies (and TV) are somewhat limited by what they can show, in that sometimes what the writer dreams up would cost more money than the studio is willing to spend on effects. Generally, though, Mind over Matter presents little problem in that Hollywood has a long history of making objects move "by themselves," beginning with such films as the first version of *The Invisible Man* (which, while not having anything to do with Mind over Matter, did allow the special effects folks to dream up ways to make objects look as though they were floating by themselves).

A discussion of films in which Mind over Matter plays a significant role would take many, many pages. As with science fiction and horror literature, films tend to show PK as a normal thing, or as a plot device to help the story along.

There have been many comedies (often *bad* comedies) made over the years where PK is the actual plot device (like *Zapped* with Scott Baio and *Modern Problems* with Chevy Chase), but the abilities shown in such comedies are not a bad thing at all. Other films show PK as an ability of a fugitive or victim, someone being chased by the bad guys (such as *Starman* and *Escape from Witch Mountain*).

Horror films display PK as an evil or destructive power, though not always (I wouldn't call *Carrie* evil, just a bit stressed out and downright destructive). In some horror films, both the villain and the hero have such powers and end up fighting it out.

Films, TV, and literature show us the dark and light sides of just about anything, and psychic abilities (or any form of extraordinary human ability, from genius to creativity to physical prowess) are often a central plot device because of their relationship to us as human beings. They both excite and frighten us, because of the sense of wonder at what one could do with such abilities that have yet to be accepted as normal, and fear of what one could do with such abilities that may set the individual apart from the norm.

But these abilities, no matter how *special* they may seem are part of the normal range of what humans can do. As such, they can be used for positive or negative reasons.

George Lucas, in the universe of *Star Wars* and the Jedi Knights that he has created shows us the true dichotomy of use of these abilities. The Force that the Jedi makes use of is the life force of all living things, of the very galaxy itself. While the Jedi philosophy seems very zenlike and appears to relate to the use of *Chi* in the martial arts, the Force is something not just in the Jedi themselves, but something to be tapped into in the environment.

Central to use of the Force seems to be acceptance and belief. To me, the scene on the planet Dagobah in *The Empire Strikes Back* where Luke is learning to use the force from the old Jedi Master Yoda is central to how psi also works. In fact, belief in oneself and one's limitations is probably the second most important tenet of the Jedi, after their belief in the Force itself.

In the screenplay by Lawrence Kasdan and Leigh Brackett, Luke attempts to move his X-Wing fighter out of the swamp on Dagobah at Yoda's request.

Luke: *(focusing, quietly)* All right, I'll give it a try.

Yoda: No! Try not! *Do.* Or do not. There is no try.[11]

Luke attempts to levitate the craft, which rises for a moment, then sinks back down into the water. He complains that it's too big, that he can't do it. Yoda replies with statements about his own size, and that his "ally is the Force. And a powerful ally it is . . ."

Luke is discouraged and states "You want the impossible."

Quietly, Yoda turns toward the sunken X-wing fighter. With his eyes closed and his head bowed, he raises his arm and points at the ship. Soon, the fighter rises above the water and moves forward as Artoo beeps in terror and scoots away.

The entire X-wing moves majestically, surely, toward the shore. Yoda stands on a tree root and guides the fighter carefully down toward the beach.

Luke stares in astonishment as the fighter settles gently onto the shore. He walks toward Yoda.

Luke: I don't . . . I don't believe it.

Yoda: That is why you fail.[12]

There are a wide range of PK abilities that work outside the body. The application of whatever Force that we use for this is apparently limited by our imaginations, by our belief in the ability itself and in our personal acceptance that we, too, have it. It is also undoubtably limited by the physics that also allow for it to work, otherwise we might all be affecting the world so often and so much that all of reality would be at odds with itself.

In any event, whether one accepts PK as a personal ability or not, people, both self-professed psychic and "normal," have demonstrated that their minds can affect matter in many different ways, both in the laboratory and in real life.

Psychokinesis, as it works outside the body, is something that most of us believe we've never observed or experienced. Most people may have a fear of anyone who displays it, or a reaction to the idea of it so strong that even if something did happen, visibly, right in front of the nose of the witnesses, it might be ignored because it challenges the belief system.

However, psychokinesis is something that may actually be an everyday occurrence for many people, though they may not recognize it as such. For while most of us never see spoons bending or glassware levitating, we do experience very odd happenings in our daily lives when it comes to using technology, and in a few other "weird" ways.

Let's move on to just how that happens. . . .

* **10** *

Human-Machine Interactions
or
How We Affect Technology Every Day

Are you one of those people who seems to have problems with machines, especially computers and photocopiers? Does there appear to be a strange, causal link between your moods and how well/poorly your computer works? Does office equipment tend to break down around you, just when you're ready to use it?

Does Murphy's Law seem to have a specific corollary applied to you alone?

Or are you a person who has a "way" with technology? Do you find that not only do machines always work well for you, machines that others have a hard time using (or complain about because they always break down) always perform for you? Are you like "the Fonz" from the TV show *Happy Days;* do machines just purr along because you touch them or tap them?

The natural outgrowth of the micro-PK work with Random Event Generators (REG) is to look at how PK might affect any machine, not just the REGs. One might suggest that PK on a REG may actually affect that part of the machine that records the random pulses from the source element, or even the display that the subject sees, rather than the source itself. In other words, PK may be working on the mechanism itself, not the random process that the mechanism records (though this is taken into account).

One of the more recent trends in parapsychological research is on a parallel course to research in a variety of other fields of technology and social science: the interaction of human beings and technology, machines, and the ways those interactions affect the humans and the machines. Human-machine interactions are being looked at in the fields of computer science, in psychology, in sociology, and even in biology and medical science.

Failure of technology can come from some problem with the technology itself, or because of human error, or perhaps because of some other, often unseen, influences (like power surges and static electricity). With computers, so commonplace in our homes and offices today, the human influences can run the gamut from poorly trained, uninformed, or merely clumsy people using the computers to problems in the software design.

Looking at such interactions, it would appear that the human factors may also relate to the emotional/mental state of the computer users and others in the setting. One explanation of this is that people who are upset or nervous or in a bad mood may be more careless than others, causing the technology to fail through careless human error. However, when computers and other mechanisms misbehave in ways that have no technical explanation, yet are misbehaving or malfunctioning at times that seem to correlate to the frame of mind of the users or especially in the case of people around the computer who don't even touch the machine, it would appear that there is some extension of the mind that acts on the computers directly.

In addition, it would appear that many of the machines that are affected are of a less electronic variety. With moving parts one would expect fewer temporary problems that can be caused by "user error" and especially ones that might relate to that could be correlated to the user's mental/emotional states (let's face it, there are not too many things that can temporarily affect the workings of a toaster).

Dr. Robert Morris, currently of the University of Edinburgh, Scotland, is one of a growing number of researchers interested in this specific area of human-machine interaction. His original connection with this came out of a series of experiments conducted while at

Syracuse University dealing with believers and nonbelievers (the "Sheep-Goat Effect"), during which it appeared that the computers curiously crashed a number of times with the "goats," necessitating restarting the computers. Morris brought up the question of whether the skeptical subjects were doing something to the computers unconsciously, allowing them to void the tests they were involved in entirely.

The first thought was actually something called "psi-missing," where the subject essentially guesses wrong on purpose in an ESP test (the subconscious knowing the correct answer, but the conscious mind gives the opposite answer) or causes the opposite result in a PK test. The reasoning behind this is that a skeptic or nonbeliever would want to make sure the results weren't positive and didn't challenge their beliefs in the nonexistence of psi. Guessing or causing the wrong answer can be just as statistically important as getting everything right (think about it: if you have a 50-50 chance to get something right, what are the odds you can keep guessing wrong again and again without first knowing the answer?).

Further investigation led him to collect anecdotes surrounding unusual failures and exceptional performances of machines such as computers and photocopiers. Morris reasoned that if there were people who caused problems with technology ("malfunction-linked" people), there must also be people who made things run smoothly (or even better than that; "function-linked" people).

There are those people who just can't seem to keep a watch going on their wrists, or who hate computers (and tend to gripe about the fact that "the stupid things are always breaking down" on them). There are also those people who seem to almost "merge" with the object of their machine interactions, whether they be computer operator or mechanic extraordinaire.

For most of us, it's the malfunction that seems to be prevalent. Given the importance of and the familiarity with computers in our society (many people today are unable to even imagine life without a computer), these devices upon which so much of the running of the world relies seems to provide great focus for studies of PK effects on technology.

I have had a number of experiences of my own with temporary

failures of technology. Back in the mid-'80s, I owned an Apple IIc, a nice little workhorse of a computer (in fact, my first three books were written on it). I rarely had any problem with it (only a broken keyboard because of my heavy-handed typing). However, on a number of occasions, the software I was using would do very odd things. For example, on one occasion, *Print Shop* suddenly started cycling through its choices, not allowing me to either make a choice of task or stop the program. I called the customer support line for the company, described the problem, and was met with a very puzzled reaction. "I never heard of *that* happening before."

He had me reboot and retry both the disk I was using (a working copy) and the original program disk. No luck. I tried another program that worked fine, then a game, which also had no problem. Back to *Print Shop,* same problem. He then told me to try the program again in a little while, and if it didn't work then, to call back and they'd send out another copy.

What I haven't mentioned is that at the time, I was under a lot of time pressure to get out a piece for a friend's workshop, and that I had a lot of resistance to doing the piece (I really shouldn't have volunteered at the time). So I called my friend, told him about the problem, and that it might be another day or two. He let me off the hook.

I calmed down and decided to try the program again. Lo and behold, it worked perfectly.

From that point on, as someone well aware of potential PK problems, I kept an eye out for any connections between my state of mind and the performance of my computer. I noticed a dramatic number of problems occurring (even in just loading a program) when I was in a hurry, or frustrated about what I was doing, or simply upset about something else in my life.

This pattern has continued since I've moved on to a Macintosh, and with the NCR laptop I use at my "real" job at LEXIS-NEXIS.

If you observe your own computer interactions and speak to friends about unusual behaviors or failures (crashes), they may be able to recall that their mental/emotional state was extreme, perhaps agitated, stressed out or in a hurry (*before* the computer screwed up, otherwise it doesn't "count"), and that the computer failures may have seemed to be just another thing to add to that frustrated, emotional state.

How I make my living outside of parapsychology (as I'm sitting here writing this in July 1995), is as an instructor of the LEXIS-NEXIS information services. LEXIS-NEXIS is possibly the premiere online full-text source of information, with legal and related materials, financial, environmental, general news, entertainment, international, and reference information from many thousands of sources. The users of the system include law firms and legal services, judges, banks and financial institutions, corporations, information specialists, advertising and public relations firms, government agencies (including the IRS, the EPA, the FBI and more), the news media, and the entertainment industry.

To give you the scope of coverage, LEXIS-NEXIS includes legal cases and publications on state, federal, and international levels; public records such as corporate filings, annual reports, property records, and professional licenses; information from medical journals and related sources; directories of people and background on places around the world; demographic information; and news information. The NEWS library alone has articles and transcripts from over 3,000 sources such as the *New York Times* (and dozens of other newspapers), the Associated Press (and many other wire services), *Time, Newsweek,* and *People* (and hundreds of others), professional industry newsletters from a variety of industries (such as banking, law, and energy), and transcripts of TV programs (such as CNN and ABC News shows), radio shows (National Public Radio), and speeches by politicians and government officials.

As an instructor (since 1984), I teach people how to retrieve information from our system. The equipment used to access LEXIS NEXIS today is any computer with a modem, but years ago this was not the case. Originally, one needed a "dumb" terminal that did nothing more than dial up and display LEXIS relayed information.

Since people have been using PCs and Macs to access the system, I have heard stories from various people I've trained (and observed firsthand on a few occasions) relating to unusual problems and crashes of computers when trying to access the data. I've also learned to ask individuals involved whether they get along with computers.

More often than not, the answers are "No, I hate them" or "Computers don't like me" or "my computer does this to me all the time, especially when I'm already stressed out."

Here's another situation I observed and participated in.

Back in late 1984, with the access points to LEXIS NEXIS pretty much limited to the "dumb" terminals (called Ubiqs), very little could go wrong with getting into the system. In fact, the only real problem with the Ubiqs might be a loose chip or board inside, which was easily fixed by picking up the front end a bit (an inch or two) and dropping it down (sort of to reset the chips, according to one of our techs).

One day, I had a class of five people (with ten Ubiqs in the training room). At the point where everyone was to go on line, I had them all switch on the Ubiqs (which would initiate an automatic sign-on procedure). All but one of the folks, an attorney from a large firm, got on immediately. The attorney (I'll call him Harry) got a message saying that the connection could not be completed.

So, I moved him to another terminal. He switched it on, same problem. As I switched him to a third one, I gave instructions to the others to enter their log-in IDs and actually begin a tutorial. None of the others had any problems with their Ubiqs.

Harry turned on the third Ubiq. Again, no connection. Before I moved him to a fourth, I switched it on, made sure the connection was intact, and brought him over.

Harry entered his ID number, pressed the enter key, and *crash,* the Ubiq kicked him off line. I switched back on one of the ones he had already tried, got it connected, had him enter his ID, and press the enter key. *Crash* went the Ubiq.

Now we had everyone's attention. His legal secretary, who had come with him to the class, was smiling (mysteriously). Everyone was curious as to why Harry couldn't stay connected to LEXIS.

I moved him to one of the other folk's Ubiqs. As soon as he touched a key, the terminal dumped him off line.

By the time Harry had tried the same thing with every connected

Ubiq in the room, the others were near amazement, his secretary was laughing out loud, and Harry was scowling.

I asked the secretary what was so funny. She told me to ask him about his attitude toward computers and why she was even attending class.

"I hate computers," said Harry, "and they hate me! She's here so she can do the research I ask for."

The secretary then went on to add that she has to keep her boss away from her word processor, because whenever he seemed to get within three feet of it, it crashed (although it was up and running a couple of minutes later).

What was happening? I believed it was psychokinesis from Harry, due to his lousy attitude toward computers. I explained what I meant by that, then pulled up an article from our NEXIS service about the human-machines interactions work that Bob Morris was working on (see "Computer Crashes: A case of mind over matter?" by John Desmond, in the June 11, 1984 issue of *Computer World*).

Harry decided to look over his secretary's shoulder, but only after reading the article on machine PK.

Since that time, I have been very interested in asking the attitudes of all who have problems with the terminals and now PCs in our training center their attitudes toward computers (and how they're doing that day).

Now of course, drawing a correlation from a perception of mood or attitude like this to the actual computer performance is very anecdotal, and certainly not based on any sort of statistical analysis or scientific experiment. It is possible that a high percentage of these cases happen because people don't watch what they're doing when they're stressed out or upset or in a bad mood.

But a percentage do appear to display a casual connection between the machine and the human.

I have had other personal encounters with the human-machine interaction effect, including some rather bizarre activities of other kinds of electronics. On two occasions, I have had a television set go on without being prompted to (in both cases, the TV set was not remote controlled; in one of them, the set was clearly unplugged!), and an unplugged stereo system switch on and play for about five minutes. I have heard similar stories from many other people around the country (and if we *could* somehow harness this ability, especially where electronics can work without any connection to a power source, think of the savings on our utilities bills).

Granted, in many cases, people are mistaken about what actually went on. People are, in general, not exactly the greatest observers when it comes to out of the ordinary events. Consequently, people may be unaware of all the circumstances that could cause a device to malfunction or work when it shouldn't. For example, other signals besides your TV's remote control can cause it to go on or off, or change channels.

And were you positive that the plug you checked (and found unplugged) was the right one? In my cases, I traced the cords back to the devices to be absolutely certain.

What's always interesting to look at when such things happen is your own mental and emotional states at the time. What were you feeling just before the devices did their weird things? Was something stressing you out? Making you angry? Or were there others in the room who could be the actual agent for the malfunction/function?

The idea here would be to look for some correlation, some pattern, to connect the mental and emotional states of the apparent "agent" of the phenomena to the actual bizarre behavior of the technology (and remember that if these things always happen when you are around, the agent might be you).

A few years ago, while visiting my family in Westchester County, New York, I was asked to visit a woman in the northern part of the county who was having apparent poltergeist problems. She reported nothing really moving around, but more unusual activity of her appliances and electronics in the house.

Her toaster would go on by itself (without being activated), her oven, food processor, electric can opener, TV, stereo and other devices would turn on and off by themselves. In addition, she reported that the countertop appliances would activate and work often without being plugged in.

As with other poltergeist cases, one pursues who the "agent" of the activity might be. In this case, although the malfunctions often happened when her husband was in the room with her, they would also happen when he was out of the room, or even out of the house. The only other person in the place at the time with her would be her infant (about eight months old at the time).

As I'd never heard nor read of a poltergeist case with an infant as the agent, and considering that this is unlikely to the extreme, the woman had to be the motivating cause of the phenomena.

Next step was to try to pin down a pattern or stress point in her mental state. That turned out to be surprisingly easy, as she was very open and up front with me.

She and her husband were only married a short time (both in their twenties) when she learned she was pregnant. Although they planned to have children, they had both wanted to wait a while before trying. When they learned she was pregnant, they decided to have the baby, even though they weren't emotionally or financially ready for that.

The phenomena actually began happening just a few weeks after she had the baby. Her husband was out working, and she had had to give up her job for a time (until the baby was old enough for affordable day care). She was bored being at home all the time, and admitted to resenting the baby and her husband a bit for her not being able to work. On the other hand, she also felt that having the baby was the absolute right thing to do (and I observed her as a very affectionate mother).

After our discussion, I concluded, with her, that the pattern of the events seemed to revolve around periods when she was especially bored. The appliances would malfunction within moments of the baby crying loudly (momentarily shifting her mental state from a bit of boredom to heightened alertness).

My suggestion to her that she was causing the malfunctions with her own mind over matter abilities was actually accepted with little other comment than "That's pretty much what I thought, too."

The "cure" for the malfunctions was for her to pick up some home activity, whether it be reading, writing, or even computer work that would chase away some of her boredom, and also to try to consciously exercise her apparent PK talents. If she could actively and consciously affect things with her mind, the situation could become exciting. So, whenever she felt the same state of mind coming on, or noticed weirdness with the appliances, she was to focus her attention on the devices and mentally push them to continue doing what they were doing (or to do even more "weird" things, such as to physically move or change to other settings).

When I checked with her a few weeks later, she was a bit disappointed that the phenomena had halted. Apparently, as soon as she would focus on a malfunctioning piece of equipment, it would stop acting up and return to its "normal" state. After a few days of trying her hand at PK, she felt bored and had to take the other bit of advice and find something else to keep her occupied at home. The phenomena then stopped altogether.

As I did not actually observe any of these malfunctions, could I ever be sure she wasn't making all that up?

Of course not. When someone, anyone, tells me their experiences, I have to judge them based on the person's apparent integrity and sincerity (and, let's face it, sometimes their apparent sanity), as well as whether the events seem to fit in with other experiences that have been reported in the history of parapsychology.

The woman's story fit well, she was quite down to earth and sincere, and she had no motive for telling me what she reported other than she wanted help.

While most people generally only experience single events of mind/machine interaction from time to time, there are those people to whom this may be a daily repeated happening.

A number of articles have appeared in the parapsychological journals dealing with the effects of the mind on machine. In general, the random event generator is typically used (rather than, say, a computer), because it is a simple mechanism and it's relatively easy to understand what could go wrong or right with it. In addition, it's much tougher to tamper with a random event generator without a quick check uncovering that.

In the March 1990 issue of *The Journal of Parapsychology,* Dean I. Radin, currently at the University of Nevada Las Vegas, pointed out the importance of determining the sources of failures in all uses of computers.[1]

Computers are complex mechanisms. What one sees on the

screen of a computer is the culmination of programming (software) and the physical construction of the computer (hardware). Any number of things can affect the performance of a computer from a glitch on the mother board to a loose connection, from a programming error to a conflict between two programs (or even a computer virus).

When looking at how PK might affect a computer, one must look at a number of levels of things that might or might not explain its performance in a given situation.

Computers today are all pervasive. They, or their components, are in a large number of homes, an incredible number of business, and even your car (depending, of course, on how new your car is). They run our bank accounts and connect us to credit companies. They allow air traffic controllers to keep track of aircraft. They help do scientific and medical research and keep track of life functions in intensive care units. They allow law enforcement to work more effectively. They run our power stations. They also run the defensive and offensive capabilities of most nations' military systems. In essence, they are responsible for many of the critical systems and functions of modern society.

While one can point the finger of fault at identifiable human or machine factors when a computer malfunctions, there are many failures that don't fit that easily. One can do a bit of detective work to help uncover the cause(s) of the failures, but the more complex systems become, the more difficult it is to track down the beginning fault that set the dominoes tumbling down.

To throw in the interaction of the human mind, whether the mind of the operator or that of a passerby, as a possible point of origin for failures really throws a monkey wrench into the workings of our increasingly more computer-reliant world.

Radin's article includes discussion of two experiments conducted to look at the hypothesis that some computer failures are the result of psi. These experiments were conducted with a custom-built circuit that could simulate the performance of a circuit that was unstable and malfunctioning. The use of such a circuit would allow the researcher to identify whether PK might be the cause of problems in the computer. Because the actual problem-piece of the system was already identified (the special circuit), one could identify what was/was not the cause of certain malfunctions.

While the experiments did provide results that seem to support the hypothesis that "some" computer failures may be the result of psychokinetic activity, Radin also cautions the reader that "some is in all probability very small, perhaps tenths of a percent of unexplained computer failures." He points out that the size of that percentage is because computer hardware is designed in such a way as to take into account certain types of errors that may happen and to correct for them, and that it is pretty tough machinery under a variety of conditions, able to hold up pretty well and continue to operate within a range of situations and operating conditions.[2]

While the devices used in experiments such as these are in keeping with the research using random event generators around the world, they are also not quite the same in operation or design as the sophisticated workings of the typical computer in the "real world" outside the laboratory. As with the very large difference in the way psi operates in the lab versus how it shows up spontaneously outside that lab, PK effects on computers and other machines are likely to be much more frequent and more robust than the laboratory testing would indicate.

On the other hand, as computer systems become more complex, as the hardware becomes more sophisticated and smaller and faster, it may be unnecessary for any sort of powerful effect to occur for the computer to crash or misbehave in other ways. A small effect on a particular chip or processor could as easily crash the system as pulling the plug.

Given the artificiality of laboratory studies, even those that try to approximate some of the conditions of "real life," the human emotional, attitudinal, and belief factors are often left out of the experiments. While some PK tests designed as games attempt to bring some of that into the situation, the experiments will not approach the context day-to-day behavior that may cause a mind to affect matter spontaneously.

Researchers in a variety of fields are becoming more and more interested in the kinds of problems and successes people have with machines, leading to what is an ever growing body of anecdotal evidence that seems to point to what may or may not be connections between a human's psychological state and the failure (or most excellent behavior) of a machine. More and more people have noticed that their computers tend to misbehave when they are in a rush or in a bad mood. Or that only some people in the office, no matter how good or bad their training is, have more or fewer problems with computers. That photocopiers break down for some people, but never cause grief for others. That some people have general problems with technology, regardless of whether the machine is a toaster, a watch, a VCR, or a computer, while others can use the machine with little or no instruction.

In many situations, one might make a case for the stress or frustration with the machine actually being a result of the breakdown or malfunction of the mechanism, rather than the other way around. However, there is an increasing awareness that our mental states—our moods, our stress levels, our emotional reactions to particular pieces of technology or to technology in general and even our beliefs and expectations related to what the machines can and cannot do—somehow affect the performance of the technology, computer or otherwise.

And when the machine is truly that, mechanical with moving parts rather than printed circuits, and the extraordinary functioning or malfunctioning still happens and cannot be related to better/worse handling by the operator, one must open one's mind to the idea that our minds not only affect our bodies, but also the extension of our bodies: the technology we use (for what is a car or computer but an extension of what we can physically and mentally do on our own?).

Clearly much remains to be studied, to be hypothesized and explained. But bringing it back to the poltergeist situation, one can easily draw parallels to these machine failures and extraordinary performances.

I like to bring that parallel home by labeling the PK effects on computers and other mechanisms a "mini-poltergeist" effect. The single event of a technological failure may be related to momentary stress or emotional outburst. However, where the poltergeist scenario may continue for weeks because of deep-seated stress or dysfunction that remains unresolved, the momentary stresses of the individual are typically that: momentary and fleeting, and thus so are the effects.

This means that a single individual can have repeated instances of problems with machines, though they are unlikely to be continual (unless the root cause, such as a fear or loathing of computers, is not addressed). A person prone to extreme emotional states or anxiety or frustrations or fears may have repeated problems with his or her computer or photocopier or VCR as the causative state repeats itself.

Perhaps the office copier tends to break down when the boss walks by; the presence of the boss creating tension among the workers in the area of the photocopier. Or perhaps the long-term discomfort with the technology in general and computers in particular keeps an individual from ever properly using a computer (thereby perpetuating the opinion that computers are not to be trusted). Whatever causes momentary or long-term stress may cause problems for people, both because of the possibility that their own PK might lash out to sensitive devices around them, and because such stresses can make people careless or lose patience with what they're doing.

Because of our increasing reliance on computers and other hi-tech devices, there is an accompanying need to completely understand how and why such devices and systems fail and to build in ways to avoid those failures. If even, as Radin suggests, only a few "tenths" of a percent of unexplained failures are psi induced, we as a technological society need to keep our perceptions open and keep considering possible detrimental effects caused by PK.

If the one failure in a million due to Mind over Matter occurs in the wrong processor, say one in a defense department computer that controls our early-warning system against missile attack, dire consequences could result. Fortunately, in such potentially dangerous settings, redundant systems provide a check against momentary failures. Such redundant systems are not necessarily in place in all systems (such as a personal computer or video game player), so while the consequence may not be all that dangerous, they can be quite frustrating and upsetting.

We are raising a highly technological generation, one that uses computers as many of us used typewriters or calculators as we grew up (or pen and paper for many). The new high technology awareness and comfort level means that it will be rare that the technology itself will be the source of our mental upsets, but as the systems become more complex, we have to look closer at how we are interacting with them.

If there is no psychokinetic effect at all, if our minds do not interact with the matter of the machines, there still seems to be that correlation between machine failures and exceptional workings that needs to be explored. So, skeptics and believers alike should encourage research in this area, so that our hi-tech society keeps flowing smoothly.

If your computer crashes or merely misbehaves (like mine does from time to time), look inward to your own moods and emotional states. You might walk away from the computer for a time and return when you feel better about yourself and your computer. You may find that the problem has mysteriously vanished, the computer "purring" for you, performing at its best.

People talk to their plants, to their pets, and to their cars to make them do better, so why not computers? Of course, as we move into the twenty-first century with new cars actually speaking preprogrammed words like "The door is ajar" or "Please buckle your seat belt," we will undoubtably encounter a time when our computers ask us "How are you feeling today?"

Don't lightly dismiss your successes and failures with technology. Whether the great functioning or malfunctioning is because of PK or because of a dumb error like hitting the wrong button, it is our minds that are affecting the matter of the machines.

Of course, it could all be Murphy's Law.

By Way of Explanation . . .

Throughout this book, you've read about extraordinary human experiences involving physical performance and apparent interactions of the mind on matter. But if one is to accept such an idea, that the mind not only interacts with the matter of the body, but also with matter outside the body, there ought to be an explanation for how it all works.

There is. Well, actually as of right now, there are a number of possible explanations, hypotheses, and theories. Most are speculation. Some are based on ideas in quantum physics. All explanations thus far have pieces that we can't quite grasp.

Skeptics and debunkers ask for proof and for an explanation for *how* PK can possibly work given the physical laws of nature. Before I give a brief overview of a few theories, let me repeat a point mentioned earlier.

If psychokinesis is Mind over Matter, and if we seek an explanation for *how* mind can affect matter, we first need to define and understand what it is we are trying to explain.

Matter (and actually we need to include energy as well): This we understand. In the world of physics, matter and energy can be defined and measured.

Mind: Uh, well, there's a bit of a problem here. We have no physical definition of mind or consciousness, and no way to measure it.

In other words, in trying to come up with a theory of how PK works, in the body or on the outside material world, we're still missing the definition and understanding of the vital part of the situation we're trying to explain. Until that time, we may have no acceptable theory of Mind over Matter. [Note to the debunkers: Just because you can't measure something doesn't mean it doesn't exist. The history of science is full of immeasurable things, from electricity to cosmic radiation, that were not defined or measurable until the technology and science of the day advanced enough to provide the means.]

In fiction, such as in comic books and cartoons and films and TV, PK seems almost like a force (sometimes even shown as a glowing energy) that reaches out from the psychokinetic to the object or person being affected. It's almost like a hand or beam composed of energy goes out and moves things, throws things, or envelopes things and people. Or perhaps it is an energetic glow that is transferred to an ill or dying (or dead) individual to bring him or her back to health.

Some theories include the idea that the mind/brain can send out energy that interacts with matter and energy in the world. If we could detect that energy, we would know what PK was.

Unfortunately, attempts at trying to measure energy from the mind/brain are hampered by not knowing exactly what kind of energy one is looking for. Is it part of the electromagnetic spectrum? If so, at what part? One needs different detectors to look for extreme low frequency waves (ELF waves), or microwaves, or photons, or magnetic fields or . . . In other words, one would need an incredible array of equipment to try to detect all ranges of the EM spectrum if one didn't have a good idea of where to start.

We don't have a good idea of where to start (if we could physically detect the mind, we would).

Then there's the issue of whether this "energy" is a different form of energy than electromagnetic, one not yet understood or measurable through our technology (science still doesn't have a good handle on *gravity*, for example). One hundred years ago, if you had told most physicists that light sometimes acts as a wave and sometimes as a particle, you'd have been laughed at. But as we know today, a photon of light can behave as either a particle or as a wave (and some have suggested that the state of the photon as it's being measured is determined by the expectation of the observer . . . how's that for a Mind over Matter connection).

In fact, quantum physicists deal with the idea of uncertainty all the time. At the quantum level, the state of whatever's being observed is affected by the act of observation. There is an interaction by the observer that helps determine the quantum states. However, it is still not appropriate to extend this to say that everything that is observed is affected this way (it is likely a tree falling in the woods still makes a sound, whether it is being observed or recorded or not).

Until we understand the energy type and form of the mind, we may not figure out what the energy is that the mind uses to affect matter. On the other hand, someone might figure out PK first, which can help track back to a good physical measure and definition of the mind (provided researchers get the funding to attempt such studies).

Some researchers and theoreticians have suggested that PK just simply *works*. That there is no force one could trace leaving the psychokinetic's body or brain, rather that the PKer thinks it and it happens. The energy of the universe, that which surrounds and suffuses the object or person being affected just reacts to the thought projected at it and the matter is affected.

If this sounds like the Force in *Star Wars,* that's undoubtably no accident (although the idea was around well before George Lucas or before psychical researchers, for that matter). Many Eastern religions have talked about the "Oneness of the Universe," and physicists have, for decades, tried to finish Einstein's unfinished theory relating to a "Unified Field" that interconnects everything (all matter and all energy) throughout the universe. Such a field ties everything together, and leads to conclusions that what goes on in one part of the universe has an effect (no matter how small) on all other parts of the universe.

It has been suggested that our minds can tap into this unified field and utilize this energy and the connections to everything else to manipulate physical objects and processes. The thought affects the field, the field causes the changes in the environment (a rather simplified example might be a child in a swimming pool slapping the water, causing a swell and minor waves that spread out and disturb other things floating on the surface).

Specific hypotheses and theories about Mind over Matter usually proceed from a couple of perspectives. This may all seem like science fiction or like something that appears in comic books, but many theories in physics can be seen in such light.

One perspective is that our minds use some currently undetected or perhaps an unknown form of energy to interact with the environment. Our minds are energy forms that reach out with invisible force to pick up objects or to muck about in computers. You could picture it as a beam of energy streaking out from the brain, wrapping itself around the object to be levitated or invading the workings of a machine like an extra arm. That energy may be either something we haven't thought to try to measure (researchers have tried a variety of measurements up and down the range—but not necessarily all forms in the range—of what is called electromagnetic radiation with no success so far), or could be a "new" form of energy for which we just haven't developed technology to measure.

A second view of PK might be that our minds create the stimulus that sparks the environment to change itself in accordance with the stimulus. In other words, like water flows around your hand when you stick it in a full bucket, or like soft clay can be molded with a gentle touch, or like our pets sometimes reflect in their behavior our own good and bad moods, there is some function of the environment in which we live that reacts to our thoughts. You think (really hard, of course) and some energy system that is in the environment picks that up. *It* (the energy of the environment) then causes the changes, whether that means an object flying across the room or a person being healed.

Some theories include the idea that our minds actually help shape the reality in which we live (that if we believed hard enough, the whole world, including our memories of what came before, would change), others that our minds can only cause changes in line with our (rather) limited thinking and acceptance (that reality can change, but only so much and according to rules set down by the limits of the imagination).

Ursula K. LeGuin, in her novel *The Lathe of Heaven,* describes a man who goes to sleep and dreams of changes in the world, something not uncommon for most of us. However in LeGuin's world, the changes the man dreams up actually have occurred. When he wakes, the world has changed according to the dream. But while he remembers what the world was like the day before, the memories and records of everyone else have also been changed so that no one else remembers a change. In other words, if your house turned green overnight, but the memory of you and everyone else was changed so that you all remember it as green, no one would consciously notice a change.

Most psychics and parapsychologists believe that if there is a reality-altering piece to psychokinesis, there is also a set of rules that we all adhere to unconsciously. One person could not change reality, because the PK of everyone else wouldn't let that change occur.

Now if everyone believed in the same change at the same time, that might be another story (I recall one of Michael Moorcock's fantasy characters—I can't recall which one—who said something like "the world was flat until everyone believed it was round").

Besides theorizing about how PK might actually work, there are those working at understanding just what factors in the brain/body and in the environment might actually affect the occurrence of psychokinesis (and other psi abilities, for that matter). Besides belief and some personality variables, the most consistent potential source for affecting psi seems to be the geomagnetic field, the magnetic field produced by the earth itself.

The magnetic field generated by the liquid iron-nickel core of our planet is subject to slight changes on a daily basis (think of this as being like the changes in our brain waves that happen throughout the day and through the sleep cycles). The changes can come because (in overly simple terms) the liquid core of the planet does slosh around a lot. Changes in a local area can happen because of movements in the earth (such as around fault lines) or because of changing weather patterns. Sunspots, solar flares, and cosmic rays can also cause fluctuations all over the world or just in some places.

There has been some research into how animals' behavior and migration patterns shift because of changes in the geomagnetic field, and there has been documented evidence that many birds and animals can sense changes in magnetic fields and react to them. Over the past twenty years, there has been growing interest in how that field may affect human behavior as well.

Researchers have noted that apparent trends in psychic performance can be correlated to the shifting magnetic field of the earth. For example, during low periods (not as much energy), people may report more telepathic or clairvoyant experiences and do better at such tasks in laboratory experiments. During higher periods, more PK activity or precognitive experiences are reported, and results in those types of experiments tend to be more significant.

There has been little funding to set up very localized sensing stations for geomagnetic activity, so the above conclusions may be a bit premature. With anecdotal evidence, where people report their experiences, researchers have tried to tie when those experiences occurred (sometimes this is, itself, only a guess on the part of the person reporting it) to the data that has been recorded all over the world by geomagnetic sensing stations. With laboratory research, the date and time information is more precise, though the measurements of the local field may not be.

But, more recently science has been looking at how fluctuations in the earth's magnetic field might affect a variety of human behaviors and activities, as well as biological mechanisms in the human body. There is some indication that the shifts in the geomagnetic field affect the temporal lobes of the brain and also production of melatonin by the pineal gland. Minute particles of magnetic material, magnetite, have been found in the human brain, providing a biological mechanism by which our brains can sense magnetic fields and changes in them.

There are a number of speculations as to the connection here. On the one hand, it has been suggested that ESP works best when there is less "noise" in the environment (when the geomagnetic field is at a low) and PK works when there are highs, more "energy" to make use of. Or perhaps, the decrease or increase may only help if there is already ESP or PK happening.

Researcher Serena Roney-Dougal has suggested that rather than the field strength itself, it is the fluctuations, the shifts from highs to lows and lows to highs that affect the production of melatonin by the pineal gland, actually affect the incidence of ESP and PK.[3]

The studies with the geomagnetic field and human psychology and biology are still in their infancy, but it is clear that there is *some* direct connection between human beings and the earth we live on that affects our connections with each other and with the environment. This area of research has spurred a lot of interest and much theorizing and will continue to do so as we search for more answers.

[For more specific information on theories and models of psychokinesis, check out some of the sources in the suggested reading list in Appendix A]

One other, rather unique idea about Mind over Matter begs discussion, especially in connection with psychic experiences in general: Do we *predict* the future (precognition) or do we *create* the future (interaction; psychokinesis)?

Do you *predict* heads or tails when a coin is flipped or do you somehow influence that coin to come up the way you want it?

This question has created some flurry of discussion and controversy when it comes to some laboratory studies that have been done with random event generators. In a random event generator using a radioactive source element, at any given moment, the mechanism is detecting whether a particle is being given off or not. In the case of a computerized system, a mathematical program will determine whether the computer has randomly chosen a "1" or a "0" at a given moment. Either way, you're talking basic coin flipping. The goal of the subject is to make more "heads" than "tails" come up, in essence to make the system less random. But chance can dictate that even in systems that are truly random, every once in a while it will look like it's not random (some people call that a run of luck—sometimes good luck, sometimes bad).

Try flipping a coin a couple of hundred times. Guess tails every time. Chance says you should get about 50 percent correct (around half . . . there should be some variation). However, you may notice that from time to time, there is a string of coin flips that are all tails, maybe five or ten in a row. Was this PK? Possibly, but random systems often have runs of what looks to be, at that moment, nonrandomness.

In the total number of coin flips, the ten tails in a row probably just helps even things out to a 50-50 chance, because maybe there was also a similar run of heads coming up on the coin tosses. But if the only time you guessed tails just happened to be the ten flips out of 200 when it showed tails every time, you might think you were very lucky, or very psychic.

Since the random event generator has a running random system, every once in a while, there's bound to be some string of what looks to be nonrandomness, of nonchance results. If the subject somehow lucks out and decides to start his or her trials at that point in time (pressing the "start" button at just the right time), it may look like some PK hits. If the subject continues to do that over time, it may look like he or she has a lot of PK ability.

Or . . . It could also be that the subject simply knew in advance when the periods of nonrandomness would occur (subconsciously, of course). This would be precognition, not Mind over Matter, since the subject is *predicting* what's going to happen, not *creating* the results.

This is a bit of a dilemma in PK research, and one not easily resolved.

In the real world (lab research on PK and ESP being artificially created situations), this confusion may also operate.

An individual who has a dream that a relative will die in a car crash may actually believe that he or she somehow caused the event when it happens a few days later. People have for decades reported predictions of a personal nature that came true along with some guilty feeling that they were somehow responsible.

Could this be PK instead of using ESP to somehow guess at the right future? I suppose it could be. But consider that there seems to be some limits as to how often and how strong PK works. It doesn't happen all the time, even in poltergeist cases, which seem to have the biggest PK events happening. It doesn't seem to allow the destruction of a house or the flip-over of a car (contrary to what you may have seen in the films *Poltergeist* and *Carrie*). It doesn't come under great control, or healers and metal-benders would *always* be able to do what they are apparently able to do sometimes. It often involves other people (and their own minds), or when a healer does healing, it would always "take" (remember that the patient has to want to get better as well) and people would have no innate defense in the case of apparent psychic attack.

There just seems to be some limitations as to how much one can do with PK, as there is just so much one can do, physically, with finite amounts of energy. These limits, whatever they are, almost *have to be* there, especially if you take into account that one would expect the survival instinct of most people might activate their own PK to prevent such accidents from happening, to save themselves.

Granted, moving an object after one states that he or she will do is hardly likely to be a prediction of an event that will occur whether the statement was made or not. This would be Mind over Matter. On the other hand, stating that one can cause an earthquake, when such statement is followed by an earth tremor, is unlikely to be Mind over Matter, and more likely to be a misinterpretation of information about the building quake received by the mind of the individual.

When it comes right down to it, one doesn't need psychokinesis to affect the future. Many psychics talk of predicting *probable* futures, the ones that are most likely to occur. In almost the same breath, they also talk about making decisions, about taking responsibility for one's actions.

You see, whether one uses PK or simply one's normal physical and mental capacities to interact with others and with the environment, we all create our own futures. Our past has brought us to where we are now. Our decisions and actions, whether conscious or unconscious, deliver us into a future (which is instantly the present) for which we are at least partly responsible.

Mind over Matter means that we, our minds, through decision or indecision, and then through our subsequent actions, can influence ourselves, others, and the world around us in a number of ways.

Ultimately, responsibility for the future lies within us all.

* **11** *

Do It Yourself
Mind Over Matter

Back in mid-1992, I was headed to Lincoln, Nebraska, to speak at
a conference sponsored by the Fortean Research Center (named for
Charles Fort, an early twentieth-century journalist who was interested in and collected reports of all sorts of unusual phenomena).
I was told the guests were to include fellow *Fate* magazine colum-
nist John Keel, UFO proponent and author Linda Moulton Howe,
crop circle expert George Wingfield, and others. Not having met
John Keel, I looked forward to the opportunity to get to know him
a bit. However, it was one other name that really excited me: Martin Caidin.

I knew of Martin Caidin mainly because he is the author of
dozens of science fiction books, including *Cyborg* (and its sequels),
the basis for the TV series *The Six Million Dollar Man* and *The Bionic
Woman*. I also knew he was a science writer, and an expert on the
space program, with his total book output over the two hundred
mark. I had also read a book called *Ghosts of the Air* (reprinted in
1995 by Galde Press), an excellent collection of case reports of encounters of pilots with ghosts, UFOs, and time slippages.

As a fan of his science fiction, he was one guy I wanted to sit
down with. What's more, in conversation with my father, Dick
Auerbach, who had a long career with NBC-TV, I was informed that

he had known Martin Caidin during the days of the Mercury and Gemini space shots, when my father was with NBC News and Caidin was covering the launches for Metromedia Television and Radio. I wanted to talk to Caidin about those "Right Stuff" days.

Two days before I left for Nebraska, I was flipping channels just before going to sleep. As I clicked on one channel, I heard the name "Martin Caidin" loud and clear. Okay, I thought, a bit of synchronicity. I sat for the next several minutes watching an episode of *Stuntmasters,* as Martin Caidin in his old, rebuilt German Ju-52 bomber *Iron Annie* set the world's record for the number of people walking on the wing of a plane in flight.

Yup, I thought. He was definitely going to be an interesting character to get to know. Little did I know. . . .

Our first evening at the conference, Marty Caidin and his wife Dee Dee introduced us to Caidin's telekinesis. As I sat and listened to the initial description of what he could do, I wasn't impressed at first. He claimed to be able to spin a small paper "cap" on a pin. But he went on. Not just one such target, but often dozens at a time. Under glass. In a vacuum, on a couple of occasions. At a great distance.

Okay, here's a well respected aviator and science journalist claiming that he's been able to turn targets with his mind. Since I have accepted psychokinesis as a reality, I was ready for anything.

But I was also skeptical (meaning I had not made up my mind about Caidin's claims). So, when Dee Dee asked for volunteers to help make the targets, the magician in me had me rush up immediately.

The targets were small, square pieces of different sorts of paper, foil, and even candy wrappers. They were folded twice and unfolded so they made a sort of pyramid shape. They were of different sizes, but none bigger than a few inches across. They were balanced on sewing needles that we set in wax as a base.

Of course, if you blew on the balanced targets even slightly, they spun. So we placed an aquarium tank over groups of targets on each of two tables. We tried blowing at the bottom of the tanks, then even shook the table to see if any of the targets would spin. No such luck (though shaking the table caused them to sway, not spin).

Marty Caidin talked about how he got started spinning the targets, and how he uses a visualization to get the targets spinning. He sat down and began to work on one of the tanks.

Nothing. He focused on the other tank. Still nothing.

Then I noticed that one of the smaller targets, positioned slightly below a taller one, was beginning to turn. And turn. And turn.

Apparently, as he related, he sometimes gets a scatter gun effect, and targets not in his direct "aim" will begin to move.

That one target, the only one to move under the tanks, turned for several minutes, while the other targets in that tank didn't move a millimeter, which one would expect due to any air currents which could disturb the one target.

During that conference, we got to know each other better. As I was able to turn Marty's pilot stories during an informal gathering to stories of the early days of the space program, I mentioned that he knew my Dad.

He stopped short, looked hard at me, and said "Not THAT Auerbach!" We've been good friends ever since.

I visited Marty the following January at his home in Gainesville, Florida, where he had a wonderful set-up for his psychokinesis practicing. On the second floor of the house, which was essentially a very large loft, he had a small room specially set for telekinetics. Three-fourths of the room was sectioned off by a wall with a large picture window and a door set in it. The doorway was surrounded by rubber sealers, the windows were painted shut and covered, and all other possible sources of air current, like heating vents and even electrical outlets were covered. There was no air-conditioning in the room, and even the fluorescent lights, at twenty watts, gave off enough energy to change the room temperature at all. A digital thermometer, visible at all times in the room, showed less than two tenths of a degree temperature variation while Marty worked at the targets at night.

With Marty sitting in the anteroom with me, I watched, amazed, as he had target after target spinning, generally with some degree of control. Several times I went into the target room, took the targets apart, put them back together in different combinations and positions, checking the room over very carefully for any possible other means of getting those targets turning. After this, we would head downstairs and wait a while for the room to become still.

Over the few days that I was there, I became convinced that something very real was happening, and that the something was likely to be psychokinesis. Yes, there was still the "how" that needed to be explored. Was it some kind of air movement, electrostatic force or what? Caidin didn't know, but that's exactly what he wants to find out.

"The targets turn in patterns that make no sense in relation to potential air currents," said Caidin. "One target out of ninety would be turning for minutes while the others stayed completely still, even though the targets next to the spinning one were practically touching it. Targets next to each other would turn in opposite directions. A pinwheel would turn points first. Pie plates to which tinsel was attached would turn rapidly, yet the tinsel stayed hanging straight down, not at an angle as one would expect on a rotating target."

In fact, I saw multiple targets spinning (as many as eighteen during one session), I watched as one target among the fifty or so he had in the room spun steadily for over an hour, with no other target movement. I saw a pinwheel spinning opposite to its normal motion (which I was only able to duplicate with a very specific directional air push, and a lot of breath).

In addition, he had me sit down with a target, first uncovered, then under a glass dome (sealed to its base with petroleum jelly), and damned if I couldn't get that thing turning.

We also connected with three scientists who had formed their own investigations group in Gainesville called The Center for Paranormal Studies: Andrew Nichols, Russ McCarty, and James Bosworth. The three of them got to also watch a demonstration at the Caidin home, and our consensus opinion was that the Caidin effect needed further study and understanding.

I kept in close touch with Marty and Dee Dee Caidin over the next few months. During that time they left Gainesville and headed back to a place Marty considered more "home," Cocoa Beach, just a stone's throw from the Cape.

Then, in the early summer of 1993, I headed back to Florida, this time with my associate Barbara Gallagher, Andrew Nichols, and a two man TV crew we were working with to shoot a pilot called *Haunted America*.

We had just spent the day and evening with Marty at a local "haunted" restaurant called Ashley's, with all sorts of unusual phenomena happening (including, unfortunately, some very weird effects on our video equipment). Then, it was over to the Caidins' place for some telekinesis.

While the setup was not ideal as in Gainesville, Marty did get some targets under glass turning, as well as teach the method to our producer/director Jude Prest. In addition, with Andy Nichols on an Agema thermal imaging video camera (which picks up temperature variations and converts it to color images on video), we could see some very inexplicable bursts of heat appearing briefly under targets just before they would begin to turn.

Was Marty causing the heat bursts which would then cause the air to move the targets? We didn't know.

The fall of 1993 brought the Caidins and myself back to Lincoln, Nebraska, for a special Caidin/Auerbach workshop. Part of the workshop was dedicated to telekinesis, as Marty taught more than 50 percent of the group (as I recall there were about 50 people there) to move targets, generally under glass. A number of attendees were on faculty or affiliated with the university there, and could find no other explanation for the targets turning at the time.

I went back to Cocoa Beach in March of 1994 for a vacation, and on one of those days I was there, my colleagues from Gainesville made it down. They brought with them a bell jar with a ground glass base, so as to eliminate any chance of air currents getting in through the bottom. They also had an electrostatic detector.

The targets turned. There was no electrostatic charge detected. There may have been some kind of microcurrents of air in the jar, yet during the "control" time periods when we just watched the jar, the target was still.

Marty sent me home from that trip with a copy of his journal from the days he first tried turning the targets. You'll be reading some excerpts from that in a moment.

Marty and Dee Dee Caidin made it out to the San Francisco Bay Area in June of 1994 for a workshop Marty and I did on Psychokinesis. We had about thirty people at the location in Marin County, and some limited success with people getting targets to spin (though not as good as the Nebraska workshop). However, a number of people were very excited about what they saw and did and continue to practice their own target turning to this day.

George Weissmann, a physicist I have gotten to know here in the Bay Area, was one of the attendees and with him, and Jon Klimo of Rosebridge Graduate School, we hope to build a suitable test "room" for Caidin's targets and get him back out here. By the time you are reading this, those initial tests will be over, during which we hope to load up the room with various sensing equipment to learn what might be causing the targets to spin (what currently known forces, that is). We will publish the results in a variety of forums and then move on from there.

For a full description of the target set up, I recommend the source of Marty's inspiration for this work, G. Harry Stine, Caidin's fellow science journalist and science fiction writer. Marty originally read about Stine's "energy wheel" in his book *On the Frontiers of Science,* which is very hard to track down. But the information is available in Stine's more recent volume *Mind Machines You Can Build* (Largo, Florida: Top of the Mountain Publishing 1992). However, take a look at the photo insert for pictures of the targets and illustrations as to how to make them yourself.

After reading about what Stine claimed about his energy wheel, that anyone could turn it with mind power, Marty got him on the phone to see how serious he was about it.

It turned out that he was very serious, and related to Marty that not only was he able to turn the target with limited success, but that there were others also able to do so. He encouraged Marty to try. "I believe you're a prime candidate," Stine said to Caidin.

"Why?"

"Among other things, you're crazy."

"No argument. Is that the best reason?"

"Sure. You're crazy like a whole den of foxes."

[from p. 6 of THE MERLIN EFFECT]

Now, let me turn this over to Martin Caidin, and excerpts from his unpublished journal of his psychokinetic learnings, *The Merlin*

Effect. The journal was written over a period of time in late 1985 to early 1986. Following the journal excerpts, Caidin will have a few more comments for us regarding learning to do this telekinetic thing. I'll add a little commentary in [brackets].

THE MERLIN EFFECT
by Martin Caidin

A journal and record of telekinetic tests and experiments that are different from anything you've ever read before.

Because they're successful.

[From the Forward]:

The PK (Psychokinesis) Factor, also known as TK (Telekinetics) is real. It's the awesome power of the mind. It refers to mind, or mental, control over the physical movement or position of physical in turning, rolling, sliding or levitating them.

There's no physical contact between the mind of the controller and the object under control. It does seem quite impossible. Common sense dictates that it's impossible. Scientists are quick to deride and ridicule the entire concept. They also said the same thing about flight and men walking on the moon.

None of this negative position matters if the facts are true. Facts are clumsy things, however, and made of silly putty or we wouldn't be updating so many "final" textbooks so often. What counts is not whether a scientist admits something is a fact, but whether or not we can again and again demonstrate the event.

TK is real. It exists. It works, and it works on demand. In this Journal on a TK venture it began without fanfare or any real hope it would succeed. Yet its success has been astounding. When you have 3,000 successes out of 3,000 target tries in a period of ninety days for just one test subject, you are very much for real.

Certain people in a tight group who perform this TK are getting better and stronger. They know very little about what they're doing, but they're doing it. . . .

[After Marty's initial exchange with Harry Stine, he sat down to try turning one of the targets; from pages 8–13]

I got a cork from the bar and we [he and Dee Dee] stuck a two-inch needle into it so it was standing straight, and cut a piece of note paper 3x3 inches, folded it over twice so it formed a sort of parasol with a central interior peak, and placed it on the needle. It balanced after a while. And it sat there.

Next, turn off the air conditioner. Close all the doors and the windows (a terrific time for me to try to be telekinetic, Dee Dee reminded me as the temperature kept climbing; it was 96 degrees outside, keep everyone the hell out of the room, light a candle and put it well to the side to be sure there was no movement of air in the room other than normal convection (which won't move a cat hair and they weigh *less* than nothing). I had bought a package of dust masks that painters wear and I blew like hell to move anything through that mask. And failed, which was good to know. So everything was right.

I sat carefully, my chair not touching the desk, and like Harry said, I placed my hands on either side of the wheel (the wheel is only for identification since the paper is a square, but Harry wrote the book and he calls it a wheel and I'll abide by that), cupped them as nicely as I could, and I thought.

I thought some more. *Move.*

It sat there.

Move. Turn! Move, you son of a bitch!

I was concentrating. My teeth were gritted, my brow furrowed, my ass as tight as wood, my stomach muscles straining, my heart pounding.

I'll kill you! Move!

It was locked in cement.

Finally I leaned back, exhausted, breathing in my own steamy air through the mask, feeling the sweat pouring down me, dripping on the chair and on my clothes and on the floor, and thought, *Here I go again with this stupid business.* I quit trying and just looked at the damn paper wheel, my hands still cupped around it *and the damn thing moved.*

Well, it *twitched.*

It wobbled a little and it twitched and then it turned again to stone. But *something* had happened, as little as it might be. Dee Dee sat about ten feet away, watching everything, and I sat a bit straighter in my chair, and I looked at that wheel with something like a strange respect for how completely it was ruling me, and I kept my hands in place, afraid to disturb anything by moving or even breathing (despite the mask), and I was holding my breath so long I felt dizzy and I was about to let it out and suck in air *when it turned.*

I'll tell you right now that there's no way to describe the feeling. It was incredible to realize I had actually moved that thing without moving my hands or body or breathing on it. *But . . .* had I really not affected it through some subconscious movement? It's like holding a pendulum and watching it move. Hell, *you can't keep it from moving,* which is why hand-held pendulums are so much crap for telling anything *except* that you can't keep your own body still.

But this was different.

Because the wheel started moving some more and then it settled down to a steady pace and it kept turning, and around and around went that wonderful son of a bitch, and I couldn't believe it but there was no way anything could be making that wheel move except whatever energy was coming out of my brain/mind and down through my hands, which maybe acted like some sort of energy antenna. I sure as hell didn't know *what,* but that wheel kept *moving.*

My God, it was actually happening. Harry had been right all the time!

I kept feeling stronger and more confident, because in those incredible moments all the doubts of all my years were washing away like wet paint sloughing off a wall in a driving rain. Dee Dee set up a chair so we could both have our shot at it, and we made four more of the square wheels, all of them from lightweight paper, all of them that same 3x3-inch size, and we had needles all over the bloody desk.

Within the hour we were spinning them steadily. We made marks on the paper so we could get an accurate count of the turns. Man, it wasn't easy. Everything was unpredictable. I got up to thirty-two revolutions of one wheel without it ever stopping. Dee Dee did thirty-five turns but we were going through crazy gyrations with our hands and we were straining and sweating and fired up like mad with what was going on. Oh, I'm sure that some hand movement brought air moving against or by the wheels, so we tried to see if we could make them move by breathing regularly on them without the dust masks, and all we could do was get a lot of rocking and wobbling and never got more than a very small partial turn, *as hard as we tried to move them this way.*

We tried everything we could short of blowing on the damn things or fanning them with our hands and we never got a half-turn out of them. Then we'd settle down and get serious about it with our hands cupped, and we discovered that when the wheels quit moving you could change position of your hands a bare fraction of an inch, lock them in place, and the wheel would take off for another dozen turns or so.

There was no control. Forget it, man! Those things just turned whichever way they wanted and that's all there was to it, and who cared? Nothing in that room short of our trying mentally to make them move and having our hands around them could affect them.

Well, could I be that sure? Would I be able to state with absolute certainty, that kind that will make Professor Doubting Thomas willing to consider seriously what we were doing? The odds were against that. Of course, there's another point. I don't give a rat's ass what anybody thinks about what I'm doing or what I say I've done, just so long as *I* know I have done or can do it. I've gone through the detractors and doomsayers and the negatives when I was setting world records with that big three-engined German bomber I flew, and when—well, when I set the world wingwalking record with the ancient, monstrous, slab sided, iron-monger of an airplane called the Junkers Ju-52/3m, as big as a B-17 bomber, and I had nineteen skydivers out on just the left wing of that airplane, starting out at 8,500 feet (of course, we came down very soon after like a raped ape) and I set the all-time world's record, even the Germans said it was impossible. Of course, that made a liar out of me and Don Yahrling, my copilot, *and* my crew chief, *and* the photographers in my plane and the other planes.

The only time the Germans fell to silence (or anyone else for that matter) was when we sent them the films and videotapes of the entire affair from takeoff to landing. We had cameras *everywhere.*

The point I make is that someone else's belief or disbelief doesn't have a damned thing to do with what *you* can do or *have* done. That's been my attitude all the way through.

Back to the desk and the incredible feelings we were going through . . .

Dee Dee was exhausted, but I like being on the thin edge of madness in hammering after things, so I kept at it and tried a variety of experiments, and when I was through I was banging on the telephone to get G. Harry Stine.

The first thing he said, without any preamble of any kind, was: "You did it." How the hell did *he* know?

I must have spouted words with all the velocity of a machine gun. "Harry, all I was trying to do after the first twitching and wobbling was to move that little piece of paper one full turn around, but I was squeezing hard enough to milk a stone and I got it maybe three-quarters of a turn around and that's the best I could do."

He sounded disappointed. "Keep trying," he said. "Frankly, I thought you could do better than that."

The light dawned in my head. I was talking about the tests I was doing *after* Dee Dee left me to carry on solo. "Harry! I'm putting things in the wrong order! We got over thirty turns. What I've been talking about with not getting the full turn is that *I moved my chair back four feet from the desk and I sat on my hands and I was moving your paper by mind control alone from four feet away!*"

I expected fireworks, cries of joy, ringing bells, solemn declarations, congratulations, huzzahs.

Harry said "Nice. Try some more." And he hung up.

[And so, Martin Caidin, in September of 1985, had embarked on another long journey of the mind. Over the next few weeks he began a series of experiments to try turning the targets in different configurations, in different directions, to start and stop them, and from different distances. He had other witnesses besides Dee Dee there as well, from time to time, and was beginning to set harder and harder tasks for himself. From page 26]:

7. *USING MIND PUSH ONLY, STANDING AT A DISTANCE OF 12 FEET FROM THE DESK, TURN THE ENERGY WHEEL (PARASOL) TO THE LEFT.*

Mind push? Hell of a phrase but I'm still not certain as to what to call it. Anyway—

It happened virtually by accident. I just felt *good*. The kind of deep-inside good that really adds up to *great!* I stood on the far side of the second desk and chair from my desk, on the far side of the row of filing cabinets, about twelve feet from my desk pad, looking at the parasol wheel standing utterly inert—*and the wheel turned suddenly and rapidly to the left, clockwise, more than halfway, then came to an instant stop.* There were several people with me in the room (Dee Dee, Ken, Gwen) when this happened and I'm not certain who was more shocked.

Dee Dee stared at it, looked at me and said, quietly, "Holy shit. Do it again."

"I don't know if I can," I told her. "I don't even know what the hell I did just *then.*"

"Do it!" she yelled. Which brings us to:

8. *THIS IS TOO HOT TO MISS. USING MIND PUSH ONLY, STANDING AT A DISTANCE OF 12 FEET FROM THE DESK, TURN THE ENERGY WHEEL (PARASOL) TO THE RIGHT.*

Did it! Got another turn of about 180 degrees. "Again," Dee Dee snapped. I managed to repeat the movement both left and right, but there was a catch. I failed to get better than an half turn at its best. Then again, who cares! When you're starving there's hardly anything better than a half-turn!

[As time progressed, Marty was able to work up to turning several targets at a time, gain some control of direction sometimes, and other times was just able to keep one target spinning through several hundred revolutions. He moved on to trying the targets under glass, as well as to working with targets of materials other than paper (such as cardboard and foil) and much heavier targets. However, while he got larger targets to spin, it was smaller targets, dense or not, that he seemed to have difficulty with. From pp 67–68]:

Weight, density, or mass—or whatever it turns out to be—is definitely a factor to be considered.

When things work, distance is not a problem.

When it does work, this case being movement generated through the glass of the bell jar, weight is absolutely a major factor. The heavier it is, the tougher it is.

My hands appear to act as some sort of antenna or focusing medium. I'm absolutely convinced of that. BUT ONLY AT CERTAIN

TIMES AND THOSE CANNOT BE PREDICTED. They are not necessary all the time. Mental crutch? Perhaps.

Mood and temperament are factors. But, once again, not always. There's no consistency here. Freshness of mind and body is important, but not always. Most of the time, yes, but not always.

[As he was learning about what worked for him and what didn't, he ran into more and more questions. Targets would turn for a time, then suddenly stop. Targets he focused on would do nothing, then suddenly start spinning. Targets he just glanced at would start without a thought. No real pattern emerged.

With more and more practice, Caidin was able to turn more and more targets. Yet it all raised more questions. There were inconsistencies in performance that kept popping up. Such inconsistencies also arose when others tried the task, yet some were able to do it. Here's Marty describing a little "how to" he gave a buddy of his, who then turned around and raised another ugly question. From pp 99–100]:

Ray Martin flew in last night. Major item for these notes. Ray is an old flying buddy, a very sharp dude, late thirties, flies fixed wings and eggbeaters, sharp as a razor, and we've flown warbird airshows and *very* tight formations for years. He's the same cat who went through self-hypnosis and took the written test for his pilot's instrument rating and scored a perfect 100 percent on the test, which is nigh well unto impossible. Point to be made: one very sharp and capable pile of folded jelly between his ears. A *perfect* candidate for the PK.

I'd shown Ray how to do things with the paper parasol wheels of 1/4th gram. He's worked on them at home with what he terms excellent results (I wouldn't expect anything less). I discussed with him this system of concentration with max output and then total relaxation. I placed the #3 aluminum (not foil) wheel on the needle. Until this point the best he'd ever done was the lightweight paper.

"Steady down," I instructed. "Don't breathe on the wheel and don't move anymore. Cup your hands. Good. Now squeeze your fingers together and without moving, bear down. Tighten your muscles as hard as you can. Concentrate so hard you're squirting adren-

alin, you quiver, you shake, sweat bursts from you. Now count back-
wards slowly from thirty, and while you're counting remember to
keep thinking TURN! When you get down to zero and you're half
wiped, absolutely *relax*. Loosen up all the way. Let your pinkies,
against the desk, slide inward slightly. Turn into a limp dishrag. Do
it."

He did exactly what I'd laid out for him. All through the hard concentration, he got nothing. Then he relaxed, and the aluminum
parasol *started turning immediately*. I was grinning at him and Ray
sat there stunned because this was a real quantum leap for him. . . .

Ray made a point I may have missed putting down here otherwise. The inertial factor has been a constant reference factor all
through these tests and notes. But I don't recall if I noted that, sometimes, when a wheel is spinning, either using hands or mind-only
control (but usually the latter), it will be going around at a really
sharp clip and then IT COMES TO A DEAD STOP JUST LIKE *THAT*.
It's rolling, snap your fingers, and in the time it takes to make that
snap, the wheel *stops*. There's no deceleration, no slowing down,
no rocking. It stops instantly. Or as much instantly as the eye can
see. Ray has seen this and so has Dee Dee and so have I, and we
have it on video tape and even at slow play it stops with a silent
crash.

[I, too, have seen this happen with Marty's targets more than once.
Such a sudden stop does not happen, however, if you get the
wheels going with an air current or by blowing on them. They go
for a bit, then slow and finally stop. There is no clash with the laws
of inertia and momentum. That is, except when they're targets of
the apparent PK.

Marty moved on to trying to get the targets to turn while he, personally, was out of the room. He and Dee Dee thought to have him
in another room, focusing on a Polaroid shot of the appropriate target. He asked her to make a target, mark it up so all four sides would
have their own distinctive patterns. From page 121]:

Well, I studied the picture. Tried to make head or tail of the mark-
ings. I simply couldn't get a good grasp on them. I glanced at Dee
Dee who looked back with doe-innocent eyes. Turned back to the

picture, angled it so that it most closely resembled the view I had of my desk from my chair. I tried to place myself in that chair and then, suddenly, it all fit like a glove. I placed my hands on each side of the picture and concentrated. Finally I knew the wheel should be turning. I hate to admit "should be" but that's the way it was.

Dee Dee went into the studio. About twenty feet from the desk. "You've got to see this," she called to me. The aluminum foil wheel was spinning steadily.

[Marty was able to turn targets from across the room, by staring at a Polaroid of the target from another room, by watching a video monitor of the targets from outside the house, even by thinking about a target from miles away.

The type of material seemed not to be too much of an issue for Marty. But size was, though not in the way one would expect. From page 125]:

I've managed to turn objects balanced on a steel needle, wood toothpick, plastic toothpick, safety pin, knifeblade point, fork tine, letter opener, metal spike, knitting needle, sharp-pointed chunk of stone, tip of needle-nosed pliers, ballpoint pens, pencils—the point is, I believe, well made.

A point of interest—small objects make for big problems:

This has been a special problem from the beginning of this effort, although it wasn't recognized at first, little understood later, and is still a baffler now, even if we can identify what is so baffling. The smaller and denser the object the more difficult it is to move. And very small objects, even when light in weight, are also very difficult to move. The why of all this lies beyond grasp (at least for now).

[While success at turning the targets was the general rule, it was (and is, today) by no means the 100 percent rule. Sometimes every target in the room could be turning, and the next day, not a thing. Marty comments on one such occasion. From page 148]:

The comedown was enormous. All the questions flew through the vacant space where only the night before I'd had a mind glowing with energy and success. Why? What was wrong? What in the hell is the matter? Is this draining oneself of this energy? Is the field somehow being blocked? Its bullshit time again, boys and girls, because there really was only one question and one question only, why did the effect I desired, vanish?

I spent most of the day appalled at what had happened. I tried the entire gamut of almost savage concentration and teeth hurting from being ground together, to that sneaky peripheral assault of "not really looking at" the targets.

I gave it up and had occasion to go through a filing drawer. I looked up casually from my work to my desk—and everything began to move. The only thing that wasn't moving was me. I didn't dare move in case I disturbed the energy flow, or whatever the hell it was that pulsed through the room.

[Over those first few weeks, he made a bit of progress, both in his own abilities and in his attitude to keep on with it. From pages 211–214]:

When you've spun up 85 grams to a whirring blur and it finally hurls itself with its rotational speed off the end of copper sheeting tracks, there's no need to return to the small and lightweight targets with which I began this testing program. Right?

Wrong. The rule of Use it or lose it stays in effect. Its like gravity. Doesn't matter whether or not you try to get up and move about, gravity is still in effect despite anything you do or don't do. The same manner of rule applies to the telekinetic ability, and the learning curve doesn't offer any free lunch. You stay with it or you experience your ability diminishing. The big reward from "staying with it" appears in unexpected ways. After the days become weeks and the weeks become months you're aware one day that you've really been hammering at this stuff long enough for the persistence to make a difference. There isn't excessive reward in constant repetition. The goals fade under those conditions, and the better you become the more difficult become the new goals and the greater their chance of failure. Which leads inevitably to the feeling of "aw, to hell with it," and let's get on with more pleasurable pursuits. That's the death-knell, the end of the line, and in this new program, like any other with real challenge to it, sticking to the effort is as important as any intrinsic or developed ability . . .

[Marty began trying to move things when the mood struck, rather than just as an experiment. From pages 225–226]:

I was now into trying different target shots whenever the mood hit, and I'd "aim" at anything. About ten feet from my desk, atop a filing cabinet, I kept the tinsel target of the inverted pie pan of 5-inch diameter and all the tape and brass center atop a tall knitting needle and the tinsel hanging down from four points. From a distance of ten feet I can just look at this thing and almost always it starts to turn. The room is dead still, no one is about, the air is turned off, the windows are closed—and this thing begins to turn and sometimes with amazing rotational speed.

Its become a "fun machine", for me. To turn around and see the target, about a foot tall, motionless, and then to stare at it and commence turning motion is an absolute gas. Sometimes I'd extend one arm, fingers stiff, and this would function as a magic wand also to bring on the turning. Then, for the hell of it, I'd turn my back to the target, study it through a mirror and then watch it begin to turn. It would often turn in spurts, stop suddenly and reverse direction. At times it would turn so fast it created a breeze in its turning and the lower part of the hanging tinsel would trail behind not as if in a wind but because they are in a wind.

These are the successful moments that make one feel like Merlin is alive and well. Its an eerie sensation, most of the time it takes place when I'm alone (but just as frequently when people are present), and having that target of Christmas tinsel and pie plate whirling about is satisfaction indeed.

[But even then, as now, the idea of *proving* this to anyone was far from his mind. From page 230]:

I am anxious to get into some deeper thinking on this entire affair, but to close out this chapter properly in the taking of notes for the journal its necessary to bring in other elements. Little by little a few elements of the scientific community have been drawn into this affair of telekinetics. Its a slow and careful procedure because, first and foremost, and although this may be repetitious it can never be over-emphasized, proving the ability to move a physical object at a distance with the power of the mind only, and no other movement or contact, is a route on which I refuse to travel. There is a vast difference between meeting the needs of honest curiosity or even inquiry, or, for that matter, even letting anyone capable of such judgment and study doing everything they want to disprove what is and has been happening.

But to prove it to try to change another person's mind?

Screw that. No way. What they think or believe is of absolutely no consequence. It is the honesty and the intent of the investigator that prompts my cooperation.

[I believe Marty and I hit it off so well because of this last point. There is something so far unexplained going on with Marty's telekinetics. I, like him, am not interested in the "if" but rather the "how" and "why." From pages 243–246]:

In attempting to understand just what is telekinetics, not does it work but how and why we've got it to work, we stumble into the mystical. The scientists reject the mystical and set up their minimum standards of repeatability and proof, and its tough (if not impossible) to fault those standards. Along comes some cat and says, "Hey, I can fly!"

Well, the scientists have been trying this scene for a long time and all they've got is busted noses, wreckage and a wrecked checking account, so quickly they dismiss this outsider and his claims with a snarl of, "Piss off." And they are absolutely right. You can either do something or you can't. If you can do it then you must be able to repeat it. If you can't repeat it the entire issue is in doubt and must be rejected. That's the law of Reality and it makes sense.

On the morning of the 17th of December 1903 every scientist and engineer in the world who insisted that man could not fly in a machine that was heavier-than-air and controllable by a man was absolutely correct in that statement. The statement was fact, as attested to (1) the wreckage of hopeful aeronauts littering the countryside (and the Potomac), and (2), the absence of any demonstrable, repeatable action of a man flying in such a powered machine.

So they were absolutely correct. That morning. Now, come the late afternoon of the 17th of December 1903, every scientist and engineer in the world who hewed to this insistence of the impossibility of such flight was dead wrong. So there seems to be something to this idea that you're wrong until you're right. At Kill Devil Hill the brothers were Wright.

Well, back to our stumbling. There would be no real justification for this journal if our experience in telekinetics were restricted to the non-repeatable on demand from a source outside of ourselves.

Therein lies the key. After several hundred repeated demonstrations of turning and moving physical objects from a distance, under glass, exposed to the air, through mirrors, on direct vision, through television monitors, around corners, by memory, through the gaze of others, and from photographs, and many other such tests—all of which have been repeated as often as it was required to be repeated—we're standing on the sandy slopes of our own Kill Devil Hill by Kitty Hawk. The TK ability we've repeated now so many thousands of times is still a ludicrous hop-skip-jump compared to what we believe it can be and will be, but then, the first fully successful flight of the Wright Flyer didn't reach from one side of a baseball field to another.

That's why we stand so firmly to our position and we dismiss the naysayers who holler, "I don't believe none of that!"

Okay. Don't believe it. It doesn't change anything.

With that stated, we're back to delving deep into science to discover the what, how and why of telekinetic movement, because at this writing, on this page of this journal, we still lack answers to those questions. And what is so damned confounding is that when we turn to the hardest, most impersonal, proof-based science for the answers, we stand before a fork in the road with seemingly infinite choices because the view before us changes constantly.

And that, friends, is the real turd in this punchbowl.

[And from page 248]:

Does this tell us, then, that all these roads must lead to a basic and simplistic universe of one, that all is a mystical poetry, and there is universal harmony? How childishly delightful and delightfully childish! If you search hard enough I'm sure you'll find a thousand eloquent phrases and turns of the words to be extracted from poet and ponderer, mystic and physicist, scientist and philosopher, all of which after intense examination and a lifetime of searching will draw you to the Inevitable Conclusion that we really don't know . . .

[From pages 256–257]:

Telekinetics is impossible. The scientists tell me this (except for a few who've stared and checked out everything we've just described) and I guess they must be right.

The atom is indivisible.

Man cannot fly.

Space travel is fantasy only and will never happen.

You can't fly faster than sound.

Braided rings about a planet are impossible (sorry, Saturn).

Okay; okay.

The point is that these things keep right on turning even when I yield to the awesome cerebral pressure of the scientists and finally I admit, yes! you're right! it's impossible! I'm going along with all that brainpower out there. I'll be good. I'll accept that its impossible. They're right and I'm wrong. I admit that a mental force cannot turn a physical object in the way I've described.

I keep telling myself that. I stick pins in my eyeballs (figuratively, of course) to punish myself for such bad thoughts as believing these things can turn. By God, I'll show those who say telekinetic energy is real in a world that demands physical measurement for everything! I'll show 'em! So now I have listened, I have trusted, I have obeyed thine commandments of disbelief and

The things keep right on turning.

Is the answer in the brain? Is the answer in the mind? Is it brain-mind or mind-brain? Damned if I know. Oh, I've gone into that area, of course. Digging, researching, studying, asking, going to the best, plumbing the depths of the best sources, and after decades of this sort of thing I came up almost empty-handed or empty-minded. Or whatever I managed to glean from the scientists who offered to represent they know how the mind works, and, how to pinpoint the source of what might be a telekinetic thrust from the mind.

I'll tell you right now and save us all a great deal of time: *these jokers do not know.*

[Of course, there have been a number of people who, over the years since the time Martin Caidin has begun his work with telekinetics, have observed, poked and prodded, but with no success as to the "how" or the "why," myself included. We have little handle on what psychokinesis can be, but unlike many of the scientists who have observed Marty, I and a few of my colleagues really want to understand, to rule out any other explanation. Scientists want repeatability, but they also have other agendas in accepting evidence as proof that relate to their knowledge base, to their standing in the society of Science, and to their interest in the phenomena displayed before them. From pages 276–278]:

The researchers have produced whole volumes on cases of poltergeists, those noisy and usually pissed-off ghosts or mental shadows (usually of children) who fling things around houses and in fields, wreck furniture and generally tear a place apart. Do *not* mistake this position of mine as saying there ain't no such thing. Plenty of solid eyewitness and personal accounts through the centuries lend great substance to such an issue, but the problem faced centuries ago and still being faced today is that poltergeist performance isn't available on demand. Who's going to tell the parapsychological entity of an angry child what to do and when and how to do it? Is the poltergeist an identifiable entity, or, is a force radiating from the subconscious of the child or adult about whom the poltergeist effect takes place? Slamming doors and windows, moving furniture, rocks flying through the air, crockery smashing itself to pieces . . . this is the stuff of which scientists grasp to heap scorn upon the events and the people involved.

You can hardly summon up spontaneous human combustion as an *order*. So the scientists who examine charred remains of bodies where even the bones of the deceased have been ground by heat to ashes, and the chair in which they sit is untouched(i), nod and harrumph and scratch their noses and their asses and really conclude nothing at all. There are scientists who have seen men and women walk barefoot across blazing coals so hot that a log dropped on them explodes in flames, yet the fire walkers emerge from their *direct* skin exposure to such heat and flame without so much as a smudge. It's happened so many times and for so many centuries that it seems impossible that scientists could still find substance of denial.

They do so because they write the books and they set the standards of belief for the vast majority of people who are not witness to such moments and events. There's the rub. It's all a matter of remembering. If you don't think so, then picture in your mind a great bombing raid of the Second World War over Europe. On one day more than two thousand American heavy bombers will take to the air to attack Germany. That's twenty thousand men in those planes. Fifteen hundred fighters will escort them. That makes the number 21,500 men. Hundreds of bombers and fighters will fly diversionary strikes to draw off the German fighters. Add another three thousand men. Now we've got just about twenty-five thousand men in one enormous air battle across Europe. Hundreds of men will die and many hundreds more will be chewed up by fire and bullet and cannon shell. The ground will be littered with wreckage. The world will shake from the thunder of thousands of engines and the crash of tens of thousands of bombs. Smoke and fury and hell and fire and—

Come back an hour later. The skies will be clean, the air will be fresh, the smoke will be gone, the great metal machines will be silent on the ground.

No one can prove that the battle ever took place. Sure as God made little green apples the best scientists who ever lived couldn't prove beans about it. Its all a matter of faith and memory. Pieces of wreckage on the ground and dead bodies prove only that you've got pieces of wreckage and dead bodies.

Martin Caidin has been ill for a few months, as of this writing (October 1995), but is coming back to full booming health (faster than the doctors expected, as I would expect). By the time you read this, I am hopeful that the first stage of a research project with Martin Caidin and others he has taught to turn the targets will be at least underway, if not over.

As of this past summer, physicist George Weissmann, John Klimo of Rosebridge Graduate School for Integrative Psychology, and myself have met a few times and have discussed the feasibility of building an enclosed space in which we can set up targets for Marty and others to try their "mind pushes." In the space, which will be glass walled and sealed, we also plan to have a number of measurement devices to check everything from temperature variations, air currents, and electrostatic fields that could otherwise explain some of the movements of the targets, and other devices such as microwave, magnetic, and radiation detectors to look for any anomalous energies that could be connected with the effects.

We're looking for the "how" and the "why." The targets turn, of that I am certain.

So, how can *you* do this? Make a few targets for yourself, starting out with a square of plain paper 3x3 inches, folded diagonally, so a pyramid form results. Put a piece of sturdy tape in the apex (so the sharp point of the pivot won't wear through). Balance it on a needle or long pin stuck into a base of cork or clay or wax. (See insert for photos and drawings of the targets).

Set the target set-up on a table or desk, preferably a sturdy one that won't vibrate much if you knock it. Place your hands, open palmed, on either side of the target, your little fingers touching the table, your thumbs on top pointed toward the sky, your palms facing the target.

Press down with your hands, lean a bit forward and breathe regularly (helps you relax). Visualize, "see", the target turning in your mind. Let your eyes drift out of focus. "See" the target moving on its own, like it is weightless. Count backward from twenty or thirty, bearing down with your hands harder, but *not* mentally concentrating or trying to push the target. As you get to zero, relax your hands, your whole body, and continue to mentally "see" the target turning.

Hopefully, what you mentally visualize will begin to happen.

Some people do better if as they relax at the end of the countdown, they think of a serene scene (like a nice forest or meadow or beach).

Keep in mind that a little turning is a good thing. "Expect some failure," says Marty. "It's no big deal. Just walk away from it, then come back and do it again."

Marty suggests a painter's mask to diffuse your breath, but you might jump right to putting the target under a thin-glassed dome, like the kind collectors use for dolls and clocks (which you can usually pick up at a crafts store).

"Get used to working with the targets in the same place, under the same conditions. It may take enormous self-discipline, with a minimum of fifteen to twenty minutes or even up to an hour a day trying. After a while, you fall into a pattern and things start turning almost immediately. Once you get into the routine of this, there's a subconscious element that takes over."

As you get some movement with your hands around the target, try relaxing them at your sides or in your lap. Keep the mental target going until the visualization is almost second nature. Then try working the target from a little further away, and start playing with multiple targets.

Marty likes to decorate the sides of the targets, making it easy to tell if one of them makes just a quarter turn or more. Try different materials, different kinds of paper stock, foil, or other materials until you feel comfortable with one or more.

A nice side benefit is that this works as a nice stress reliever, provided you don't make the task of turning the targets stressful in and of itself.

"If they try very hard and strain to 'push,' it won't work. You'd be blocking it by trying so hard. If you fight it, push it, you get angry at it, you're not going to get anywhere.

"You must become part of, merge with, what you're going to do." This is something I've also heard from various martial artists.

"Once you either see someone else do this, or you get some movement yourself, your skepticism starts to break down and let's your belief start to happen. Once you start doing this and stick with it, it'll get better."

As with other forms of physical and mental performance, confidence is important. "Doubt and disbelief hamper things. The only key seems to be belief."

Does Martin Caidin believe we are simply rediscovering something our primitive ancestors had a better handle on? Or is this a new faculty to which we're evolving?

"I do not believe, as many scientists say, that this was once the province of the primitive mind, that Man, a long time ago, uncluttered by the modern world as he is now, was more capable of telekinetics or other powers of the mind. I think that that's so much bushwah!

"The very fact that kids today at ten years old know more than people who had lived their entire lives before, the ability to learn, to communicate with one another, the benefit of all the scientific and cultural achievements before us, gives us the chance to use the brain better than we have before.

"And I believe we're reaching a point, if man doesn't wipe himself out in a nuclear war, if man remains on this planet for a while, he will gain the ability through his mind to begin to cure his own body."

As you read earlier in the book (Chapter Five), Caidin has not only worked wonders on his own body, but also has taught and written about a technique to lower blood pressure that many, many professional pilots swear by. But it is belief in at least the possibility of success that works its wonders on the mind.

"All you're doing in telekinesis is freeing your mind. Not everyone can do it." Meaning, not just the TK, but not everyone is able to easily open their minds up to new ideas, to break down programmed belief-driven barriers.

"The key is this: If you think it's impossible, you're not going to turn a damned thing. If you believe it's possible, you're on your way. Let your mind be free. Let it be unfettered. Cast off the shackles that our society and our science puts on ourselves because they're protecting themselves [from new ideas] and amazing things will happen.

"But it all takes place in that great, great long journey between your right ear and your left ear.

"And that's what I tell people, and it works!"

Faking It

"That's all well and good," says the debunker, "but any magician worth his salt can duplicate those psychokinetic effects. That invalidates them as evidence. What you saw *could* have been fraud."

That argument has been used by debunkers and disbelievers, many of whom incorrectly call themselves "skeptics" (which indicates an open, undecided perspective, rather than one where disbelief is the rule). There's some validity to that argument, as parapsychologists (and magicians) have learned over the years. But there are also flaws in that argument.

Just because something *could* have been fraudulently produced does not make it so. It may decrease the value of the evidence as proof, given that the circumstances under which the effect of, say, metal-bending or computer influencing would have to be carefully scrutinized to eliminate the probability of fraud and any opportunity for it. One can never completely eliminate fraud as a possibility, since there's always the chance that the experimenter or observer or reporter had lied about what he or she witnessed.

Of course, experimenter fraud occurs in all fields of science. Incompetence also occurs in all fields. In fact, I would like to think that parapsychologists, because of the potential for fraud by subjects, and because of the difficulty in trying to accumulate proof of psi phenomena, have been more watchful of one another.

Fraud does occur in the performance of psychic feats. Of that there is no argument. People who put themselves forward as "gifted" subjects have, over the decades, caused severe headaches for parapsychologists and others observers. Fraud has been uncovered in many circumstances, and suspected in many others.

However, the idea that because fraud *can* happen it always *does* happen is absurd.

Over the years, I have investigated many, many cases of apparitions, poltergeists, and hauntings. My colleagues and I always look for the "normal" causes first, which may include fraud. I personally have encountered fraud on the part of the people reporting the situation only a very few times once I have gotten to the investigation stage (many of the calls I get I have to dismiss because of there not being enough to the case to investigate, or because the motives of the people are to gain publicity and/or money and that leads me to suspect they may be making most, if not all, of the situation up). Those cases that I did investigate that involved fraud showed me that the fraud was perpetrated on other members of the family, not on the scientist/investigator.

Many people claiming psychokinetic abilities, whether they be bending metal, healing someone, or levitating an object, have been caught at fraud over the years. Others have been accused of fraud but never caught, their skills never duplicated under the same conditions.

For example, Ted Serios, who was able to affect film and somehow cause images to appear, was well researched under excellent controlled conditions by psychologist Jule Eisenbud. While the effect of getting an image on film was duplicated, it could not be duplicated under exactly the same conditions that Eisenbud tested Serios.

Does the duplication of a reported psychic effect mean it doesn't *really* happen? Hardly, though one must always watch for such possibilities.

Taking this idea of duplication eliminating the possibility of reality outside of the paranormal, one would have to question most of reality today. Magicians have for decades been able to create the appearance of miracles, some of which mimic scientific realities.

Special effects artists have clearly been able to duplicate not only that which exists, but also things that lived millions of years ago (in *Jurassic Park*) as well as things that exist only in the imagination. Does the fact that the movie *Earthquake* simulated a real quake mean that earthquakes don't exist? Does the *Earthquake* ride at Universal Studios mean that because we can duplicate such an event it doesn't happen?

The films *Apollo 13* and the older (predictive) film *Marooned* effectively duplicated space flight on film. Does this mean films of the Apollo spacecraft shot by NASA are phonies? Hardly.

Granted that some of what the skeptics say is true: one must always be on the careful watch for fraud or (more commonly) for more "normal" explanations that may be perceived as paranormal ones. However, the possibility of fraud or duplication does not invalidate a phenomenon. It merely means that with human "performers" involved, one must question the events more and observe them more carefully, with insight.

As I discussed earlier in this book, while some magicians such as the Amazing Randi, and Penn & Teller are clearly in the debunker camp, disdaining the idea that psychic phenomena might actually be real, most magicians are not averse to that idea. Some have gone on record that they either accept the possibility of ESP and PK or that they have had some psi experiences of their own.

In 1983, a panel of magicians and mentalists convened by sociologist and skeptic Marcello Truzzi at the Parapsychological Association Convention discussed a number of issues connecting conjuring, fraud, and psychic phenomena. On the panel was noted critic and magician the late Milbourne Christopher, the Amazing Randi, Anthony Raven (mentalist), Scott Gordon (mentalist), the late Jack Malon (mentalist), Robert Cassidy (mentalist) and myself. As I recall, Malon and Raven discussed having psi experiences of their own, and Raven, Gordon, Cassidy, Truzzi and Malon (and me, of course) expressed their support of work in parapsychology.

Subsequent to that panel, other conventions have included presentations by magicians, including Boston area mentalists James

Rainho and Ray Goulet, and Cornell psychologist and mentalist Darryl Bem.

Because of the flurry of accusations of fraud surround the '70s superpsychics and because of the media latching on to the statements of the skeptics and debunkers, researchers have been aware of the need to watch out for fraud. The fact that I am a performing magician is due to this trend, since the master's degree program I graduated from at John F. Kennedy University included a one-unit course on psychic fraud and magic (which I taught for a few years on my return as a faculty member there in 1983).

Researchers are on their toes with respect to suspected fraud, but many I have talked to are more concerned about fraud conceived and executed by debunking magicians such as James Randi and colleagues than they are about off the street phony psychics. In other words, given the circumstances of research today, researchers have had a concern that skeptics might try to "set them up," as opposed to being especially worried about a self-professed psychic being a fraud. Researchers have gotten much smarter, and I and other magicians (generally friendly, open minded ones) have consulted with a number of them over the years.

But the real issue is not the researchers being taken in, for that leads to very little in the way of monetary loss by anyone. The real problems occur because members of the general public are taken in with non-entertainment situations.

Perhaps the biggest problem with fraudulent PK is that the average person can be easily taken in by it, merely because it exists within a mysterious realm. If PK were accepted as a real part of human experience/ability, it would become quite "normal," and there might be less motivation to even perpetrate such fraud.

As mentioned in Chapter Nine, Uri Geller is perhaps the most controversial figure in the recent history of psychic performers. I pretty much said my piece about him in that chapter, so let me turn to another recent figure on the scene.

In April 1994, I had the opportunity to observe another Israeli claiming psychic powers, my first report appearing in the November, 1994 issue of *Fate* magazine (part of the following is drawn from that article).

Claiming such abilities as metal-bending through mind over matter, clairvoyance of contents of sealed boxes, levitation of small objects, and the ability to drive (or read) while blindfolded, Ronny Marcus offered to be the subject of controlled experiments and demonstrations in Berkeley, Santa Cruz and Concord, California, as well as in other parts of the U.S. His goal, apparently, was to prove to several researchers that he could do all he claimed through psychic means.

Before his arrival in this country, I was contacted by a few people who had been referred to me because of my dual expertise in parapsychology and as a magician. I was provided with a list describing some of Marcus's talents. I read them over, undoubtably rolling my eyes as I did.

To be honest, I have long been concerned that some of the skeptics might try an attempted set-up of researchers (there had been such a major setup in the early 1980s). So when I read the descriptions of Marcus's achievements, which included a description of him bending metal, "reading" with his fingertips and driving around blindfolded, I couldn't decide whether to be interested, to laugh, or to be worried. Actually, all three reactions were appropriate (together).

The blindfold effects were particularly interesting from the magician's standpoint. While not the easiest of effects to fake (if you have bad vision and don't wear contacts, that is), reading something while blindfolded is a common effect amongst mentalists (performers whose "magic" simulates psychic powers, such as mind reading). Driving while blindfolded is a common and long-standing publicity stunt by mentalists.

While I can't reveal the method for professional reasons, suffice it to say that the following speaks for itself:

"SIGHTLESS VISION"
Revello

You've read about it. You've heard about it. You've seen it. Now it's yours. The blindfold act that's been baffling television audiences. Just think, the audience places a piece of cardboard over your eyes

then plasters it with putty, dough, etc. and covers that with cotton and then adhesive tape. A blindfold is then placed over all this and if that isn't enough a black hood is laced completely over your head and tied around your neck. Yet with this super method, you can drive a car, write and duplicate numbers and names written on a blackboard, play pool, ride a bike, pick out colors named and scores of other impossible feats. Full instructions including hood.
L-177 . . . **$10.00**

. . . From *Tannen's Catalog of Magic* #17, Louis Tannen, Inc., New York, NY

TEN DOLLARS???

Hopefully, without giving away a secret, I have at least given you the idea that this is not an impossible feat of psychic prowess. Most of the other descriptions read like descriptions of magic and mental effects as well.

I was extremely surprised that Ronny Marcus would actually claim this kind of blindfold effect as psychic when he had to know that sooner or later he'd run up against a magician or two who would know instantly what was going on. To my mind, if he were truly psychic he should have know not to use this kind of effect for his psychic demonstrations.

So you might say I was a bit biased against him as a "genuine psychic" right from the start. But, I was still interested in seeing his stuff.

Before he arrived in Northern California, I spent time on the phone providing suggestions to a couple of the scientists who would be observing Marcus. My suggestions to a group in Berkeley who would be seeing him first were fairly minor, since they had thought out some interesting controls against fraud based on the descriptions of Marcus's talents. I was asked to come to the University of California at Santa Cruz for Marcus's second appearance, but was unable to, due to work conflicts. However, I did provide a few suggestions to my contact there, which included having some other magicians who were knowledgeable there to observe.

It turned out that the guys I suggested were also suggested by others, so Santa Cruz was well covered. I was to be informed of

Marcus's performances in both Berkeley and Santa Cruz before he would come to the third site, Rosebridge Graduate School for Integrative Psychology in Concord, where I would be on hand.

After a very disappointing showing for a group of physicists in Berkeley on April 3rd, wherein he was unable to produce any effects under controlled laboratory conditions, Ronny Marcus tried his best to convince the second group at UC Santa Cruz on the 4th.

Unfortunately for Marcus, physicist-magician David Knapp of Lawrence Livermore Laboratories and sleight of hand expert Steven Youell of Martinez, were on hand throughout the session. As time got closer, I was involved in full discussion with Youell and Knapp, both very good friends of mine and, I truly believe, unbiased toward single events being "real" or "fraud. In other words, I trust them to keep their minds open when observing ostensible psychic phenomena. They also acted, I believe, in a non-adversarial way during the session in Santa Cruz. If he couldn't perform, for Dave and Steve to keep low key throughout would help avoid any claim by Marcus that his psychic abilities were hampered by their negative behavior.

So, Marcus was given "free reign" so the researchers could see what he could do. What Knapp and Youell saw was a lot of simulation, and nothing they could construe as other than magic effects and manipulation. "And he wasn't even good at it," said Youell, referring to Marcus's sleight of hand technique.

Marcus did a bit of spoon bending, attempted to clairvoyantly see inside sealed boxes, and levitated a matchbox off his palm. Blindfolded, he walked around the room, then "read" the serial numbers off a dollar bill. "We had a guy do the blindfold drive bit in Concord, California" said Youell, "at a magic convention a couple of years ago." He and Knapp pointed out how the blindfold routine is a very common one in mental magic acts. "And you can buy it for ten dollars," added Youell.

Youell, by the way, appeared more annoyed by Marcus being a "lousy magician" (my interpretation of what he said) than being a phony psychic, and at Marcus not willing to admit to what he had done once he was clearly caught. After I watched Marcus, I thought Steve had been kind in that assessment. The man is no entertainer.

One of the things we had discussed prior to their observation of Marcus was the man's motives. If Marcus, up front, admitted that he was gearing up for an entertainment career, then while we all would have been as careful in checking him for fraud in an experimental setting, we would also handle things a bit differently in our final evaluation, possibly even supporting him as a good entertainer (without supporting his claims of psychic powers, of course).

But his motives were not for entertainment. Neither, apparently, was his skill.

I received reports from witnesses at both the Berkeley and Santa Cruz sessions before my own session with him. Youell, Knapp and I had a lengthy conversation as to their interaction with and observations of Marcus in Santa Cruz and I felt well prepared.

The third session with Marcus in the Bay Area occurred the 5th of April at an open session at Rosebridge Graduate School in Concord. Marcus was originally to come in and do demonstrations for a group, but due to his miserable performance the two previous sessions, he offered only to lead the group in their own metal-bending. I was there to observe, along with my associate Barbara Gallagher, and several colleagues such as Jerry Solfvin, Jon Klimo, and fellow JFKU graduate Mike Smith. In addition, I had a video camera with me to capture Marcus on tape (one of three cameras there, actually).

What I saw (and taped) was amazing. Marcus led the group in a very subdued session where he talked them into closely focusing in on their utensils in hand. He held a spoon himself, and at the end of a lengthy period of time, he showed the spoon apparently bending in his hand.

What I saw, and what my camera captured, was Marcus, over an approximately 20 minute time period, physically bend and twist his spoon, while most eyes were focused on their own metal pieces. At one point, Marcus met my eyes and I nodded, which, I believe, prompted him to come over to me at a break.

He asked me why I was taking notes (I was noting the time code on the video as to when he actually did the bending so I could rewind to it directly), whether I was a journalist. I told him I wrote for *Fate,* that I was also on faculty at Rosebridge as a parapsychologist, but that my notes were of what actions he did. I then told him I was also a magician and that "the two guys you met yesterday are good friends of mine." He didn't appear very happy.

After the break, he began by talking about his own bending, how little happened with everyone else (there were a few others who had bent spoons, including a man seated next to me whose spoon sure looked to me like it bent over by itself). He then spoke of a "chain" that was the group, and that the group "energy" could only be as strong as its "weakest link," and that there was a "weak link" in the crowd (that would have been me). Therefore, his performance, and the audience's wasn't the best.

After a short dressing down by Jon Klimo with regards to this evident cop-out, I spoke up as the "weak link." I had not intended to redress Marcus in front of the crowd, but as with what he did with my friends the day before, he forced me out. I spoke to him and the audience of my background as a researcher and investigator who had both experienced and observed PK, then stated flatly that what Marcus did was clearly not PK, but physical manipulation.

The audience reaction was mixed. Many spoke up saying Marcus couldn't have faked it, because they were watching. A couple of others said they saw what I described very clearly. Marcus first denied it, then kept quiet. As things broke up, I was happy to replay the video to show the doubters that he could have manipulated the spoon as I described. Then, I bent a key from my key ring, repeatedly (it was bent to begin with), to illustrate that even close up one may not be in a position to see what is hidden unless one knows where to look.

Marcus left the Bay Area, canceling some other appearances.

Does Ronny Marcus have any real PK or clairvoyant abilities? As far as the Bay Area is concerned, the answer is no. He could perform nothing under even light controls, and when left to his own devices, he clearly faked the phenomena. And based on his choice of tasks as a psychic, I have to say he's not terribly imaginative, given that those tasks are clearly available to magicians and mentalists.

But does such a fraudulent situation mean that all PK is fraud or misperception?

Many debunkers would have us believe that. My question is, does a fraud in the medical field invalidate all doctors? Does someone pretending to be an expert or a performer of any kind mean no one is genuine at what they do?

Of course not. It just means that there are phonies out there, not that everyone is a phony. It just means we have to take each person, each event, and each reported phenomenon separately.

Two months later, I was working with author/investigator Martin Caidin in a workshop in Larkspur, California, where he was teaching people to turn targets on pivots, even under glass. While not all our attendees were able to affect the simple targets, about half had some (or much) movement, and I've heard from a few of them that they are still able to affect the targets they took home. Further research is planned to see just how good people can get in learning Caidin's PK tasks.

But how was it possible for Marcus to convince most of the group at Rosebridge that what he was doing was "real"? That answer's not a simple one, since it involves a few issues.

First and foremost is that people who come to see a demonstration of reputed psychic ability (or a demonstration of anything) might be biased for or against what they expect to witness. Believers in the reality or probability of PK, who are coming to watch PK, are more likely to unconsciously miss any suspicious moves or behavior, partly because without being educated in what kinds of moves might be considered "suspicious," there's no way to consciously, properly catalog what is being seen. Disbelievers or people predisposed to the nonexistence of PK, may also not see or identify suspicious movements for what they are, but are more likely to disbelieve or be suspicious of what they're seeing because of their bias.

I would guess that most of the attendees at the session were biased in the "PK does exist" direction, since this was an invitational event not advertised to the public.

The second reason why the majority of people at the Rosebridge session might have been "fooled" by Marcus is that he was misdirecting them to watch their own spoons. In other words, most people, focused on their own hands rather than Marcus's, could hardly have been aware of any suspicious or overtly fraudulent moves he might have made.

In observing any apparent demonstration of ESP or PK, people's beliefs, knowledge base, and expectations work together to allow for the acceptance or nonacceptance that what they are seeing is really psi. In addition, I think most people want to believe that an individual presenting them with any information or demonstrations is who and what he/she says. I know I'd like to believe people are inherently honest and good, though I know better.

Faking something like metal-bending has become part and parcel of the literature and apparatus of the magician and mentalist. There are several books on the subject and a number of magic effects one can buy that either helps in the bending of keys and utensils, or simulates the process.

I, myself, still keep that bent key on my key ring, and have probably "bent" it hundreds of times. In fact, in the photo insert you can see a brief progression of shots showing me doing just that.

Metal-bending on the fraudulent (entertainment) level involves 1) the assumption that a key held in the hand is straight, especially if the performer can show it that way to begin with, 2) the assumption that the fingers of the hand are not strong enough to bend the key or utensil, and 3) the ability of the performer to hide a bend in the key or utensil that he or she put there, revealing the bend slowly so it looks like it's actually bending in the hand.

How does it bend and what's the exact method of revelation? I'm afraid the ethics of my art prevent me from revealing the various methods in this kind of book. However, I will say that the principles rely heavily on perception, the expectations of the audience, and the ability of a performer to understand the psychology of both of those.

People often question the "ethics excuse" that magicians and mentalists use, as I did above. There are a couple of reasons why magicians don't like to reveal their "secrets."

One of them is that we're trying to protect trade secrets that, if they were known by all, could allow other magicians to copy an effect or an act that a performer may have spent long hours learning and perfecting.

Secondly, such revelation would cause the audience to lose interest in watching magicians perform. Some people go to magic shows to figure things out, others to watch because they are amazed and *can't* imagine how things are done. There's a major element of the *sense of wonder* that we all feel when we watch stage and close-up magic being performed.

Revealing secrets of magic often cuts at that sense of wonder. People would be disappointed *because* they now know the secrets and the audience, the vital part of the reason for performing, could itself vanish. If people are no longer amazed and in wonderment at the magic, they may have no reason to hire or pay money for a magician.

When it comes right down to it, *anyone* can walk into a magic shop, plunk down some cash or credit card and buy whatever is for sale. There are plenty of books on how to do magic in your local public library, and some at the book store. *Anyone* can read those books.

But, of course, to make the effort to find the books or to buy and learn the effects does require the effort. That would indicate a real interest in how and why magic works, an indication that it's unlikely that the person learning the "secrets" is doing so for no good reason, and an indication that such a person will have an appreciation for the methods themselves.

My friends often ask whether I get bored watching other performers, since I know how things are done.

First of all, *no one in magic and mentalism knows how all effects are done!* New methods and new twists on old methods are constantly being looked for and released to the magical community (generally for purchase). If not, no one would buy any new magic effects, and there are many new ones on the market every month.

Secondly, one can have an appreciation for the performance of one's own art form. Strange that I've never heard the "aren't you bored?" question asked of writers or actors or dancers or athletes. One can appreciate the performance of another in all sorts of arts and sciences, so why not in conjuring?

In fact, the method, the secret is hardly the "all" of a magic performance. Just how the magician actually *presents* the effect is at least half of what a good magician is. I have seen (too) many magicians who are technically excellent at what they do, with moves or methods that are near undetectable, but who are lousy in the presentation skills department. Those people are not terribly interesting for non-magician audiences. They are not entertaining.

So, in looking back at Ronny Marcus, I'd have to say he was a "bad" fraud. His methods were a bit weak (easy to spot, if you had any understanding of the methods at all), but more importantly, he'd make a lousy entertainer. His presentation skills, his enthusiasm and ability to convince an audience of even his sincerity of belief in his own powers and his excitement (lack of, in his case) in sharing these abilities were just not there.

Whatever one wants to say about the reality or trickery of Uri Geller's psychic abilities, he is an *exceptional* entertainer and presenter. His enthusiasm and his sense of wonder at psychic abilities, his own or those of others, is contagious and makes believing him that much easier.

The methods of PK fraud therefore rely on more than sheer mechanics for the abilities to be believed. But, since PK is a physical thing, to someone watching a performer of PK, knowing some of the methods of fraud is handy.

There are a number of ways to levitate a small object. Most often, magnets and so-called "invisible threads" are used. Objects which look to be nonmagnetic may be gimmicked in some way so that there is a magnetic attraction or repulsion possible. Very fine threads, usually nylon, can be secretly attached to objects, and depending on the lighting, one would have a near impossible chance of seeing them, even if you knew what you were looking for.

Electrical fields can be used to simulate PK. One of my students at JFK University once did a project to simulate PK in this manner. Believe it or not, he attached a battery to his pants leg, so that there would be a minor charge running through him (don't try this at home, folks!). The charge created a static electric build up, which he could direct with his hands.

With the battery connected, he proceeded to turn the pages of a phone book and cause a pencil to move away from his hands without coming closer than a half inch near to the book or the pencil.

Another method might involve the use of a confederate, a helper in the audience. An audience member shouting that the keys on his key ring bent while the "psychic" was concentrating would do two things: 1) reinforce the amazing abilities of the psychic (who, after all, bent not only the key he was concentrating on, but also those of an audience member), and 2) allow the performer a moment where the audience attention is focused away from him (a perfect opportunity to do a little hands on manipulation without being seen by the audience).

There are other methods for moving objects or levitating things that rely on where the focus of attention is.

Try this sometime. While sitting with friends (and discussing psychic phenomena or strange happenings, to set the stage), wait for a distraction from outside the room (could be a car backfiring or a loud noise of some other kind) or ask a helper to create a distraction (breaking something or dropping something that makes a clatter is good).

While people are distracted, grab something from off the table or from a nearby shelf (or have something in your lap), and toss it high into the air (keep it to a small, non-heavy, preferably non-breakable object). If it hits the table or floor just as the others bring their attention back to you, then you may notice their eyes widening and perhaps their jaws dropping (make sure you act amazed, as well).

As a child, I read about a method to cause a table to rise up when doing a seance.

You and a helper should be prepared with long sleeve shirts or jackets. Up the sleeves you should have a sturdy ruler or wood or metal dowel or rod. Keep them hidden. As you and the seance crowd sit around the table, bring your hands to your laps and allow the rods or rulers to slip out slightly from the sleeves. Place your hands on top of the table, flat, but make sure the ruler/rod goes under the lip of the table.

Wait a while. Then, as you or someone else attempts to "contact" the spirits, give your helper a signal and lift up. Because everyone's hands are on the table in full view, it will look like the table is rising on its own.

Make sure, when you're done, to slide the rulers/rods up the sleeves again.

You also might get into the habit, as I have, of taking automatic credit for every odd flicker of light or strange sound or movement that happens around you. Saying "I did that" when something falls off the wall or when the power goes on and off (especially signif-icant if you are talking about PK or ghosts at the time) makes peo-ple begin to wonder about you. . . .

Not all physical effects that might be PK—but are not—are fraud-ulent. In other words, there are plenty of unusual things that can happen which people automatically categorize as psychokinesis, but are not. Unless, of course, you expand the definition, as we have in this book, to include any conscious or unconscious effect of the Mind on Matter.

Take the use of a pendulum to help answer questions, for ex-ample. Most people have done this sometime in their lives. A pen-dulum, hanging straight down, will start swinging left/right for a "No" answer, or up/down for a "Yes." Or perhaps it will go in a cir-cle for a negative and swing back and forth for a positive response to a question asked.

You can buy a number of crystals or talismans on a chain or string which are supposed to have mystic powers. Or, you can use just about anything, including a favorite pendant for this.

The pendulum does appear to swing of its own accord, since you would try to hold it as still as possible, and certainly not move it consciously. But in reality, while it may seem like you are not mov-ing it (or your hand), there are minute muscle impulses respond-ing, moving it, due to subconscious direction.

The idea that we have unconscious movements of our muscles is hard for some to understand. But magicians and mentalists have long understood this. In magic jargon, this is called "muscle-reading" or Hellstromism (named for Axel Hellstrom, one of the earliest and most famous performers of this).

Muscle-reading, which takes lots of practice to learn, involves the performer holding the hand or arm of the volunteer and perceiv-ing slight movements of the muscles which can give away a direction to move (to find a hidden object) or the answer to a question (as with the pendulum).

Today, the Amazing Kreskin is probably the best known (and quite likely the best) performer of this art. I have seen Kreskin both in person (only a few times) and on TV (many times) utilizing muscle-reading to locate a hidden object somewhere in the theater or building in which he is performing. A signature of his act has been to have his paycheck for the event hidden without his knowledge. He grasps the hand or arm of the individual who hid it (often while he, himself, is blindfolded) and leads the volunteer around this way and that, until he has a feel for the right directions to head in, and generally finding the check in only a little more time than if he knew right where it was.

The mind provides, even unconsciously, the information to the muscles, and one can learn to interpret such impulses in another person.

As with the pendulum, the Ouija Board may rely on such unconscious movements of muscles, the subconscious playing the mind over body game. With your own or yours plus the fingers of others placed on the moving piece of the Ouija Board set (the planchette), questions can be asked and the planchette will move around the board, spelling out answers or comments.

Several things are important to remember about the Ouija Board, since many people have concerns about them.

First of all, keep in mind that it's easy for one of the "players" to give an extra, conscious, push without anyone else being aware. A little fraud is easy to do with the Ouija Board.

Secondly, the muscle impulses that move the planchette, when you're playing by yourself, come through the unconscious, as with the pendulum. So, this can be one way to communicate with your inner self. But remember that sometimes the unconscious mind works with metaphor and symbols, so don't take any Ouija advice literally. Interpret it as you would interpret one of your own dreams.

When playing with others, remember that there's no absolute way to determine *whose* unconscious is moving the planchette at any given time, so again be careful in how you take the information. If you have to interpret the information if it came from your own subconscious carefully, be that much more careful when interpreting information that could come from someone else's mind.

Many believe that spirits can come through in this way, and that the Ouija Board can open up pathways for evil spirits and demons to come through. The evidence is to the contrary, with the likelihood in almost all cases that it is the mind of a player that is saying or doing good or bad things with the Ouija Board.

It is Mind over Matter, in the same way any body movements are mind over matter.

In general, one must be cautious in looking at many psychic effects with a physical component, since there can be any number of alternative explanations that have to be considered, from fraud to misinterpretation of "normal" phenomena.

If you are really interested in the methods of the PK fraud (or any other psychic fraud), whether that's because you want to be a better educated consumer, or because you are interested, as I am, in being able to sort out the normal from the paranormal (so you can study the real paranormal events), head out to your local magic shop, read some of the sources I've mentioned in Appendix A, and always think, when you see a demonstration of PK, that there *could be* another explanation.

One final note on behavior once you know the "secrets":

Always remember to consider *why* a person claims magic or psychic powers. If they are performers, entertainers, magicians, mentalists or the like, don't *ever* be like the ten-year-old boy and stop the show in the middle (or at the end) with a comment like "I know how you did that!" That's childish and spoils the fun for others, especially if you then go on to say how it was done (or how you think it was done—you could be wrong on the method, after all).

Learn to recognize and appreciate good performance. That way your sense of wonder about the real phenomena hasn't a chance to vanish.

On the other hand, do be careful as to how you openly accept all claims of paranormal phenomena. There are (too) many phonies out there. Be an educated consumer, but again, don't jump to conclusions that what you're about to see is fraudulent.

After all, just as the performance of a martial artist can seem "impossible," sometimes psychic phenomena can look just like a magic trick.

We're all capable of extraordinary performance. How you judge and whether you accept such performance in others may affect how far you can push past your own "limits."

∗ **End-Game** ∗

What Does This *Really* Mean to You?

So just what has all of this meant to you, personally? What conclusions have you reached after reading about what I've covered here? What are the implications for the future of all of us?

The experiences and talents and performances I've discussed throughout the book run a wide spectrum. We've gone from excellent performance in sports and the martial arts, through unusual, perhaps anomalistic performances by human beings and people who came to be called by special titles like "saints" and "mediums."

We've looked at fire-walking and other accomplishments by people who simply try to do the "impossible." We've explored mental healing and its opposite, the negative affect of the mind on the body.

What did all those things have in common? The fact that the mind can directly affect the body, that we set and break perceived limits of what we can and can't do all the time.

Of course, by "we" I mean humans in general. Individually, we all have varying degrees of what we believe is "possible" and what we believe is "impossible." The first few chapters cover topics of human experience and performance that may be more easily related to in how we can constantly break limits.

The lesson of sports, martial arts, healing and the other examples of the mind-body connection is that our minds do act directly on physical matter. In those instances, I am really talking about the physical matter being that of our own bodies. Of course, while the mind of the individual may be capable of both setting and overcoming its own limits as they relate to the body, the major source of those limits is not the individual.

Society and culture set limits. If most people believe it's impossible to run the three-minute mile, and that's essentially put out as "fact," it will take someone like Roger Bannister, who defied the "fact" of the limit of the four-minute mile, to show us all the error of the limitation.

Human history is filled with examples of people who, through physical performance or through invention, have defied limits set by science, by religion, and by culture. Sometimes the world isn't quite ready for new ideas (as with the case of Galileo and his predecessor, Giordano Bruno, both of whom set about to change the view of the earth's place in the universe, one of whom was jailed, the other executed for their defiance of "fact.").

But when it comes to human physical performance, when a person can truly demonstrate an impossibility, it may convince some more people to try the same, and that impossibility simply becomes a "difficult" task.

Modern medicine has finally had to face up to the idea that it may not have all the answers, that some of the traditional ideas in cultures around the world may, in fact, have more to say to human health. What many of those ideas speak to, and perhaps part of why medicine has to rethink its outlook on them, is that the mind plays a strong role in the healing process, that the mind of the patient can dramatically affect the eventual outcome of the healing process, positively or negatively.

If a patient is told he has eight weeks to live, there might be a couple of reactions.

The patient may take that as "fact," go home and prepare himself to die, emotionally as well as financially and legally. But during that eight week period, the person is *dying,* in both body and mind.

Eight weeks rolls around and the person may be merely "hanging on."

Let's take the opposite reaction. After hearing the sentence of death, the patient decides he's going to fight it, that he won't accept that number of weeks. After all, just how do the doctors know it's "eight" weeks vs. "five" or even "fifteen"? For the next few weeks, that patient tries to have "hope" that the doctors are wrong, and may even seek out other forms of treatment to lengthen the pronounced sentence. In any event, that patient *lives* for those last few weeks.

When the eight weeks rolls around, the patient may still die, though depending on the illness, it could have been a little sooner or a little later. But, there is case upon case on the books of people who have beaten such a sentence of death, who have willed themselves to live past the deadline, even if only for a short time, but sometimes for years to come.

Unfortunately, there are more who have died around the predicted time.

Can I say with total conviction that mental attitude *caused* the beating of the clock or the adherence to the deadline? I can't prove that. But I can say that, at least on the surface, it sure looks like the *will to live,* that fighting the illness sure couldn't hurt, and certainly looks like it may physically help, and pushes the person to die while *living* rather than while dying.

We can *will* ourselves to accomplishment, both physically and mentally, provided we accept that it is our own beliefs that push us forward (and backward). Granted we may believe that God or some magic is aiding us in extraordinary performance, or some Evil force (or even a bad experience in our lives) is holding us back or causing us harm.

But it is our own minds that create the beliefs, and the acceptance or rejections of the beliefs, that affect us physically and mentally.

Mind affects body. The body is matter. Mind over Matter.

For many, it is a leap to believe that the Mind that can truly affect the matter of the body can reach out past the physical body and affect things around it. Direct mental connection with the environment is what most people have typically thought of when hearing the phrase "Mind over Matter."

Can we do it? In the latter part of the book, I presented my own views and some of my personal experiences, as well as the experiences of others. I addressed the scientific evidence for Psychokinesis, for Mind over Matter (beyond the body).

Does it happen? I firmly believe it does. I believe I have experienced it. But I also believe (and here's where I'm probably setting limits on my own psychokinetic abilities) that it has some limits, both on when it can happen (connected to state of mind) and how much it can do.

There are undoubtedly limits to just how much one can physically do with the body, no matter what the Mind believes and how it affects the body. A three-minute mile may be physically impossible for the current configuration of the human body, just as someone lifting a car and incurring no injuries to bones, ligaments, tendons, or muscles is beyond the limits of the physical body.

But wait a minute . . . people have done the latter.

So, it would appear that the Mind can shore up the body, can affect matter in a way that allows it to outperform it's supposed limitations, sometimes, and under extreme circumstances. I believe that's also the case with psychokinesis.

We can affect our own bodies in ways that seem impossible.

Our minds can affect matter outside the physical connection to the body.

In extreme cases, especially under life-threatening or stress-inducing conditions, our Minds can bust through some limits and lift cars or throw objects around or screw up computers or heal others or make things work that shouldn't or . . .

But what's really doing it? *WE* are; our own minds, that is. *We* are *responsible* for ourselves and our actions, since we have the choice to think about things in a certain way and to take or not take action.

Just as we need to have a responsible attitude toward *how* we affect ourselves, we need to think about a responsible attitude toward how we think about, and potentially really affect the world around us with our minds.

As attitudes change about what is *possible* for human performance, people bust through limits. The implications are that we, as human beings, using the power and imagination of our minds, have many, many more things we can do which are currently impossible.

As impossibilities become reality, we look for more and more impossible things to beat, and we strive to beat them. As the impossibilities become reality, human beings change their beliefs as to what we can and can't do, and this shifting belief system allows for more and more accomplishment.

With an acceptance that health is more than just a matter of taking pills or undergoing surgery, there is an implication that self-healing, that mental healing of others, will become part of the medical process, and that people will be healthier for it.

Much of psychokinesis, as identified by parapsychologists, is done by the subconscious. But if people like Martin Caidin can show others that not only is it possible for him to do it (move objects), but for others to do it as well, psychokinesis might eventually leave the realm of the subconscious, and become part of our conscious, day to day, lives.

Does this mean we'll all be able to levitate ourselves to work every day? I'd say I doubt it, but then you could say I'm setting limits on what's possible.

I do believe that accepting psychokinesis, especially where we personally accept responsibility for "odd" things happening around us, can push us in the direction of being generally more positive in our outlooks on the world, better in accepting our own personal "power" (that we as individuals do have both an effect and a responsibility), and perhaps give us more of a connection to the world in which we live.

Of course, personally speaking, that means I have to admit that I'm often a psychokinetic klutz.

If more and more people cannot just accept (and believe) the *possibility* of psychokinesis outside the body, but its *reality,* we might all have a bit more fun in our lives.

However, the key is to accept that you, too, can do this. And that you must be responsible not only when trying to do psychokinesis, but also when witnessing it in others.

There are charlatans out there who will try to take advantage of your beliefs in the reality of psychic healing and psychokinesis. There are too many phonies. They exist in the psychic related fields, but they also exist in the medical and alternative health fields (and even in the field of psychology). One must always examine any individual claim with a critical eye, especially if money is involved.

I'm certainly not saying one should dismiss claims. After all, curing a person with a new medical procedure is possible, and even probable. Moving an object is possible, and even probable under certain conditions. But that doesn't mean that the person making the claim can really do what he or she claims. As with doctors diagnoses, it doesn't hurt to always consider a second opinion.

Is it possible to saw a person in half and restore them? Not with present science. But certainly a magician can make it look that way.

Special effects and magic can duplicate real, proven events.

Does that mean that what we declare impossible or improbable cannot happen? No, but we should be careful not to accept claims on the surface, especially where our health is concerned, where our wallets are pulled out, and where we might give up personal responsibility for decisions that affect our lives, both immediately and long term.

Human beings are seemingly obsessed with knowing how things work, and sometimes not using techniques or substances that work without knowing the reason why. Yet under certain conditions, we do get past the *why* and just *do* (to paraphrase the great Jedi philosopher Yoda). We don't know how placebos work, yet they (generally) do.

So if one tries to apply certain healing techniques and there is a positive benefit (and no threat to health because one is avoiding other forms of healing), is it a bad thing that we may not yet know how it works? Or that it is not a societally acceptable form of treatment?

If one extends the idea that we can mentally influence plants to grow to the use of such a technique in agriculture, would it be a bad thing for the farmers to do both the physical work and mentally *push* the crops to grow? Or to believe that they mentally affected the plants if the crops grow better than before?

Where there could develop problems around Mind over Matter would be if people could learn to use the abilities in ways that approach what appears in science fiction novels and movies and in comic books.

The military in the U.S. and Russia has had long-standing interest in using psychic abilities for military applications. Imagine if one could disable a nuclear warhead from a distance? Or cause the computer that would launch the missiles to crash? Or, on the downside, cause the missiles to explode while in their silos? Or assassinate political leaders from a distance?

So far, the range and sheer power of psychokinesis seems to fall short of accomplishing any of those things, with the possible exception of the computer operator having an inadvertent effect on the computer he's working at a military base (thank goodness for redundant systems).

Right now, the only truly powerful examples of psychokinesis come from poltergeist cases, which seem to be so related to stress and the subconscious, that it's unlikely that the above scenarios are even possible.

But in the future, where we all might accept, believe and practice some psychokinetic activities, who knows. I do know that in that kind of future, while there will be better performers (as in athletics), there will be enough of an influence by everyone with PK (provided most have a responsible attitude) that we really shouldn't worry about that now.

We should, however, concern ourselves with accepting responsibility for both our own actions and for understanding the claims and the actions of others.

Seek out second opinions about healers, as one would with a doctor. Don't accept claims of individual psychics as examples of why they are *better* than the average person at what they do. As with a star athlete, look at their accomplishments.

Fire-walking brings many questions and possible explanations with it. But the main reason it is used in motivational or self-esteem training has less to do with why someone can do it without burning their feet than the confidence that one can overcome fear of being burned, that one can do a potentially dangerous action and succeed.

The mind of the fire-walker has decided there will be no harm, even if doubt and fear had previously been involved. The mind of the fire-walker may know that there is an explanation that involves temperature variance and not anything psychic, but it still has to overcome any fears and doubts. The mind needs to push to do the fire-walk, to take the first step toward achieving the goal.

But to take the first step, the fire-walker must *believe* he or she can do it. Yoda's lesson in *The Empire Strikes Back* was that you may try all you like, but there is really only the outcome . . . you do it or you don't do it. But believing you can't generally accounts for the failure.

Mind over Matter means *believing in yourself.* Mind over Matter means *taking responsibility for your actions, your inactions and even your thoughts along the way.*

Your mind has power over you. *Your mind* is what you use to interact with people and with the environment around you. *Your mind* is what allows you to have an impact on the world around you, or to stand away from the world and let it pass you by. Your *mind* is what influences your health and well-being. *Your mind* is what can push you to new heights or sink you to new lows, both physically and mentally.

Your mind is what matters.

So, what comes next?

Hopefully, two things . . .

First, I hope I have gotten you thinking about the incredible, wondrous thing that is the mind, and that you, personally, can use the power of your mind to influence your life and the environment in which you live.

To that end, if you think more responsibly about what you do and how you interact and about your own self-image, than I will have accomplished something I set out to do.

Second, and just as important, I hope that I have caused you to have more questions, to increase both your curiosity and your sense of wonder about what is possible if we put our minds to it.

To that end, I have included some further reading for you (to get you thinking even more), and some other resources that will answer some questions and undoubtedly bring up more.

May the Force (of your Mind) Be with You.

CHAPTER NOTES:

Sources of Quotes and References

Chapter 1:

1. Stapp, Henry P. *Mind, Matter and Quantum Mechanics.* Berlin: Springer Verlag, 1993, page 239.

2. Ornstein, Robert. *The Evolution of Consciousness.* New York: Prentice-Hall Press, 1991, page 2.

3. *Psychology Today: An Introduction,* second edition. Del Mar, CA: CRM Books, 1972, page 731.

Chapter 2:

1. Dong, Paul and Esser, Aristede H. *Chi Gong.* New York: Marlowe & Co., 1990, page 1.

Chapter 3:

1. Walsh, Michael, editor. *Butler's Lives of the Saints.* San Francisco: HarperSan Francisco, 1991, pages 294–295.

Chapter 5:

1. Sorelle, Ruth. "Texas Medical Center to Study Benefits of Alternative Medicine" *Houston Chronicle,* October 18, 1995.

2. Weaver, Peter. "Consider the Alternative." *Nation's Business,* October 1995, page 82.

3. Rogo, D. Scott. *Mind over Matter*. Wellingborough, Northamptonshire, England: Aquarian Press, 1986.

4. Bullard, Janice. "A Boy's Best Friend: Dog Nudges Boy Out of Coma." *USA TODAY*, November 20, 1991, page 3A.

5. Tighe, Theresa. "Giving Human Health a Helping Paw, Claw Conference Exploring Pet Therapy Opens" *St. Louis Post-Dispatch*, October 7, 1993, page 1B.

6. Dossey, Larry. *Healing Words: The Power of Prayer and the Practice of Medicine*. New York: HarperCollins Publishers, 1993.

7. Condor, Bob. "Pursuing the Healing Power of Prayer; Dr. Larry Dossey Sees it as a Medical Issue." *Chicago Tribune*, September 18, 1994.

8. Quote from transcript retrieved through the LEXIS-NEXIS information service.

9. Pelletier, Kenneth R. "Between Mind and Body: Stress, Emotions, and Health" in *Mind Body Medicine: How to Use Your Mind for Better Health*, edited by Daniel Goleman, Ph.D. and Joel Gurin. Yonkers, NY: Consumer Reports Books, 1993, page 21.

Chapter 6:

1–3. Berry, Lynn. The Associate Press, January 29, 1995. Article retrieved through the LEXIS-NEXIS information service. Lead: "They often lead secret lives, sometimes using two different names, wary of outsiders. For good reason. They often are stereotyped, as in Cher's 1971 song "Gypsies, Tramps & Thieves." Now America's 1 million Gypsies are seeking to shed that image."

4. Yoors, Jan. *The Gypsies*. New York: Simon & Schuster, 1967, page 169.

Chapter 7:

1. Kaye, Marvin. *The Handbook of Mental Magic*. New York: Stein and Day, 1975, page 32.

Chapter 9:

1. Rhine, Louisa. *Mind over Matter*. New York: Collier Books, Macmillan Publishing Co., Inc.: 1972, page 2.

2. Ibid., page 3.

3. Ibid., pages 3–4.

4. Rogo, D. Scott. *Mind over Matter*. Wellingborough, Northamptonshire, U.K.: The Aquarian Press, 1986, page 75.

5. Eisenbud, Jule. *The World of Ted Serios*. New York: William Morrow & Co., 1967, page 24.

6. Lyons, Arthur and Truzzi, Marcello. *The Blue Sense: Psychic Detectives and Crime*. New York: The Mysterious Press, 1991.

7. Myer-Czetli, Nancy and Czetli, Steve. *Silent Witness: The Story of a Psychic Detective*. New York: Birch Lane Press, Carol Publishing Group, 1993.

8. Katz, Richard. BOILING ENERGY: *Community Healing Among the Kalahari Kung*. Cambridge, MA: Harvard University Press, 1982.

9. Gersi, Douchan. *Faces in the Smoke: An Eyewitness Experience of Voodoo, Shamanism, Psychic Healing, and Other Amazing Human Powers*. Los Angeles: Jeremy P. Tarcher, Inc., 1991.

10. Morgan, Marlo. *Mutant Message Downunder*. New York: HarperCollins Publishers, 1994.

11. Attias, Diana and Smith, Lindsay, editors. *The Empire Strikes Back Notebook*. Screenplay by Lawrence Kasdan and Leigh Bracket. New York: Ballantine Books, 1980, page 89.

12. Ibid., page 89.

Chapter 10:

1. Radin, Dean I. "Testing the Plausibility of Psi-Mediated Computer System Failures." In *The Journal of Parapsychology,* March 1990, volume 54, number 1.

2. Ibid., page 15.

3. Roney-Dougal, Serena. *Where Science & Magic Meet*. Rockport, MA: Element, Inc., 1991.

APPENDIX A:

RESOURCES

1. BIBLIOGRAPHY AND FURTHER READING

Chapter 1: What Is Mind Over Matter? General Readings in Consciousness, the Mind and the Body

Ackerman, Diane. *A Natural History of the Senses*. New York: Random House, 1990.

Dennett, Daniel C. *Consciousness Explained*. Boston: Little, Brown and Co., 1991.

Jahn, Robert G. and Dunne, Brenda J. *Margins of Reality: The Role of Consciousness in the Physical World*. San Diego: Harcourt Brace Jovanovich, 1987.

Murphy, Michael. *The Future of the Body: Explorations into the Further Evolution of Human Nature*. Los Angeles: Jeremy P. Tarcher, Inc., 1992.

Ornstein, Robert. *The Evolution of Consciousness*. New York: Prentice-Hall Press, 1991.

Penrose, Roger. *Shadows of the Mind: A Search for the Missing Science of Consciousness*. Oxford, England: Oxford University Press, 1994.

Restak, Richard. *The Brain has a Mind of its Own*. New York: Harmony Books, 1991.

Scott, Alwyn. *Stairway to the Mind*. New York: Copernicus (Springer-Verlag), 1995.

Stapp, Henry P. *Mind, Matter and Quantum Mechanics*. Berlin: Springer Verlag, 1993.

Wolf, Fred Alan. *The Dreaming Universe*. New York: Simon & Schuster, 1994.

Chapter 2: Outstanding Human Physical Performance

Alexander, Colonel John B. Groller, Major Richard and Morris, Janet. *The Warrior's Edge*. New York: Avon Books, 1990.

Butt, Dorcas S. *The Psychology of Sport*. New York: Van Nostrand Reinhold, 1976.

Chow, David and Spangler, Richard. *Kung Fu: History, Philosophy and Technique*. Burbank, CA: Unique Publications, 1977.

Dong, Paul and Esser, Aristede H. *Chi Gong*. New York: Marlowe & Co., 1990.

Fiennes, Ranulph. *Mind Over Matter: The Epic Crossing of the Antarctic Continent*. New York; Delacorte Press, 1993.

Lee, Bruce. *Tao of Jeet Kune Do*. Burbank, CA: Ohara Publications, Inc., 1975.

Millman, Dan. *The Warrior Athlete: Body, Mind & Spirit*. Walpole, NH: Stillpoint Publishing, 1979.

Murphy, Michael. *Golf in the Kingdom*. New York: Viking, 1972.

Murphy, Michael and White, Rhea A. *The Psychic Side of Sports*. Reading, MA: Addison-Wesley Publishing Co., 1978.

Murphy, Michael and White, Rhea A. *In the Zone: Transcendent Experience in Sports*. New York: Penguin/Arkana, 1995.

Nideffer, Robert M. *The Inner Athlete*. New York: Crowell, 1976.

Orlick, Terry. *In Pursuit of Excellence: How to Win in Sport and Life Through Mental Training*. Champaign, IL: Leisure Press, 1990.

Payne, Peter. Martial Arts: *The Spiritual Dimension. London:* Thames and Hudson, 1981.

Reid, Howard and Croucher, Michael. *The Way of the Warrior: The Paradox of the Martial Arts*. Woodstock, NY: The Overlook Press, 1983.

Chapter 3: The Powers of Saints, Prophets, and Other Spiritual Figures:

Brandon, Ruth. *The Spiritualists*. Buffalo, NY: Prometheus Books, 1984.
Gauld, Alan. *Mediumship and Survival*. London: Heinemann, 1982.

Hall, Trevor H. *The Spiritualists*. New York: Helix Press, 1962.

Hall, Trevor H. *The Enigma of Daniel Home: Medium or Fraud?* Buffalo, NY: Prometheus Books, 1984.

Kelly, Sean and Rogers, Rosemary. *Saints Preserve Us!* New York: Random House, 1993.

Nieman, Carol. *Miracles: The Extraordinary, the Impossible, and the Divine*. New York: Viking Studio Books, 1995.

Rogo, D. Scott. *Miracles: A Parascientific Inquiry into Wondrous Phenomena*. New York: The Dial Press, 1982.

Walsh, Michael, editor. *Butler's Lives of the Saints*. San Francisco: HarperSan Francisco, 1991

Chapter Four: The Unusual and the Bizarre

Burkan, Tolly with Mark Bruce Rosen. *Dying to Live*. Twain Harte, CA: Reunion Press, 1984.

Danforth, Loring M. *Firewalking and Religious Healing*. Princeton, NJ: Princeton University Press, 1989.

Houdini, Harry. *Miracle Mongers and their Methods*. Toronto, Ontario: Coles Publishing Co., 1980.

Jay, Ricky. *Learned Pigs & Fireproof Women*. London: Robert Hale, 1986.

Vilenskaya, Larissa and Steffy, Joan. *Firewalking: A New Look at an Old Enigma*. Falls Village, CT: The Bramble Co., 1991.

Chapter 5: Mental Healing

Acterberg, Jeanne. *Imagery In Healing: Shamanism and Modern Medicine*. Boston: Shambhala, 1985.

Barasch, Marc Ian. *The Healing Path*. New York: Penguin/Arkana, 1993.

Borysenko, Joan. *Minding the Body, Mending the Mind*. New York: Bantam Books, 1988.

Carlson, Richard and Shield, Benjamin, editors. *Healers on Healing*. New York: G.P. Putnam's Sons, 1989.

Chopra, Deepak. Creating Health: *How to Wake Up the Body's Intelligence*. Boston: Houghton Mifflin Co., 1987.

Dossey, Larry. Healing Words: *The Power of Prayer and the Practice of Medicine*. New York: HarperCollins Publishers, 1993.

Goleman, Daniel and Gurin, Joel. *Mind Body Medicine: How to Use Your Mind for Better Health*. Yonkers, NY: Consumer Reports Books, 1993.

Kraft, Dean. *Portrait of a Psychic Healer*. New York: Berkley Books, 1982.

Krippner, Stanley and Villoldo, Alberto. *The Realms of Healing*. Millbrae, CA: Celestial Arts, 1976.

Krieger, Dolores. *The Therapeutic Touch*. Englewood Cliffs, NJ: Prentice-Hall, Inc., 1979.

Moskowitz, Reed C. *Your Healing Mind*. New York: Avon Books, 1992.

Moyers, Bill. *Healing and the Mind*. New York: Doubleday, 1993.

Rogo, D. Scott. *New Techniques of Inner Healing*. New York: Paragon House, 1992.

Villoldo, Alberto and Krippner, Stanley. *Healing States*. New York: Simon & Schuster, Inc., 1987.

Wallace, Amy and Henkin, Bill. *The Psychic Healing Book*. New York: Dell Publishing Co., 1978.

Weil, Andrew. *Spontaneous Healing*. New York: Alfred A. Knopf, 1995.

Chapter 6: Psychic Attack

(see also books on the occult, below, and on parapsychology in general).

Denning, Melita and Phillips, Osborne. *Psychic Self-defense & Well Being*. St. Paul, MN: Llewellyn Publications, 1983.

Ebon, Martin, editor. *The Satan Trap: Dangers of the Occult*. Garden City, NY: Doubleday, 1976.

Fortune, Dion. *Psychic Self-Defence: A Study in Occult Pathology and Criminality*. Wellingborough, Northamptonshire, Great Britain: The Aquarian Press, 1987.

Franklyn, Julian. *Death by Enchantment*. London: Sphere Books, Ltd., 1975.

Hope, Murry. *Practical Techniques of Psychic Self-Defense*. New York: St. Martin's Press, 1983.

Leland, Charles Godfrey. *Gypsy Sorcery and Fortune-telling*. New Hyde Park, NY: University Books, 1962. {Note: this book is currently available from several publishers]

Yoors, Jan. *The Gypsies*. New York: Simon & Schuster, 1967.

Chapter 7: Manipulating Nature: The Occult Perspective

The following are general readings on the occult and magic, as well as some excellent anthropological resources that deal with magic and sorcery.

Angoff, Allan & Diana Barth, eds. Parapsychology and Anthropology: Proceedings of an international conference held in London, England, August 29–31, 1973. New York: Parapsychology Foundation, Inc., 1974.

Elkin, A.P. Aboriginal Men of High Degree: *Initiation and Sorcery in the World's Oldest Tradition.* Rochester, VT: Inner Traditions International, 1994.

Evans-Pritchard, E.E. *Witchcraft, Oracles, and Magic Among the Azande.* Oxford: Clarendon Press, 1937.

Gersi, Douchan. *Faces in the Smoke: An Eyewitness Experience of Voodoo, Shamanism, Psychic Healing, and other Amazing Human Powers.* Los Angeles: Jeremy P. Tarcher, Inc., 1991.

Gregor, Arthur S. *Witchcraft and Magic: The Supernatural World of Primitive Man.* New York: Charles Scribners' Sons, 1972.

Kaye, Marvin. *The Handbook of Mental Magic.* New York: Stein and Day, 1975.

Katz, Richard. *Boiling Energy: Community Healing Among the Kalahari Kung.* Cambridge, MA: Harvard University Press, 1982.

Kiev, Ari, editor. *Magic, Faith, and Healing.* New York: The Free Press (Macmillan), 1974.

Lieban, Richard W. *Cebuano Sorcery: Malign Magic in the Philippines.* University of California Press, 1967.

Long, Joseph K., ed. *Extrasensory Ecology: Parapsychology and Anthropology.* Metuchen, NJ: The Scarecrow Press, 1977.

Marwick, Max, ed. *Witchcraft and Sorcery: Selected Readings.* Harmondsworth, Middlesex: Penguin Books, 1970.

Metraux, Alfred. *Voodoo in Haiti.* New York: Schocken, 1972.

Middleton, John, ed. *Magic, Witchcraft, and Curing.* Garden City, NY: The Natural History Press, 1967.

Morgan, Marlo. *Mutant Message Downunder.* New York: HarperCollins, 1994.

Rose, Ronald. *Living Magic. New York:* Rand McNally & Co., 1956. (a later edition of this excellent book is called *Primitive Psychic Power.* New York: Signet Books, 1968).

Rush, John A. *Witchcraft and Sorcery: An Anthropological Perspective of the Occult.* Springfield, IL: Charles C. Thomas, Publisher, 1974.

Wilson, Colin. *The Occult:* A History. New York: Random House, 1971.

Wilson, Colin. *Beyond the Occult.* New York: Carroll & Graf Publishers, Inc., 1988.

Wolf, Fred Alan. *The Eagle's Quest: A Physicist's Search for the Truth in the Heart of the Shamanic World.* New York: Summit Books (Simon & Schuster), 1991.

Chapter 8: Poltergeists and Ghosts: A Few Suggestions

Auerbach, Loyd. *ESP, Hauntings and Poltergeists: A Parapsychologist's Handbook.* New York: Warner Books, 1986.

Baker, Robert A. and Nickell, Joe. *Missing Pieces: How to Investigate Ghosts, UFOs, Psychics & Other Mysteries.* Buffalo, NY: Prometheus Books, 1992.

Caidin, Martin. *Ghosts of the Air.* St. Paul, MN: Galde Press, 1995.

Cavendish, Richard. *The World of Ghosts and the Supernatural: The Occult, the Unexplained, and the Mystical Around the Globe.* New York: Facts On File, 1994.

Gauld, Alan and Cornell, A.D. *Poltergeists.* London: Routledge & Kegan Paul, 1979.

Guiley, Rosemary Ellen. *The Encyclopedia of Ghosts and Spirits.* New York: Facts On File, 1992.

Iverson, Jeffrey. *In Search of the Dead: A Scientific Investigation of Evidence for Life After Death.* HarperSan Francisco, 1992.

Lewis, James R. *Encyclopedia of Afterlife Beliefs and Phenomena.* Detroit, MI: Visible Ink Press (Gale Research), 1995.

Mackenzie, Andrew. *Hauntings and Apparitions: An Investigation of the Evidence.* London: Paladin Books, 1982.

Owen, Iris M. with Margaret Sparrow. *Conjuring Up Philip: An Adventure in Psychokinesis.* New York: Harper & Row, 1976.

Peach, Emily. *Things that Go Bump in the Night.* Wellingborough, Northamptonshire, Great Britain: The Aquarian Press, 1991.

Price, Harry. *Confessions of a Ghost Hunter.* New York: Causeway Books, 1974.

Price, Harry. Poltergeist: *Tales of the Supernatural.* London: Bracken Books, 1993.

Rogo, D. Scott. *An Experience of Phantoms*. New York: Taplinger Publishing Co., 1974.

Rogo, D. Scott. *The Poltergeist Experience*. New York: Penguin Books, 1979.

Rogo, D. Scott. *Life After Death: The Case for Survival of Bodily Death*. Wellingborough, Northamptonshire, Great Britain: The Aquarian Press, 1986.

Roll, William G. *The Poltergeist*. Metuchen, NJ: The Scarecrow Press, 1976.

Time-Life Books. *Hauntings*. Mysteries of the Unknown book series. Alexandria, VA: Time-Life Books, 1989.

Time-Life Books. *Phantom Encounters*. Mysteries of the Unknown book series. Alexandria, VA: Time-Life Books, 1989.

Tyrrell, G.N.M. *Apparitions*. New York: Collier Books, 1963.

Underwood, Peter. *The Ghost Hunter's Guide*. London: Javelin Books, 1986.

Wilson, Colin. Poltergeist: *A Study In Destructive Haunting*. New York: Perigee/Putnam Publishing, 1981.

Chapter 9: The Force is With You
and
Chapter 10: Human Machine Interactions

Sources and suggestions for these two chapters are combined since both deal with psychokinesis and with parapsychology in general. I will break these books down into two categories:

a. General Readings about the field of parapsychology

Auerbach, Loyd. *Psychic Dreaming: A Parapsychologist's Handbook*. New York: Warner Books, 1991.

Auerbach, Loyd. *Reincarnation, Channeling and Possession: A Parapsychologist's Handbook*. New York: Warner Books, 1993.

Berger, Arthur S. and Joyce. *The Encyclopedia of Parapsychology and Psychical Research*. New York: Paragon House, 1991.

Broughton, Richard. *Parapsychology: The Controversial Science*. New York: Ballantine Books, 1991.

Duncan, Lois and Roll, William G. *Psychic Connections: A Journey into the Mysterious World of Psi*. New York: Delacorte Press, 1995.

Ebon, Martin, editor. *The Signet Handbook of Parapsychology*. New York: New American Library, 1978.

Edge, Hoyt L., Morris, Robert L., Rush, Joseph H., & Palmer, John A. Foundations of *Parapsychology: Exploring the Boundaries of Human Capabilities*. Boston: Routledge & Kegan Paul, 1986.

Gauld, Alan. *The Founders of Psychical Research*. New York: Schocken, 1969.

Gittelson, Bernard. *Intangible Evidence*. New York: Fireside Books, 1987.

Grattan-Guinness, Ivar (editor). *Psychical Research: A Guide to Its History, Principles, & Practices*. Welingborough, Northamptonshire: The Aquarian Press, 1982.

Guiley, Rosemary Ellen. *Harper's Encyclopedia of Mystical and Paranormal Experience*. San Francisco: HarperSan Francisco/HarperCollins Publishers, 1991.

Inglis, Brian. *Natural and Supernatural: A History of the Paranormal*. Bridport, Dorset, Great Britain: Prism Press, 1992 (distributed in the United States by Avery Publishing Group, New York).

Irwin, Harvey J. *An Introduction to Parapsychology*. Jefferson, NC: McFarland, 1989.

Kurtz, Pau, editor. *A Skeptic's Handbook of Parapsychology*. Buffalo, NY: Prometheus Books, 1985.

Rhine, Louisa E. *The Invisible Picture*. Jefferson, NC: McFarland & Co., 1981.

Rogo, D. Scott. *Parapsychology: A Century of Inquiry*. New York: Dutton, 1977.

Rogo, D. Scott. *Psychic Breakthroughs Today*. Wellingborough, Northamptonshire, Great Britain: The Aquarian Press, 1987.

White, Rhea. *Parapsychology: New Sources of Information, 1973–1989*. Metuchen, NJ: The Scarecrow Press, 1990.

Wolman, Benjamin. *Handbook of Parapsychology*. New York: Van Nostrand Reinhold, 1977.

Zollschan, Dr. George K., Dr. John F. Schumaker and Dr. Greg F. Walsh, editors. *Exploring the Paranormal: Perspectives on Belief and Experience*. Bridport, Dorset, Great Britain: Prism Press, 1989 (distributed in the United States by Avery Publishing Group, New York).

b. Books on psychokinesis

Braude, Stephen E. ESP and Psychokinesis: *A Philosophical Examination*. Philadelphia: Temple University Press, 1979.

Braude, Stephen E. *The Limits of Influence: Psychokinesis and the Philosophy of Science*. New York: Routledge, 1991.

Brown, Michael H. PK: *A Report on Psychokinesis*. Blauvelt, NY: Steinerbooks, 1976.

Eisenbud, Jule. *The World of Ted Serios*. New York: William Morrow & Co., 1967

Geller, Uri and Playfair, Guy Lyon. *The Geller Effect*. New York: Henry Holt and Co., 1986.

Hasted, John. *The Metal-Benders*. London: Routledge & Kegan Paul, 1981.

Panati, Charles, editor. *The Geller Papers: Scientific Observations on the Paranormal Powers of Uri Geller*. Boston: Houghton Mifflin Co., 1976.

Rhine, Louisa. *Mind over Matter: Psychokinesis*. New York: Collier Books, Macmillan Publishing Co., Inc.: 1972.

Robinson, Diana. *To Stretch a Plank: A Survey of Psychokinesis*. Chicago: Nelson Hall, 1981.

Rogo, D. Scott. *Minds & Motion: The Riddle of Psychokinesis*. New York: Taplinger Publishing Co., 1978.

Rogo, D. Scott. *Mind over Matter: The Case for Psychokinesis*. Wellingborough, Northamptonshire, Great Britain: The Aquarian Press, 1986.

Time-Life Books. *Mind Over Matter*. Mysteries of the Unknown book series. Alexandria, VA: Time-Life Books, 1989.

Chapter 11: Do It Yourself Mind Over Matter

Caidin, Martin S. *Natural or Supernatural: A Casebook of True, Unexplained Mysteries*. Chicago: Contemporary Books, 1993.

Mishlove, Jeffrey. *PSI Development Systems*. New York: Ballantine Books, 1988.

Rogo, D. Scott. *Our Psychic Potentials*. New York: Prentice-Hall Press, 1984.

Sanders, Pete A. *You Are Psychic!* New York: Fawcett Columbine, 1989.

Stine, G. Harry. *Mind Machines You Can Build*. Largo, FL: Top of the Mountain Publishing, 1992.

Chapter 12: Faking It:

Some of the books listed below deal with the art of magic and conjuring, some specifically with mentalism effects in mind. Those that do so are generally available only through magic shops and dealers.

Abrams, Max (compilation and commentary by). *Annemann: The Life and Times of a Legend*. Tahoma, CA: L & L Publishing, 1992.

Alcock, James E. *Parapsychology—Science of Magic: A Psychological Perspective*. New York: Pergamon Press, 1981.

Becker, Larry. *Larry Becker's World of Super Mentalism*. Brooklyn, NY: D. Robbins & Co., Inc., 1987.

Berger, Eugene. *Spirit Theater*. Richard Kaufman and Alan Greenberg, 1986.

Berger, Eugene and Neale, Robert E. *Magic and Meaning*. Seattle, WA: Hermetic Press, 1995.

Blackstone, Harry Jr., with Charles and Regina Reynolds. *The Blackstone Book of Magic and Illusion*. New York: Newmarket Press, 1985.

Booth, John. *Psychic Paradoxes*. Los Alamitos, CA: Ridgeway Press, 1984.

Christopher, Milbourne. *Mediums, Mystics, and the Occult*. New York: Thomas Y. Crowell, 1979.

Christopher, Milbourne. *ESP, Seers and Psychics*. New York: Thomas Y. Crowell, 1970.

Corinda. *Thirteen Steps to Mentalism*. New York: Louis Tannen, 1968.

Houdini, Harry. *A Magician among the Spirits*. New York: Arno Press: 1972.

Kaye, Marvin. *The Handbook of Mental Magic*. New York: Stein and Day, 1975.

Keene, M. Lamar as told to Allen Spraggett. *The Psychic Mafia*. New York: Dell, 1976.

Lesley, Ted. *Ted Lesley's Paramiracles*. Seattle, WA: Hermetic Press, 1994.

Marks, David and Kammann, Richard. *The Psychology of the Psychic*. Buffalo, NY: Prometheus Books, 1980.

Minch, Stephen. *Mind & Matter*. Calgary, Alberta, Canada: Hades Publications, 1987.

Nelson, Robert A. *"Hellstromism."* Calgary, Alberta, Canada: Hades Publications.

Randi, James. *The Truth about Uri Geller*. Buffalo, NY: Prometheus Books, 1982.

Randi, James. *The Faith Healers*. Buffalo, NY: Prometheus Books, 1987.

Sharpe, S. H. *Conjurer's Psychological Secrets*. Calgary, Alberta, Canada: Hades Publications, 1988.

Steiner, Robert A. *Don't Get Taken!: Bunco and Bunkum Exposed; How to Protect Yourself*. El Cerrito, CA: Wide-Awake Books, 1989.

Walker, Mark. *Key Bending*. Calgary, Alberta, Canada: Hades Publications, 1979.

Waters, T.A. *Mind, Myth & Magic*. Seattle, WA: Hermetic Press, 1993.

PUBLICATIONS:

The Journal of the American Society for Psychical Research

Refereed journal published by The American Society for Psychical Research (see below). Covers parapsychological research and investigations, as well as book reviews of scientific and popular publications.

The Journal of Parapsychology

Refereed Journal published by the Institute for Parapsychology, Rhine Research Center (see below). Covers parapsychological research and investigations, as well as book reviews of scientific publications.

The Journal of the Society for Psychical Research

Refereed journal published by the Society for Psychical Research (see below). Covers parapsychological research and investigations, as well as book reviews of various publications.

The Journal of the Society for Scientific Exploration

Refereed journal published by the Society for Scientific Exploration (see below). Covers research and investigation in a number of fields, including parapsychology, UFOlogy, cryptozoology, and studies of other anomalous phenomena.

Fate magazine

P.O. Box 64383, St. Paul, MN 55164. Monthly newsstand publication with popular coverage of psychic phenomena and study, UFOs, cryptozoology, supernatural beliefs, and many other anomalous phenomena. Loyd Auerbach has a column, "Psychic Frontiers" that appears every other month, and often writes feature articles.

2. ORGANIZATIONS AND INVOLVEMENT

a. Research & Information Organizations:

Here's a few that will get you to other sources of information. Several of these organizations have some form of membership.

THE AMERICAN SOCIETY FOR PSYCHICAL RESEARCH
5 West 73rd Street, New York, NY 10023. Phone: 212-799-5050.
Publishes a Journal and Newsletter. Conducts lectures and conferences. Extensive library and archives. Provides information and research services. Membership organization.

THE CALIFORNIA SOCIETY FOR PSYCHICAL STUDY
P.O. Box 844, Berkeley, CA 94704. Phone contact through the Office of Paranormal Investigations (415) 553-2588.
Provides monthly lectures and occasional workshops. Publishes a newsletter, IRIDIS. Membership organization.

THE INSTITUTE OF PARAPSYCHOLOGY, RHINE RESEARCH CENTER
402 North Buchanan Blvd., Durham, NC 27701-1728. (919) 688-8241.
Fax: (919) 683-4338.
Publishes *The Journal of Parapsychology*. Does extensive research in psi phenomena. Conducts an eight-week Summer Study Program which provides extensive educational grounding in parapsychological research. The program takes 12–15 students each year. Also provides a public information service and offers classes and workshops locally through a community education program. Recently added membership to support research.

ORGANIZATION FOR PARANORMAL UNDERSTANDING AND SUPPORT (OPUS)
P.O. Box 273273, Concord, CA 94527. (510) 689-2666. E-mail:
opus@awaiter.com
A new referral network for people who have an anomalous or psychic experience and need someone to talk to about it. Network is composed of researchers, investigators, licensed counselors and therapists, psychologists, physicians, and others with some interest and/or expertise in the paranormal, UFOs, psychic phenomena and other anom-

alous or unusual human experiences. Holds monthly meetings and is establishing local groups in California.

THE OFFICE OF PARANORMAL INVESTIGATIONS
P.O. Box 875, Orinda, CA 94563-0875.

Loyd Auerbach, director. Barbara Gallagher, associate director. Established in 1989, this group of investigators was set up to look at cases of apparent hauntings, poltergeist phenomena, apparitional sightings, and other psychic phenomena, as well as to provide information and consulting services to the media and the general public. Also provides consulting to researchers (and others) on psychic fraud. Check out the OPI site on the World Wide Web (see below). Primarily conducts investigations in northern California, but has affiliated field investigators in a number of locations around the U.S.

THE PARAPSYCHOLOGICAL ASSOCIATION
P.O. Box 3695, Charlottesville, VA 22903-3695.

Only professional organization of parapsychological researchers around the world. Holds annual conference and publishes papers of the conference, and disseminates research findings to other branches of science. Affiliated with the American Association for the Advancement of Science. Membership organization with strict criteria for various membership levels.

THE PARAPSYCHOLOGY FOUNDATION
228 East 71st Street, New York, NY 10021. (212) 628-1550.

The foundation supports research and writing in parapsychology, holds an annual conference (and publishes proceedings), offers research and student grants, and has an extensive library.

THE PSI CENTER (Parapsychological Sources of Information Center)
2 Plane Tree Lane, Dix Hills, NY 11746.

Rhea White is the director. The center offers services aimed at pulling together information for researchers and laypersons. It publishes *Exceptional Human Experience.*

THE SOCIETY FOR PSYCHICAL RESEARCH
49 Marlowes Road, Kensington, London W8 6LA, England.

The oldest parapsychological organization in the world, it publishes a journal and other materials, and maintains an extensive library and archives. Membership organization.

THE SOCIETY FOR SCIENTIFIC EXPLORATION
P.O. Box 5848, Stanford, CA 94309-5848.
Publishes a journal and a newsletter. Organization promoting the scientific study of anomalous phenomena, including, but not limited to, psi phenomena, UFOs and cryptozoology. Holds an annual conference. Membership organization.

b. Educational Opportunities:

Besides the Summer Study Program offered by the Institute for Parapsychology, there are, unfortunately, few educational opportunities in parapsychology. Here's two to start with:

ROSEBRIDGE GRADUATE SCHOOL FOR INTEGRATIVE
PSYCHOLOGY
This state-approved grad school, primarily aimed at high quality clinical psychology education, has expanded out to include several degree tracks for clinical and experimental parapsychology.

Now in place at Rosebridge Graduate School for Integrative Psychology in Concord, CA, is a graduate program offering Psy.D. and M.A. in psychology specializing in parpasychology. The degree program offers a licensing track and a research track, and provides one of the most ambitious sets of courses offered by any university anywhere in the world.

The licensing track involves much of the same training a licensed therapist or psychologist needs to take, plus parapsychology. In this track, the graduate can get licensed as a psychotherapist and practice psychological counseling (undoubtably specializing in counseling people with some psi-related problems). This, of course, provides one with a career as well as an education. One may call this the "Clinical Parapsychology" track. Rosebridge is the only school in the world focusing on clinical parapsychology.

The research track includes a core of psychology classes with the majority of work done in parapsychological research and investigation. This will give graduates an excellent education as a researcher.

Bachelor's degree programs are also being developed at the school, though the time frame for the offering of those programs is undetermined at this time.

One other project for Rosebridge is the development of distance learning programs, more than likely using the Internet and the World Wide Web, as well as phone bridges, to deliver coursework and to stay in contact with students.

Rosebridge has plans to build a research laboratory as funds come in to do more "conventional" psi research, but would like to specialize in field research and studying spontaneous psi experiences, as well as in healing research and complimentary medicine.

Contact Dr. Jon Klimo, Rosebridge Graduate School for Integrative Psychology, 1040 Oak Grove Road, Suite 103, Concord, CA 94518. (510) 689-0560. Fax: (510) 689-4456. Check my Web page (see below) for more current information on the status of Rosebridge's electronic presence.

UNIVERSITY OF EDINBURGH, KOESTLER PARAPSYCHOLOGY UNIT

Long a bastion of parapsychological research in the British Isles, the psychology department houses the Koestler Chair of Parapsychology and conducts extensive research in psi functioning. One may do graduate studies at this university in parapsychological research.

Contact Dr. Robert Morris, Department of Psychology, University of Edinburgh, 7 George Square, Edinburgh EH8 9JZ, Scotland, UK.

3. THE ELECTRONIC CONNECTION
The Internet and the World Wide Web

Whether you have a computer or not, if you watch TV, listen to the radio, or read just about any regular newspaper or magazine (not counting *The Weekly World News*), or even keep up on the current movies out there, you can hardly miss hearing about a couple of new terms in the English (and undoubtedly other) language: INTERNET (a.k.a. "the Net") and THE WEB (short for the World Wide Web).

Developed originally for academics, the Internet is a rather nebulous network of computers all over the world which hook into various telecommunications services. Through the Net, people have been able to send electronic mail or create or participate in discussion groups on all sorts of topics. Discussion groups literally run a vast range from TV and movie groups to scientific discussions, from the paranormal to conversations about sex (the most popular topics on the Net, I have been told, are sex and the paranormal, though not necessarily in the same discussion group). However, the Net has been a nightmare to navigate through until fairly recently, with the development of the World Wide Web.

The Web makes things quite easy if one has a "Web Browser" such as Netscape. Through the searching of what's called a "Web page," one can get basic information on people, places, and things, and can be pointed to other sources of information. A Web page is usually a combination of graphics and text. They may provide significant information, such as a reprint of a scientific paper, or background on a new TV program, or even artwork and photos one can download or print. They provide automatic links to other topic-related Web pages or even to Internet "news groups" (these are the discussion groups mentioned above), and may even include links to electronic mail (E-mail) so one can send an immediate note to the subject/author of the Web page or to appropriate resources and experts.

People and companies are putting up Web pages all over the place (including yours truly). The future of information sharing, in fact, looks to be with the Internet and the World Wide Web.

As the paranormal is such a hot topic among users of the New and the Web (with over thirty million users of the Net out there, there are tens of thousands—by some estimates over two million—people interested in some paranormal topic or other), it's no surprise that there are so many Web pages up already, with more seemingly every week, besides the paranormal newsgroups that have been on the Net for quite a while. CompuServe has an "Encounters" forum that boasts more than forty thousand visitors.

In the next couple of pages, I will describe a few "Web Sites" you may want to visit. These will, of course, lead you to other sites I may not go into here (merely for lack of space). I've only been on the Web for a few months, myself, so I'm still exploring. In fact, I'd appreciate it if anyone out there who knows more sites that may be of interest forward them to me at my E-mail address (esper@california.com).

First of all, let me mention the sites on the Web that have been put up by the publisher of *Fate* magazine, seeing as how I write regularly for that publication. Llewellyn Publications has a Web site (http://www.llewellyn.com/) which provides information on many of its publications, as well as a way to reach the publisher. Linked to that is the *Fate* Web site (http://www.llewellyn.com/fate.html), which gives you access to selected articles and columns from and to descriptions of the current and past issue of *Fate,* to *Fate* writer's guidelines, to subscription info, and will eventually be set up to take reader feedback.

If you go through the often visited Yahoo Web site (Yahoo provides a variety of topical sites) on the paranormal (http://www.yahoo.com/Entertainment/Paranormal__Phenomena), you'll gain access to an amazing list of links to topics all over the Web. Included in the list of links are topics such as altered states of consciousness, astral projection, astrology, skeptics organizations, the FORTEAN TIMES on line, various folklore sites, healing, mysticism, psychics, UFOs and even indexes to other sites, resources and networks.

One of those other sites is called "Archive X" (http://www.crown.net/X/). According to the Web page, "Archive X is a series of Web pages devoted toward Paranormal Phenomena. It is a portion of The Virtual Library. Information is gathered from various news groups as well as submissions from interested parties and case histories from officially documented hauntings and paranormal activities. Archive X gives you access to some experiences people have reported on ghosts, angels, channeling and UFOs, as well as links to related movie and TV sites (such as the X-FILES). It also provides links to a variety of newsgroups that discuss paranormal topics (one of the most extensive being the ParaNet (alt.paranet)).

The X-Files home page is a very fun place to visit (http://www.delphi.com/XFiles/xfsecret.htm), and it will link you to info on the show and the actors and staff, as well as background information on the paranormal, and of course, to other discussion groups (including ParaNet) covering specific topics such as alien abductions, ghosts, dreams, conspiracy theories, the paranormal in general, and skeptics newsgroups. It also links you to newsgroups discussing horror and science fiction.

On the scientific side, there are a number of organizations (including some mentioned above) that have established their own Web sites. First check out the "Parapsychology Sources" Web page at http://www.dundee.ac.uk/~fmsteink/for.htm. That will provide links to a wide variety of other sites. You can find the Society for Psychical Research (http//www.ed.ac.uk/~parapsi/spr.html) and the Koestler Parapsychology Unit of the University of Edinburgh (http//www.ed.ac.uk/~parapsi/kpu.html) online, as well as the Rhine Research Center (http//world.std.com/~rhinerc/).

One of the more interesting scientific Web pages is unique just in the way it even looks and welcomes you in. The home page of the Physics and Consciousness Research Group (http://www.hia.com/hia/pcr/webhole.html#index) comes up with a message that says: "You have just fallen into and out of a webhole" and then continues with links to very interesting topics related to Consciousness and the New Physics, including research papers, info on proposed warp drives (a la *Star Trek*), scientific discussion of Time and Space, and even to a bunch of other "cool sites" related to leading edge physics and consciousness research (http://www.hia.com/hia/pcr/new.html).

One of the links takes you to a fairly new site which will give you plenty of info on frequently asked questions (FAQ) about parapsychology, as well as links to other sites (http://eeyore.lv-hrc.nevada.edu/~cogno/para1.html). According to that particular Web page, "This FAQ was compiled by an ad-hoc group of scientists and scholars interested in parapsychology, the study of what is popularly called "psychic" phenomena. The disciplines represented in this group include physics, psychology, philosophy, statistics, mathematics, computer science, chemistry, anthropology, and history."

This particular information site was compiled (and is constantly evolving, as with other Web sites) by a group, the majority of whom are members of the Parapsychological Association (PA).

As with other fields of science, there is not always agreement on answers to all questions so, according to the compilers, "the group aimed for consensus on each FAQ item, but as in many intellectual pursuits, especially in young, multidisciplinary domains, there were some sharp disagreements. In spite of these disagreements, the authors believe that because of burgeoning public interest in parapsychology, the relative lack of reliable information, and the many myths and distortions associated with this field, it was important to put some basic information on the World Wide Web sooner rather than later."

Compilers include Editor Dean Radin, Ph.D., Consciousness Research Laboratory, University of Nevada (which has its own Web site at http://eeyore.lv-hrc.nevada.edu/~cogno/cogno.html), Carlos Alvarado, MS. of the University of Edinburgh, Scotland, Dick Bierman, Ph.D. of Anomalous Cognition at the University of Amsterdam, Charles Tart, Ph.D., University of California, Davis and a number of others in psi research.

There are links to other organizations, including the PA, the Society for Scientific Exploration, and the Society for Psychical Research. There are additional links to a variety of journals, and of course, to a number of laboratories and university departments all over the world. In fact, one can access psi experiments (and even participate) from the University of Amsterdam, with promised experiments coming from other labs.

In a nutshell, that should be enough to get the seeker started. The most amazing thing about the Web, I think, is how as you link up from one source to another, you continuously get links to new and exciting sources of information on the Net. In fact, starting with one site like Yahoo, you can stay on for hours and never visit the same site twice.

While my own Web site is currently under construction, as well as related Web sites for the Office of Paranormal Investigations and Rosebridge Graduate School, they will all be maintained by Global InfoNet, Inc., whose Web page will provide information as to how to go to their own paranormal Web sites, including mine (http:/www.california.com).

Planned for my page will be links to information about (and generated from) this book and my others, links to my columns written for *Fate* magazine (with the kind permission of *Fate*), and to a variety of other information sources.

The Office of Paranormal Investigations page, as well as my own page, will include a link to a form you can fill out right on the Web that will allow you to report your paranormal and extraordinary experiences, which we'll attempt to respond to. These experiences will receive a bit of editing (and a masking of your identity if you desire) and will then be available to all visitors to the Web sites.

Finally, I want to mention that Larry Loebig of Global InfoNet and I are in the process of putting together an exciting project for the Web. We plan for a special online-only "magazine" that will feature articles, columns, photos, artwork, sound files, video clips, and other bits dealing with paranormal topics. Our goal is to "wow" our audience with the amount and quality of information.

The subscriber restricted magazine is targeted to be online before the release of the book you are holding, so go check out the Global InfoNet site (http://www.california.com) for more information.

TO CONTACT ME ON THE NET OR VIA "SNAIL-MAIL":

In the meantime, you can contact me on E-mail (esper@california.com) or by writing to me at P.O. Box 875, Orinda, CA 94563-0875. Please include a self-addressed stamped envelope and be a bit patient if using regular mail. I do prefer E-mail since it's an easier process to respond in a timely manner to people.

You can also call the Office of Paranormal Investigations (415) 553-2588 to get a message to me.

I am extremely interested in experiences like those you've read about in this book. In fact, I encourage you to fill out the following questionnaire, and to either mail it to me via regular mail, or preferably send it to me on E-mail.

APPENDIX B:

Mind over Matter Survey

One of the things I and others in my field have noticed over the years is the fact that people, once they know they will be listened to and taken seriously, often have experiences they would like to share in the realm of psychic or anomalous phenomena. Often surveys are done by organizations such as Ropers or Gallup or by sociologists, all of whom try for a random sampling of the population to look at overall belief and experiential factors.

One skeptic told me that by trying to do a survey of psychic experiences, it might be a bit biased since people who don't believe in such things would probably not fill them out or answer questions such as many of those below. He noted that surveys such as these don't accurately reflect how many people do or don't have the experiences, since those who don't are often uninterested in filling them out.

I countered by suggesting that if the skeptics really wanted to show that fewer people than surveys in the past have suggested really have such experiences, then it's up to the skeptical and disbelieving members of the populace to stop ignoring them, to actually go out of their way and fill such surveys out.

So, whether or not you believe in psychic phenomena, in Mind over Matter as defined in any section of this book, whether you've had an experience or not, providing information about your beliefs and experiences is useful. Pass it along to others, as well (especially those who might be skeptical) to get their perspectives included.

Of course, the fact that you are reading this book already may mean you are interested in the phenomena, and therefore even biased that it exists. The data gathered from these surveys is not so much to gauge how much of the populace has had experiences, but to help find common factors in those experiences that can help us understand and explain them.

If you are using regular mail, please send the survey to:

LOYD AUERBACH
PK SURVEY
P.O. BOX 875
ORINDA, CA 94563-0875.

I would appreciate inclusion of your name and address on the survey, though the anonymity of all concerned will be preserved. In the future, we may want to contact you with further questions (so please be sure to answer the last question) as well as to provide you with information on publications and events that may be of interest to you. If you do not wish to put down your name and address, please still fill out the questionnaire (though it would be a big help if you give the city and state in which you live).

As you answer these questions, if you have experiences to report, please feel free to write (legibly, please), type, or word-process them. Answer "yes," "no," "not sure" or "n/a" (not applicable) to the questions, and, if possible (with the "yes" answers, of course) provide an example. Some of the questions do require more of an answer, by the way.

E-MAIL YOUR SURVEYS. . . .

If you have access to E-mail, please use that for your surveys. If you'd like an electronic form to fill out (rather than typing your answers in by the numbers), contact me at my E-mail address (esper@california.com). Also, take a look at the home page on the World Wide Web for Global InfoNet (http:/www.california.com) for a link to a survey form you can fill in right on the Web.

PART ONE: MIND OVER MATTER AND HUMAN PERFORMANCE

1. Do you believe that the mind can influence the body (yours) directly?

2. Have you ever mentally pushed yourself beyond what you thought were your physical limits?

3. Have you seen others do extraordinary physical actions?

4. Have you ever seen an athlete do what you considered an "impossible" feat?

5. Have you ever taken martial arts classes/training? If so, what kind and to what level?

6. Have you ever seen martial artists do physical actions that you felt were beyond "normal" limits of the human body?

7. Have you ever seen someone walking on hot coals? What did you think of that?

8. Have you ever seen people pierce their bodies with sharp objects, yet not suffer pain or extensive bleeding?

9. Have you seen people do other such "bizarre" feats that seem to defy explanation? If so, what kind?

10. Do you believe that individuals can have the power to levitate themselves?

11. Do you believe that individuals can have the power to teleport themselves through space?

12. Do you believe that individuals can have the power to produce objects without sleight of hand?

13. Do you believe that individuals can have the power to heal themselves?

14. Do you believe that individuals can have the power to heal others?

15. Do you believe such powers come from God?

16. Do you believe such powers come from Spirits?

17. Do you believe such powers come from the Devil or demons?

18. Do you believe such powers come from the individuals themselves?

19. Do you believe such powers come from some other source? If so, what?

20. Have you ever felt you healed yourself from an injury or illness through sheer willpower?

21. Do you believe you have the ability to affect the health of your body?

22. Do you know others who have done this for themselves?

23. Have you ever felt that someone else (a healer) was able to help heal you?

24. Have you seen healers work on others?

25. Do you believe others have the ability to use their mind's to harm you physically?

26. Has this ever happened to you or someone you know?

27. Do you believe spirits or other "nonphysical" entities have the power to harm the living?

28. Do you know of such an instance where this happened?

29. Do you believe you have the ability to prevent such harm from coming to you, personally?

30. Do you believe you can train your mind to affect your body, either positively or negatively?

PART TWO: PSYCHIC EXPERIENCES

1. Have you ever witnessed object movements or sounds which had no "normal" physical explanation that you could discover (psychokinesis)?

2. Do you believe people have the ability to move objects with their minds alone?

3. Do you believe people have the ability to levitate objects?

4. Do you believe people have the ability to teleport objects?

5. Do you believe people have the ability to affect machinery such as appliances and computers (either positively or negatively) with their minds?

6. Do clocks, appliances, computers, office machines, or other technology tend to function differently for you than for others (better or worse)? If so, what kinds of technology?

7. Have you witnessed occasions when such devices have functioned in an unusual/ non-normal way which had no discernible "normal" physical explanation?

8. Have you felt that you, personally, were responsible for an unusual physical effect (such as described in question 1, 6 or 7)?

9. Have you ever known about a future event before it happened?

10. Have you had dreams of future events?

11. Did the event(s) check out as predicted?

13. Were you aware that the dream, feeling, or vision was of a future event at the time you remembered the dream or had the experience? Can you recall how you knew?

14. Do you believe the future is predetermined, that predictions that really come from the future have to come true?

15. Do you believe that you (and everyone else) have the ability to make decisions that affect the future?

16. Have you ever felt that you received information psychically about an event (or person or location) in the "present" that was out of reach of your senses or logical inference?

17. Did you try checking to see if those events were real?

18. If it matched an event, how and when did you learn that?

19. Have you ever felt you "picked up" information from the mind of another person?

20. Did you check the information with that person?

21. Have you ever felt a "psychic" connection to another person?

22. Have you ever had the same dream (the same night) as another person?

23. Have you ever had, awake or asleep, the feeling that you were located outside of or away from your physical body?

24. Have you ever had a near-death experience (that is, one in which you were thought to be physically dead, and then came "back to life")?

    a. Do you have any memories from the time you were thought to be dead?

    b. Did you experience seeing a light?

    c. Did you hear a voice? What did it say?

    d. Were there other beings present?

    e. Were you aware of things going on in the location where your physical body lay? Or away from your body?

25. Have you ever dreamed of encountering a person who you knew was dead?

26. If so, did you feel that person really visited your dream?

27. Have you ever had, while awake, a vivid impression of seeing, hearing, smelling, sensing, or being touched by someone or something which you could not explain by normal means?

28. Have you ever "seen" (or "heard" or "smelled") a person or persons who you would consider to be an apparition?

29. If you've had contact with an apparition, did you feel the apparition was aware or conscious of you (did you have a sort of two-way communication or interaction with the apparition)?

30. Have you felt physically threatened by an unseen force or entity?

31. Have you ever witnessed a poltergeist outbreak (with many objects flying around or being destroyed)?

32. Do you believe such major manifestations exist?

33. Do you believe a living person is responsible (psychokinesis)? If not, what else do you think might be responsible?

34. Have you ever been to a location you would consider "haunted"? If so, did anything unusual happen there to you or others around you?

35. Do you believe haunted locations are relaying historical information to those sensitive enough to pick it up?

36. Do you believe in past lives (reincarnation)?

37. Do you believe you have had a past life (or more than one)? If so, why?

38. Have you ever been to a professional psychic, healer, shaman, channeler, or spirit medium?

39. Have you ever felt the need to talk to someone about these type of experiences?

    a. If yes, have you actually done this?

    b. Who did you talk with (relationship to you)?

    c. What kinds of experiences did you talk about?

    d. What was the person's response to your experience(s)?

40. For each of the categories listed below, please indicate ("Y" or "N") whether you would consider going to such a person if you ever felt the need to talk to someone about experiences like those in this book or questionnaire.

_____Friend   _____Parapsychologist

_____Relative   _____Psychologist (or other therapist)

_____Minister/Priest/Rabbi   _____Psychiatrist

_____Doctor (M.D.)   _____Professional Psychic

_____Channeler   _____Spirit Medium

_____Hypnotherapist   _____Other scientist

_____Professional Magician   _____Other (please specify)

PART THREE: PSYCHIC FRAUD

1. Have you ever been to a psychic, healer, channeler, or spirit medium?

2. Did you believe the practitioner was genuine? If so, why? If not, why not?

3. Do you believe there are genuine psychic practitioners?

4. Do you believe psychic abilities can be faked?

5. Do you believe you can tell the difference between real psi and fraud? If so, what makes you think so?

6. Do you believe all magicians are opposed to the existence of genuine psychic ability?

7. Have you ever conversed with a magician about psychic abilities?

8. Have you ever been to a skeptics' group meeting? Are you a "member" of such an organization?

9. Have you read books/articles which debunk psychic phenomena (such as those that might appear in the *Skeptical Inquirer* or materials written by individuals such as the Amazing Randi or Martin Gardner)?

10. Do you think parapsychologists can tell if someone is a phony psychic or not?

PART FOUR: ABOUT YOURSELF

1. Please provide the following information:

NAME:

ADDRESS:

CITY/STATE/ZIP/COUNTRY:

AGE:

SEX:

MARITAL STATUS:

DO YOU HAVE CHILDREN:

OCCUPATION:

RELIGION/SPIRITUAL BELIEFS:

FAVORITE KIND OF FICTION:

FAVORITE SUBJECTS IN NON-FICTION:

FAVORITE KIND OF MOVIES:

FAVORITE KIND OF TV SHOW:

DO YOU OWN A VCR?

WHAT KIND OF COMPUTER DO YOU HAVE:

DOES IT HAVE CD-ROM CAPABILITY?

E-MAIL ADDRESS:

DO YOU USE THE INTERNET?

DO YOU USE A WEB BROWSER?

DO YOU SUBSCRIBE TO AN ONLINE SERVICE (AMERICA ONLINE, COMPUSERVE, PRODIGY, LEXIS-NEXIS, DIALOG, OTHER)?

2. Would you be interested in participating in future surveys or studies?

3. Do you want to receive information about parapsychologically related events, videotapes, publications or products?

4. Do you prefer future contact by a) regular mail or b) E-mail?

Again, thanks for your time and I hope you enjoyed this book. Your responses will be totally anonymous, but you may see your experiences (the names and other personal facts changed to ensure your anonymity) available to others in future publications or on-line.

1. Regular mail: Send the survey to:

Loyd Auerbach

PK Survey

P.O. Box 875

Orinda, CA 94563-0875

2. E-mail the survey to: esper@california.com

May the Force (of your Mind) be with You (and Matter to you and those around you)